THE
SEXUAL
SELF

Also by Avodah K. Offit, M.D.

Night Thoughts: Reflections of a Sex Therapist

THE SEXUAL SELF

How Character Shapes Sexual Experience

REVISED
EDITION

Avodah K. Offit, M.D.

JASON ARONSON INC.
Northvale, New Jersey
London

THE MASTER WORK SERIES

1995 softcover edition

Copyright © 1995, 1983, 1977 by Avodah K. Offit, M.D.

All rights reserved. Printed in the United States of America. No part of this book may be used or reproduced in any manner whatsoever without permission from Jason Aronson Inc. except in the case of brief quotations in reviews for inclusion in a magazine, newspaper, or broadcast.

Library of Congress Cataloging-in-Publication Data

Offit, Avodah K.
    The sexual self : how character shapes sexual experience / by
Avodah K. Offit
        p.   cm.
        Originally published : Rev. ed. New York :   Congdon & Weed,
c1983. With new introduction.
        Includes index.
        ISBN 1-56821-548-7 (alk. paper)
        1. Psychosexual disorders.   2. Sex (Psychology)   3. Personality.
    I. Title
    RC556.O33   1995
    616.85' 83—dc20   95-22483

Manufactured in the United States of America. Jason Aronson Inc. offers books and cassettes. For information and catalog write to Jason Aronson Inc., 230 Livingston Street, Northvale, New Jersey 07647.

To Sidney Offit

Contents

Author's Note   ix
Preface to the Revised Edition   xi
Acknowledgments   xiii
Introduction   1

PART I: BEING AND BECOMING

1. The Bonding Touch   13
2. Attachment and Separation   24

PART II: PERSONALITY TRAITS AND SEXUAL BEHAVIOR

3. Dependency: Sexual Reliance   39
4. Histrionic Display: Sexual Theater   49
5. Narcissism: Sexual Egocentricity   58
6. Compulsiveness: Sexual Obsession   65
7. Passive Aggression: Sexual Strategy   76
8. The Paranoid Approach: Sexual Espionage   81
9. Schizoid Withdrawal: Sexual Avoidance   87
10. Aggression: Sexual Conquest   93
11. The Affective Factors: Sexual Mood Trends   103

PART III: PSYCHOSEXUAL DISORDERS

12. Disorders of Desire   113
     Aversion   116

    Indifference   118
13. Disorders of Arousal   122
    Avoidance and Ambivalence   122
    Excessive Sexual Arousal   129
14. Male Maladies   133
    Disorders of Excitement   133
    Orgasmic and Ejaculatory Disorders   142
        Premature Ejaculation   142
        Inhibited Orgasm   150
        Impaired Orgasm and Ejaculation   153
15. Female Maladies   155
    Sexual Excitement Disorders   155
        Inhibited Sexual Excitement   155
        Vaginismus   165
    Orgasmic Disorders   167
        Inhibited Orgasm   168
        Impaired Orgasm   178
        Inhibition of Multiple Orgasm   183

PART IV: PSYCHOSEXUAL THERAPY

16. Techniques: Pushbutton Panaceas   189
17. Power and Intimacy   202
18. Sexual Fantasy   217
19. Women's Web   231
20. Psychosexual Change   246

PART V: SEXUALITY TODAY

21. The "New" Impotence   255
22. Female Sexual "Liberation"   269
23. The Old "New Sexuality"   293
    Epilogue   309
    Index   311
    About the Author   317

Author's Note

In society as in marriage, the passion for sex waxes and wanes. When *The Sexual Self* was first published in the 70s, society revelled in sex like any newly bonded couple in the throes of their first amours. As an author praising the delights of sexual freedom, even then I counselled a weather eye to the clouds of sexual storm. Personality traits concealed in courtship could emerge to deluge sex later in marriage. And just as sex might be quelled by the emergence of hidden traits, the sexual revolution began to subside when the hidden virus of AIDS appeared in the early 80's.

In 1983, I revised *The Sexual Self* for a second edition after paperbacks, book club and foreign versions had been printed. Certain new concepts were included, as well as words of caution about AIDS, which was thought by most people then to be rare. AIDS, of course, has become such a national disaster that sex, today, frequently occurs in the disembodied milieu of cyberspace. To elucidate this phenomenon, I wrote a novel called *Virtual Love*, published in 1994 by Simon & Schuster. It makes the point that with or without physical encounter, the characterological traits examined in *The Sexual Self* work their mischief and magic. Readers who wish to discuss these or other issues may contact me at Virtualove@aol.com.

For this reprinting by Jason Aronson, I have chosen to make no revisions to the second edition. The main point of

The Sexual Self—that the way we relate as well as the way we behave sexually reflects our fundamental attitude to life—remains unchanged. There has indeed been a sexual backlash in society as we continue to try to deal with the plague. While there are a few references to greater sexual freedom than most of us permit today, to fine-comb the text for them would be pedantic.

Similarly, references to women as less economically empowered than they are today have also been retained. Women still have to struggle for their financial and emotional selfhood. Reminders of where they recently have been—and where many remain—are still relevant.

While other minor corrections might be made, perhaps the greatest change since the Preface to the Revised Edition of 1983 is in my children's accomplishments. Dr. Kenneth Offit is no longer in his medical residency. He is Chief of the Clinical Genetics Service at the Memorial Sloan-Kettering Cancer Center. My younger son, Michael, remains in finance at Goldman Sachs. I have also acquired two remarkably able daughters-in-law and five grandchildren. Among other new friends—people who feel like family—I wish especially to thank Jason Aronson, Ruth Brody, and Michael Moskowitz for selecting *The Sexual Self* to continue its good long life in print.

In 1995, I continue to find character a guide to sexuality, if not sexual dysfunction, although the successful treatment of dysfunction generally relies on an accurate assessment of character. Knowledge of the sexual self serves to enhance the therapist's skill, the patient's recovery, and the general reader's alertness to the problems as well as the ecstasies of love.

Avodah K. Offit, M.D.
February 1995

Preface to the Revised Edition

Since *The Sexual Self* was first published in 1977, the sophistication of those who are concerned with sexual science, psychology, and manners has vastly increased. I have tried to encourage this enlightenment not only in professional periodicals such as *Contemporary Psychology,* but in a variety of popular ones as well, among them *Vogue, Glamour, McCall's,* and *Self.* But it is in my books, *The Sexual Self* and *Night Thoughts: Reflections of a Sex Therapist,* that my fundamental ideas are preserved. As good editors remind me, books have lives of their own, and for that reason I am particularly grateful to Congdon & Weed for the opportunity to revise *The Sexual Self.*

The additions to the text have not altered the original premise: that character shapes sexuality and especially sexual difficulties. They serve only to reinforce the thesis. It may be of interest to readers to observe how such recent topics as the Grafenberg spot, extended orgasm, herpes virus, and acquired immune deficiency syndrome (AIDS) relate to the variety of personality responses. I have also introduced several problems identified by the terms "sexual hypochondria," "supersex," and "sexual dyskinesia" or "sexual learning disability." These, too, reflect the book's major concern with individual character.

The chapter "The Old 'New Sexuality'" is rewritten as well as revised. Other revised chapters concern inhibition of sexual desire and inhibition of sexual excitement. Avoidance of once pleasant sexual relations was a significant topic of general discussion in the original edition. I have rechristened the problem "sexual arousal disorder" to emphasize the difficulties so many couples have with both desire and excitement. In addition, inhibited male orgasm and ejaculation are regarded in a new light.

This is not a revision in the sense of altering ideas to fit new circumstances. It is rather an attempt to fit some of today's concepts into the original thesis. Though discoveries about sexual function are multiplying rapidly, I am no less committed to the proposition that disorders of the sexual life reflect the psychological variations of the sexual self.

Avodah K. Offit, M.D.
April 1983

Acknowledgments

Writing a book, like serious lovemaking, owes an intricate debt to the past. When an author cares as much about language and ideas as any true lover committed to authenticity and grace, the education is long and sometimes painful. With words as with touch, we enhance our impulses by daring to imitate, experiment, and fail before arriving at a style we may, perhaps, call our own. Aspiring to the significant sentence, as to the enduring touch, leads to diverse experience of joy and anguish. It is for such reasons that my acknowledgments are so various.

As an undergraduate at Hunter College and the University of Chicago, I read the classics and practiced the construction of sentences. I was fortunate to encounter Professors Mildred Kuner, Robert Halsband, Irene Samuels, and Marian Witt, scholars of different disciplines, but singular in their respect for words.

Since my studies at the New York University School of Medicine, I have been particularly indebted to Dr. Lewis Thomas for his literary reminders about the compassions that nourish the healing arts.

As a psychiatrist in full-time private practice, I have been most fortunate in the voluntary hospital affiliations that have enabled me to teach and to learn by giving treatment. At Lenox Hill Hospital, I am grateful to Dr. Michael S. Bruno, Director of the Department of Medicine, and to Dr. Hugh R. K. Barber, Director of the Department of Obstetrics and Gynecology, for the opportunity to create and be in charge of the Sexual Therapy and Consultation Center during the decade of its service to the needy. To Dr. Allen Collins, Dr. Loren Skeist, Dr. Larry Goldblatt, Dr. Lenard Jacobson, and Dr. Damir Velcek, I wish to express my enthusiasm for their continuing support of psychosexual education for physicians.

In the early 1970s, I especially appreciated the foresight of Dr. William T. Lhamon at The New York Hospital, who—although he was skeptical of psychosexual therapy as a discipline—permitted me to initiate that activity in the Department of Psychiatry. Later, a sexual treatment program was formed, of which I became for a time the associate director.

In my private practice, the doctors with whom I have exchanged friendship are too numerous to name; the patients who are indirectly responsible for the observations in this book cannot be named, although, perhaps, they deserve the most gratitude for revealing themselves so generously to me. Among doctors, I thank particularly Dr. John Astrachan, Dr. Marvin Zuckerman, Dr. Seymour Grossman, Dr. Lisa Tallal, Dr. Colter Rule, Dr. Thomas Argyros, Dr. Stewart Orsher, Dr. Peter Bruno, Dr. Marvin Kaplan, Dr. Howard Bogard, Dr. Alvin Donnenfeld, Dr. Sidney Kreps, Dr. Harry Fein, and Drs. Ruth and Bertel Bruun. I also thank Dr. Harvey Klein, Dr. Arnold M. Cooper, Dr. Richard Glass, Dr. Ira Glick, and Dr. Lawrence A. Downs. Dr. Marilyn Karmason supported my choice of psychiatry as a profession, and Dr. David Clayson predicted the path of my career.

Within the therapeutic field, I have felt close over the years to Dr. Shirley Zusskind, Dr. Maj-Britt Rosenbaum, Dr. Alexander Levay, Dr. Jon Myers, Dr. Robert Kolodny, and Dr. Clifford Sager. For her kindnesses in recent years, I wish to thank especially Dr. Virginia Sadock. On several occasions, Dr. Benjamin Sadock has given me excellent advice.

This book was first encouraged by Martin Goldman, former editor of *Intellectual Digest* and recently publisher of *New Harvest*. From the original outline to the galleys, I knew I had the support of my editor, Beatrice Rosenfeld, and my literary representative, Candida Donadio. Dr. William A. Frosch scrutinized the manuscript with a friendly but judicious eye. To Thomas B. Congdon, Jr., friend and publisher, who has seen fit to renew the life of this book, I offer my fond appreciation.

This list of my gratitudes suggests what must be the most demanding rigor of all—living with an author-doctor. In this my blessings have been abundant: my sons, Dr. Kenneth Offit, Princeton '77, Harvard Medical School '81, and currently a medical resident at Lenox Hill Hospital; and Michael Offit, Brown '79, Columbia Business School '83, and now employed in banking. My gratitude, too, must be expressed to my mother, Carrie Komito, for enduring my long silence; I hope this book explained the reason. For Sidney Offit—teacher, novelist, editor, commentator, writer of children's books, and always my very best friend—there is no need here to spell out the feelings without which this book could not have been written. He knows; he knows.

THE
SEXUAL
SELF

Introduction

Who are we? What is to become of us? Perhaps the most lavish source of insight into human nature lies in sexual personality. Sexual attitudes, activities, and fantasies constitute the most graphic measure we have of character. In our sexual lives, we express our basic relations to others. We show whether we fundamentally prefer to go it alone or to act in concert. We display our tastes for submission, domination, dependence, conquest, or cooperation. In sex, a person's generosity or selfishness, sense of responsibility or carelessness, may be so easily defined that it is small wonder so many people prefer to have sex either in anonymity or as a profound commitment of trust. We are chary with information about our bedroom lives, even to best friends, but not because genitals are private parts by virtue of being covered most of the time. We simply don't enjoy being psychologically naked.

Certainly we demonstrate character profiles in business, as parents, or in civic and social situations. But when a businessman takes pleasure in outwitting a competitor, or a glib performer enjoys stealing the social scene, there are convenient rationalizations and rewards for less than altruistic behavior. In sex, when a man reaches orgasm with the fantasy of whipping his partner or a woman is stirred by a vision of herself as a busy prostitute, these dreams—and the reasons for them—may not be acceptable fireside recollections. Not only fantasies, but all the multiplicity of

1

curious sex acts with unlikely partners, are matters we tend to keep secret from others, even from ourselves.

If we are to fathom ourselves, the questions must be rephrased. Who are we sexually? What will become of us unless we understand our sexual selves?

This is not a book about how to assume the best new sexual positions or play the latest games in order to enhance sexual joy. It is not a manual purporting to enlarge upon and modify clinical techniques for curing sexual ailments. The intention of this book is to illuminate what has been so assiduously avoided in the impersonal textbooks and the sterile joy books: that sex involves character and philosophy. We can tell who we are and what we believe by observing how we act, think, dream, and feel sexually. We may even become moved to make changes based on what we have observed. No how-to book can help us to make such changes. We may either search deeply for our own best way or enlist the services of a trusted professional to guide us.

In an absolute scientific sense, we know very little about sex. We have discovered gonadotropins, hormones, and pheromones, but their precise relationship to human sexuality remains to be fully elaborated. Perhaps the most important advance was made in 1954, when we discovered that electrical stimulation of the limbic area of the brain produces sexual feelings. Indeed rats like these feelings so much that, when they can turn themsleves on by pressing a lever connected to electrodes implanted in their brains, they do so enthusiastically for hours. People might do likewise. Electricity is the final aphrodisiac. If we could all walk about with electrical implants in our heads, we might be perfectly sexy, or perfectly happy, or whatever we choose to be. We could negotiate life with a panel of control buttons at our fingertips. However, this does not seem to be an immediate solution. Remote control by others might replace individual freedom, and besides, not much else would get done.

Since nature did not intend us to respond automatically to the primitive demands of the limbic system, we are provided with a sophisticated new growth of brain cells, the neocortex. This is probably the site of character development. Without a neocortex, we should all act like rats or lizards, having sex without much thinking about it. What we say to ourselves, the permissions and restraints we impose, the controls we exercise over the ancient limbic requirements for mating (and eating and fighting), are all governed by the learning stored in the neocortex.

We cannot yet dissect out and decode this information about character. The best we can do is to have a look at our thoughts before, during, and after acting, and to note our opinions of ourselves for behaving as we have.

Our ability to see ourselves, to integrate the learning of the new brain and the demands of the old, is generally referred to as "ego function." Ego psychology has concentrated recently on studying aggressivity, also primarily situated in the limbic system, capable of being turned on by electricity, and subject to modification by the neocortex. It is now time to examine sexuality. The sexual ego can be our most treasured guide in the classic quest for being and becoming.

What we do, think, and feel sexually represents the entire spectrum of our personality traits. A skilled fortune teller may be able to tell what people are like—their warmth, coolness, assertiveness, shyness, compliance, defiance—merely by the way they shake hands. Is the hand cold, trembling? Is it offered palm up, down, or sideways? Is the grip firm or flaccid? Does the contact last long, or is it brief and tenuous? How much more we can learn about ourselves by the ways in which we do or do not unite our genitals, with whom, under what circumstances, and for what reasons!

We express our most fundamental natures through our sexual choices. A person's sexual pattern is not, as a rule, anything else but what he or she is. The way we have

sex, and with whom, is just as much a part of ourselves as
how we spend money, take vacations, do our work. Understanding our sexual selves before opting for married or
single life, or even coming to terms with sexuality as marriage progresses, could prevent the enormity of sexual despair now wracking so many lives.

We may fear pleasure or seek it without constraint. We
may give our souls to establishing a sexual ethic or have not
the slightest insight into how morality and sex could possibly be related. Suspicion and fear of lovers' motives may
dominate relationships, or blind trust can protect us from
knowledge of all human perfidy. We can derive the most
basic information from whether or not we experience sexual feelings, commit them all to one relationship, feel
obliged to have an apple in many baskets, or are driven to
collect a sexual empire.

As a psychiatrist, I help people not only to observe
their sexual patterns but also to discover the meaning sexuality has to them. Sexuality is what we conceive it to be: a
valued or worthless commodity, a means of procreation, a
defense against loneliness, a form of communication, a tool
of aggression (control, power punishment, submission), a
sport, love, art, beauty, an ideal state, evil, good, luxury,
recreation, reward, escape, a source of self-esteem, a means
of expressing affection (maternal, fraternal, paternal, or
simply human), a way of rebellion, a source of freedom, a
duty, a pleasure, a communion with the universal, a mystical ecstasy, a death-related wish or experience, a road to
peace, a cause, a mode of pioneering and exploring, a skill,
a biological function, a manifestation of psychic health or
disease, or a simple sensory experience.

How we come to regard sexuality is a product of what
we have learned in our relationships to others. The first
two chapters in this book offer the hypothesis that fundamental sexual feelings and attitudes are based on early life
experiences. Analysts have been saying this for years, and

before the analysts, playwrights and novelists wrote as though they took it for granted. Religious thinkers have always sensed it and have tried to prescribe the feelings and actions which would nourish sexually appropriate development.

What early life experiences shall we study, however, for information about our sexual selves? Shall we try to unravel our Oedipal complexities, attempt to reconstruct our birth trauma, seek our archetypal heritage, observe the ways our spirits have been crushed by authority, or assume that societal codes have done us in or brought us out?

The experiences I feel one must examine are those involving trust and body contact. When trust is violated or body contact unreliable for comfort, children develop defenses against being hurt. Defenses—attitudes of excessive self-sufficiency, self-love, self-hate, blame taking or blame giving—cluster to form a nidus that creates, from very early on, a personality. We all develop defenses: there are no parents so perfect, or children so endowed, that defenses are unnecessary.

A troubled mother can handle her infant so nervously that the child may develop a permanent repugnance to being physically close. Later life may produce, perhaps, a highly "intellectual" man or woman, a person who considers sex and affection a "low" form of communcication. Obsessional behavior, isolation, withdrawal may occur. Sexual feeling, love, and trust may be significantly damaged.

Forming defenses is an ego activity. We are, in a sense, the product of our ego's effectiveness. Personality is defined as the totality of an individual's characteristics, especially as they relate to other people; it is an integrated group of emotional trends, interests, and behavior tendencies based largely on defensive maneuvers. We are all a bit strange.

The second section of this book will examine how major personality types respond sexually. We bring to sex all our defenses, disorders of trust, attitudes toward love and hate. We cannot come to terms with our sexuality until we know what sort of people we are. Our sexual life is the most sensitive barometer of personality, our defenses against emotional pain, and our means of coping with it. Do we withdraw and avoid? Are we moody and change-able, dramatic, exhibitionistic, egocentric, selfish, manip-ulative, passive, aggressive, orderly, miserly? What we do, think, imagine, and feel during the sexual act itself can reveal our natures more emphatically than any other single human activity.

In this section the reader may find clues as to how to identify himself or herself and, perhaps, decide whether there is something so radically wrong that change is called for. I say "radically wrong" because most of us have some anxieties which occasionally shut off the mental electricity we can generate by ourselves to stimulate the lusty old limbic system. We can put up with these minor troubles, but when no signals at all get through, or too few, we may need to open new doors, make new connections. Most of us want to approach sex without feeling abused by it, using it to hurt others, being afraid of what it will reveal, or consid-ering ourselves inadequate. The ability to take pleasure in sexuality, a pleasure consistent with the sensible dictates of our neocortex, conscience, intelligence, or superego, is a highly civilized art. It may take some hard work to achieve.

In Part III, I offer the reader such insight as I have acquired into the relationship between sexual disorders and personality traits. Although anyone may have any sex-ual disorder, the cause of the underlying anxiety is quite individual. At least as much as the symptom itself, the cause requires understanding and treatment. We have learned to treat impotence, for example, by teaching a man to distract himself from "performance anxiety." Yet I have not yet encountered two men who suffered this anxiety for pre-cisely the same reasons. One man might feel anxious about not being a sexual athlete, in response to parental demands for perfection; another might fear that his "performance" will offend the madonna beneath him; a third could be afraid of losing his identity as his penis disappears into a vagina. The source of sexual anxiety relates intimately to the wellsprings of life's other difficulties.

Whereas the second section of this book suggests what sort of sexual lives people with differing personality traits may be expected to experience, the section on sexual disorders offers a reverse perspective, one that has only become richly possible through my clinical experience in dealing directly with sexual problems. These chapters attempt some insight into the variety of personality traits that people with differing disorders may be anticipated to possess. No broad generalizations can cover any one disorder, however. Just as we cannot conclude that all shy men are impotent, so we cannot conclude that all impotent men are shy and fear self-assertion. We cannot pass the verdict that all passive-aggressive women are nonorgasmic, or that all nonorgasmic women are passive-aggressively withholding their pleasure. Nevertheless, there are significant patterns which sensitive readers may identify in themselves, or therapists may find helpful in working with their patients. If the reader is not personally suffering sexual complaints, these chapters may offer an empathetic view toward those who are: husbands, wives, lovers, or friends. In sex more than any other life transaction, anxieties play like unhampered microbes on a helpless body. To be compassionate is to recognize our identity with suffering, even if we are fortunate enough not to bear such afflictions ourselves.

The fourth section of this book describes an approach to better treatment techniques for the people who are in despair, methods which attempt to incorporate all that is known about alleviating psychosexual misery. Analysts know how to help people understand their problems, but are often unable to help them learn new patterns. Behaviorists offer new patterns, often without commensurate self-understanding. Analyzing dynamics is not enough; offering behavioral prescriptions that encourage human beings to neglect their principles and values in the service of being able to press the psychological equivalent of an aphrodisiac lever is also insufficient.

On the purely behavioral model, "sex clinics" have sprung up throughout the land like so many laundromats. They dispense techniques for release of sexual inhibition and improvement in sexual function which appear to work on the coin-op principle. Put in money and come out clean of dirty old scars after a few revolutions in the tumbler. A little patience, the right strokes, enough touchy-feely, and a dose of porno promise freedom from the tattletale blood of sexual wounds. Baptized in the waters of liberation, we shall all become instantly pure, regaining sexual innocence and delight. It is, quite clearly, not so simple. We need a better intrapsychic vehicle in which to travel toward Eden.

Why do two people choose to mate? What are their chances for sexual success? For remaining paired? For separating amicably if cleaving unto each other is not a primary intention or even a secondary possibility? Some researchers have observed that if one person supplies what another lacks, there is a tendency to join and stay joined. Others note that relationships which provide a lot of honest battle tend to be more interesting and durable. These conclusions, however true and general, neglect the sexual essence of a union as it reflects each partner's entire personality.

People who depend on others like to have sex with someone who can be relied upon. They also enjoy doing business and having regular fun that way. Other people, whose defensive systems operate to value self-sufficiency and independence, like to have sex with equally free-spirited partners. In business, they prefer not having bosses. For fun, they try out different sports in widely ranging places. We cannot expect the compulsive mate—whom we admire for steadfastness, integrity, and, perhaps, a dedication to approach perfection in either art or commerce—to be rambunctious, experimental, indeed even indiscriminate. Personality, as it reflects a fundamental orientation to life, determines the viability of sexual encounter.

A psychotherapy of sexual disorder must do more than create automatons who can function at a pre-moral level of sensory pleasure, although liberating that ability is often a priority. It must do more than help people to understand why their sexual energies are tangled in childhood conflicts, although such knowledge is a prerequisite for emancipation. Given that it takes all kinds of people to make a world, psychosexual therapy should aim at freeing people to attempt to become the best of their kind. This usually calls for change.

Few of us reach our potential or even know that we have any. We cling to our uncertainties and confusions. A therapist ought to have an eclectic view of what might be best for his or her patients, help them define it, and offer guidance and support through the complexities of self-realization, whenever that is possible.

While this is not a novel ideal for a psychiatrist, I feel that it ought to be an imperative for anyone who practices "sex therapy." Too many psychiatrists are relinquishing their tradition of healing the mind in favor of quick sexual "cure." Too many nonpsychiatrists who have become "sex therapists" never even entertained the thought that sex is considerably more than a body function like urinating or defecating.

In Part V, I consider the complexities of sexuality that range far beyond whether or not people can have orgasms, alone or together. The interest of the twentieth century in sexuality neglects far deeper structural enigmas. The twentieth century did not discover sex, but we do appear to be more confused by sex than any former generation. Just as a man or woman must develop sexual attitudes on reaching adulthood, so our society must eventually come to terms with changing sexual mores. The last section of this book raises some questions peculiar to contemporary Western society and offers a few preliminary answers.

Did the sex therapy of the sixties cure impotence for all time, as Masters and Johnson hoped? What was the effect of "liberation" on female sexuality? Has the "new sexuality" of unrestricted partnership been an answer to the miseries of monogamy as attested to by our rising divorce rate in the seventies? What can we expect as we move through each new decade of our sexual life in the eighties?

The "sex revolution," for all its liberating qualities, tended to confuse, frustrate, and even pain the people who subscribed to its simplistic identities. The purveyors of eroticism cushioned in pop culture seemed to say that there were two ways to relate to sex and, by inference, two kinds of people: those who were free to explore its endless varieties, and the inhibited and repressed, trapped in a Puritan ethic. The naked ladies and gentlemen who testified to the boldness of the new sexual freedom (for a fee) challenged credulity and even fantasy. We did not need the new sexual journalism to record for us the extravagances of the sexually preoccupied. Such verbal and visual excursions provided entertainment, perhaps, but only bewildering sexual guidance. Sexual personality is not so conveniently defined as hot or warm, liberated or inhibited. Illustrated manuals offered new games to play, but they presented us with no vocabulary ior searching out our individual sexual identity. It is only when the individual has a true sense of self that he or she takes the first step toward becoming sexually fulfilled. There is no competition, no better or best performer, when one understands sex as a part of the total personality and accepts it in oneself as well as in those one loves. Only then do we move toward harmonious sexual relationship.

Part I
BEING AND BECOMING

1

The Bonding Touch

Scholars in the field of human sexuality have instructed us that mature adults may sensibly and responsibly provide mutual satisfactions by placing their genital organs in proximity. Yet in our first young rushes of passion—and in the echoes of those early intensities which reverberate periodically—we do not think of sensible, mutual satisfactions. The need is so strong, so urgent, that the union seems essential to our fulfillment as beings.

We touch here on one of the profound mysteries of sex as it relates to love. People today, as ever, take preposterously contradictory views on the subject. For every heart which sighs that "falling in love" is the ultimate aphrodisiac, there is a cooler head which advises that eros resides in the next new body, preferably nameless. While many laud the supremacy of reliable domestic delight, many more love and lust and sin, and give secret statistics to sex researchers.

How can we resolve the dichotomy between our ardent sufferings and the commonsensical view of the scientists who tell us we must aspire to mature mating? While "immature" love may be painful, unrealistic, and sometimes self-destructive, it frequently feels immensely good. It is certainly a rite of passage most of us experience, not only in adolescence, but through each of our decadal crises as we advance toward old age.

But psychosexual maturity involves "outgrowing childhood dependency needs," establishing the "primacy of the genitals." Only when "infantile motives are surrendered," we are taught, can sex become real sex.

In spite of the admonition, however, sex simply felt much more exciting in those first few uncertain infatuations, or love affairs, or whatever they were—and sex often plainly feels more exciting in later recapitulations of those pubertal ecstasies—than it does in regular, reliable marital interaction. Whether or not orgasm, ejaculation, or perfect mechanical conjunction occurs, there is certainly elation in these spontaneous couplings.

Adults ask, troubled married couples ask, even psychiatrists who have all the answers ask, in private: Can it feel that way again? Should it? Is it infantile to feel so thrilled? Is there something better?

Most theorists answer emphatically no to the first two questions, yes to the second two. They say that adolescent sex, whether experienced at fifteen or fifty, feels so splendid because it offers the excitement of the forbidden, a delight mature people should do without. Or they may talk of transferring too many needs onto inappropriate objects and trying to satisfy impossible longings. We should not search for those feelings again because they are embarrassingly juvenile.

The mystery is that sex, accompanied by the full gamut of mankind's dependency needs, is—for many— life's most heightened and sensual experience. This is the way it should be. And it is among the wonders of nature's cycles that those needs were exceptionally intense during late adolescence. The keenest sexual experiences of later life resonate to and form a harmony with the earlier ones. Sometimes these later raptures do indeed occur within a marriage; more often they bloom suddenly outside.

A path to solving the dilemma would seem to lie in the relatively recent studies of "attachment behavior" and "separation anxiety." These cumbersome terms, developed by researchers intent on demonstrating that people are systematized and programmed, like computers, nevertheless do provide a welcome shorthand for revelation of familiar feelings. When we are small, we feel cozy and safe in the presence of a good mother. Like Lilliputian warriors, we fight to stay close. As William James wrote, "The greatest terror of infancy is solitude."

Parents may be warm and affectionate, distant and rejecting, punitive or lenient, or generally inconsistent. Their attitude strongly affects what sort of person a child will become. Since I believe that varying personalities enjoy sex most under very different circumstances, this book presents the hypothesis that attachment and separation responses greatly influence the sexual ego, a term I use to describe a person's capacity for sexual pleasure at maturity and his or her ability to understand the optimal characterological conditions for finding it.

Scholars of the psyche have relentlessly instructed us that our sexuality forms a separate part of ourselves. Religious sages insisted it was, under most circumstances, a sin to be cleansed away. Philosophers divided us into neat sections containing reason, spirit, and passion. They argued the merits of each for centuries. Psychoanalysts felt sex belonged to the "libido," an outgrowth of that often unsavory and bestial mass of life tendencies known as the "id." Although the word means "it" in Latin, some scholars feel that "id" is an abbreviation for "idioplasm," a term that biologists used before they discovered DNA. It meant "germ plasm," that portion of cell protoplasm supposed to determine the character of the species. Whether "id" is a neuter Latin pronoun or a truncated Greek prefix, its use is still an attempt to compartmentalize us after the scientific fashion.

Even more modern theoreticians discard sin, passion, and libido-producing ids in favor of the computer model.

We are formed by "affectional systems." The sexual is one such system, quite emphatically separate from all the rest. Of course, the theoreticians admit reluctantly, there are overlaps between the sexual system and others. Feelings from the early "attachment system" tend to intervene. How infants relate to parents and how parents relate to children get all mixed up with sex. The mix-up is an area requiring much further investigation, scientists confess. There seems to be no doubt that we are computers with a lot of crossed circuits. So much for computer theory.

In fiction and drama, it has been taken for granted for millenniums that people have basic "characters" which govern what they do and feel. Parents, environment, and heredity influence character. Therefore, it seems worthwhile to pursue the relationship of sex to character or personality. Freud's most interesting contribution to psychiatric "science" was taken from the play *Oedipus Rex* by Sophocles. Had Freud developed more theories from theater and drama, he might have told us all we need to know.

Warm, secure, consistent parents, theoretically, create "rational-altruistic" children who are considered "normal." The first task, therefore, should be to inspect the development of the sexual ego in such children, who are raised by kindly, supportive, helpful parents and live serene lives in which one growth step succeeds the next without fuss and trauma. Having never treated—or even met—anyone in this category, I confess myself unable to trace "normal" growth and development. Biased as I am by literature, it seems to me that everyone is a bit daft. We all have odd quirks of personality which make great sense to us but perplex and bewilder others. So long as we are able to function in the world without disturbing the peace too emphatically, we are considered "within normal limits," which are very wide indeed.

Most of us have one major personality trait and several minor ones. Classifiers of our character, suddenly realizing this old truth, have recently engaged in massive studies of personality, trait by trait, in the attempt to define the very smallest particles of our being. Atom-smasher theory threatens to replace computer theory. If you divide people into small enough parts, perhaps the secret of life will become clear. We may all be composed of charm and quark. Since "quark" is a word taken from James Joyce's *Finnegans Wake* ("three quarks for Muster mark"), the new studies in physics and personality science may be a further tribute to our literary heritage. However, dividing people into minimums will probably not provide any final answers. At least, one would hope not.

Fortunately, the scholars of the American Psychiatric Association have not yet succumbed entirely to computers and atom smashers. They still recognize the existence of character, of fundamental personality—and they define approximately eight key traits. When people suffer exaggerations of these traits or patterns, they have a personality disorder. They have simply gone too far, and we must treat them because they are making themselves absolutely impossible. Preferably, they are in enough emotional pain to request help themselves.

This book will be concerned not so much with the pathological personality as with the trends and tendencies we all have. As defined and continually undergoing redefinition, these traits are: dependence, aggressiveness and passive-aggressiveness, paranoia, schizoid withdrawal, histrionic display, compulsiveness, and narcissism. Excessive affective responses, such as depression, will also be considered. The intention will not be to survey the consequences of such tendencies in all areas of life, but rather to restrict discussion to their sexual implications. When people have not sufficiently developed their key traits, or do not understand how best to live with them, they are immature and inadequate. Some psychiatrists still postulate an "ideal personality," a warm, responsive person always altruistically in control and highly successful. This is the image of the perfect doctor, and we have all encountered many such façades. However, different sorts of humans (the vast majority of us) are perfectly acceptable.

People who mate heterosexually, homosexually, or bisexually have essentially the same personality traits. Whether male and female sex organs interlock, or there is interplay between man and man or woman and woman, seems independent of other characteristics. Efforts to prove that male homosexuals, for example, are all paranoid have not met with any great success. Certain patterns do assert themselves with greater frequency: male homosexuals do tend to have sexual relations which are freer of dependency bonds, and perhaps female homosexual pairs have a higher ratio of long-term dyadic bonding than the male homosexual norm. This can reflect either a constitutional or a cultural predisposition: men have sex more for conquest and reassurance, women more for security. Nevertheless, all manner of people engage in all kinds of sexual unions for every variety of reason.

One cannot tease out "the homosexual personality" or "the heterosexual personality." Given that some men are sexually attracted to other men, that some women are sexually appealing to other women, and that often men and women find each other irresistible, we may take a step beyond that primitive impulse and examine what sorts of relationships they get themselves into, why, and what would make them happier. As many men may become trapped in the shifting transience of homosexual tradition as other people become jailed in the limits of heterosexual monogamy. And homosexuals are at least equal to heterosexuals in their capacity for sexual dysfunction.

In the absence of firm scientific data indicating whether or not homosexuality is biologically predetermined, it seems to me that we should accept it as a choice that people make in much the same way that they decide to become firemen or nurses. Inheritance and the hormonal vicissitudes of pregnancy may contribute; circumstance assists. If homosexuals are pleased with their choice, they do not need help.

For purposes of this book, it must be considered that anything stated about heterosexual relations may also be true of homosexual relations. No distinctions are made, because character belongs to all of us. Men and women engage in dominance-submission pacts; so do homosexuals, and for the same reasons.

Treatment procedures for homosexuals with dysfunctions—impotence or impaired orgasm—proceed along very much the same lines as methods for heterosexual improvement. Performance anxiety, hidden anger, and the negative effects of societal pressure are universal inhibitors. Homosexuals have a more troubled path, since they not only have to overcome more ordinary fears of sexuality but also the societal bias against their life-style. Some homosexuals have as much guilt about heterosexual fantasy as heterosexuals do about homosexual fantasy. Beyond these phenomena, specific to the homosexual situation, people and their sexual lives fall into similar classes no matter what their choice of gender in a partner. Perhaps all my pronouns should be genderless. However, since it has been difficult enough to write a book without saying "he" when I mean "he or she," it might have been impossible to contrive a volume about sex without any gender definition at all.

We develop personality characteristics largely in response to the way our parents treated us. The one that most of us have in common, either as a major characteristic or a minor theme somewhere in the substrate of ourselves, is dependence. At the extreme which causes trouble, we may base our entire life-style upon it, doing as little as possible for ourselves. At the other end of the dependency scale, we may fear asking even small favors. On the whole, we tend to depend on others for feelings of emotional security. We often form sexual attachments which reflect dependency bonds. These frequently lead to marriage, even today when that venerable institutionalization of dependence has fallen into some decay and disrepute.

Why are sex and dependency linked? Should they be? Are they, necessarily?

It is difficult to have good sex without touching another person. It is alo virtually impossible to sustain life without having been touched by someone else. We form our greatest dependence on the person who touches us the most as infants. The progression of experience is simple and familiar. The baby's desire is to be skin to skin, mouth to breast, buttocks to lap, penis or mons or belly to mother's chest. Father will do as well if he is gentle and knows how. Denied this body closeness, babies have been known to die of a condition identified as marasmus. At Bellevue in the early 1940s a physician was concerned with the great numbers of infants who were expiring, for no apparent health reason, on the wards. They simply lost interest in life and died. This perceptive doctor ordered that each baby be "handled" several times a day, and the death rate fell to zero.

We live to be touched. We need to be touched, at least as infants, in order to live. Our primal dependency is reenacted in the fusion that enables humanity to survive. Touching is a prerequisite not only for life but for procreation. Sexually, the initial urge is not to have an orgasm, but rather to have contact.

Most of us now accept that sexuality exists all through human life. Although babies cannot identify their sexual feelings as such, we do not doubt that they have them. Baby girls may have orgasms. Infant boys have erections and orgasms, but no ejaculations. The affectional contact between mother and child (or child and any other being by whom it is held and loved) must be the foundation for later physical intimacy. While I do not believe that "sex" is the basis for all human relations, I do think that touching is the basis for all sexual relations, and that the emotion of dependency often occurs simultaneously, whether it is appropriate or not. Sexual excitement emerges when people feel (or want to feel) safely close, unpressured, cared for. Lovers relax best by holding each other before sleep. The touch of mother's arms, breasts, and body had to be an early ecstasy for which we search again. Were it not for custom, most of us would stay close to our mother's bodies until we found some warm replacement. As it is, we are laid crying to rest by ourselves, left to learn very slowly that being alone is not a death. Anyone who has ever made love, and had to separate from a lover before the need for intimacy was sated, knows about dependency feelings.

What I shall call "touch bonding," then, seems to be the first requirement for the establishment of sexual feelings. It is also necessary to the creation of one's first dependent attachment. The road map to old-fashioned marital joy requires a firm relationship between dependence, touching, and sexuality. Warmly nurturant parenting is thought to groom us into becoming delightful lovers and dedicated parents ourselves. If we begin life properly in that domestic snuggery where mother's breast pours contentment into the kiss of our infant lips, all the rest of our days may pass in safe transitions to teachers, friends, and passionate votaries. We can attach, without quite so much touching, to surrogate figures: baby-sitters, nurses, teachers. Later, friends are enough, providing a parent is safely at home. When we are ready to leave home, we will find someone with whom to recapitulate the old securities. We will "fall in love." Progressing chronologically beyond the trial separations of childhood, let us look at that first exquisitely painful and highly concupiscent moment in life when one "falls in love" for the first time. The separation anxiety is intense. It will never, can never be like this again. The ties to childhood are breaking; the act of falling in love is the giant step in renouncing parental security, in becoming an adult. To fall in love is to leave the physical image of one's parents and turn to a new person.

One falls in love with joy and longing, fear and anger, helplessness and abandonment. Frequently one chooses a most unsuitable person for the first breaking away; otherwise it would seem too final. Sexual excitement is inspired by the rage to leave, to start one's own life, to touch the new person. The need to be close to the protecting lover as parent and, conversely, the need to reciprocate the role of protecting parent are justified by the demands of the genitalia. The sexual can even become the conspicuous, but actually secondary, motive for the high fury.

Erotic gratification alone could not provoke such stormy feelings. Most people who fall in love have masturbated for a considerable time, and are accustomed to quick, reflex satisfaction whenever they want it. Most of us have also been exposed to a wide variety of other sexual stimulation which has not led to falling in love. Adolescents today kiss and fondle and have all manner of experimental sexual activity, frequently including intercourse. Yet we do not fall in love until we suspect we are ready to leave our parents, and unless we are capable of making a new, dependent attachment. Many people feel that the act of falling in love frees people to give sexuality its most unified meaning.

In the ideal progression, if marriage results, any threat to the union will deepen it. Separation anxiety will intensify the longing to be together, whip sexuality to its most sensual expression. Apartness caused by work will intensify reunions. If a person has to travel to sell a product, perform a part, lecture or speak at a conference, the return home will stir the most poignant and voluptuous feelings. Difficulties with children will only create a firmer bonding. Each separation may give rise to the same compelling, primitive need for a pleasurable, comforting, and reassuring union through sex.

As the child experiences the anguish of separating from parents, so, in time, the parent faces what appears to be desertion by the child. The young adult leaves home for college, for marriage, for parenthood. Mother and father, left behind, hold on to each other in special devotion. The empty nest may become a new and sexier boudoir. Parents may truly begin to know each other, alone together after so many years.

Our final severance occurs in death. The deaths one may experience in the course of life are so various as to be entirely bewildering. Death can project us into a state of emotional nakedness that rivals any newborn, meconium-covered infant, slippery and red in the doctor's hands. Grandparents, parents, children, friends, brothers, sisters, uncles, aunts, cousins—each year exacts its lives; passing time invites new sicknesses and terrors.

Perhaps the greatest intimacy of an ideal marriage is to turn to sex in death and loss and grief. To go to a funeral is to have sex afterward, if you can. Sex in marriage is the darkest and the best, a celebration of life's most capricious glory and its most permanent sorrow, when one faces separation from existence itself.

2

Attachment and Separation

Perfect marriage, in which sexual ardor increases along with the years that bring the philosophic mind, seems rather hard to come by. Packing suitcases to leave home apparently keeps people busier these days than accumulating the wisdom to stay there.

We are familiar with the height of the divorce statistics, the range of marital discord, and the estimate that at least 50 percent of all existing marriages suffer sexual despair. Why can't we all remember our infantile bliss, depend on each other appropriately, and help each other to survive in permanent pairs?

The fact is, we don't even know if mankind is a pair-bonding species of animal! Scientists, familiar with radio signals from distant stars, interplanetary voyages, and the mutations of time, have given us no answer as to whether or not we go, or should have gone, two by two into the ark. Before we destroy ourselves with our complex weaponry, it does seem as though we ought to be able to murmur something more definitive about our mating preferences to the intelligences of the future who will inspect our time capsules. Even if we are so ignorant and bumbling that we can't figure out how we are put together and what makes us work, after so many thousands of years of being here we ought not still to be muddling through such basic issues as our mysterious mating patterns.

To suggest an approach, the quality which distinguishes us from cows, lions, amoebae, and baboons, is that we probably have no fixed, biologically programmed pattern. Our sexual habits appear to be governed, or influenced, more by what goes on around us and what we think than by some implacable timetable. Whether this sets us above other animals, or only confuses us more, is a dilemma. Certainly it gives us an opportunity to invest our joy with meaning and grandeur. I suppose we each have to judge for ourselves whether that is carrying *hubris* too far.

Our sexual paradise does not become automatic because—as humans—we habitually invent such odd ways to defeat nature. We must be so ingenious to survive without fur or fangs, wings, claws, or prehensile tails that we sometimes get too clever and make ourselves miserable. One of our tendencies has been to attempt to keep from touching our young. We are gradually learning that keeping our hands off accomplishes very little. But it is characteristically human to have to learn this rather than to have known it all along.

With our dim-witted brilliance, we devised the most complicated and tortuous systems to reduce the powerful imprint of early touch bonding. Of course, we are coming around to discarding them now, but that only proves how far we are from being in harmony with our "nature." For years we have removed infants from their mothers at birth and placed them in sterile isolation. We have actually thought it an advance to feed them a substance called "formula" from bottles with rubber nipples. For sleep, we threw away the cradles and invested in motionless beds with bars. We forbade our young to sleep near us lest we should wish to have sexual relations with them or they should later wish to have sexual relations with us. We put them in playpens and harnesses and toted them about in plastic carriers, like packages. If someone hadn't protested, we should probably have raised them in laboratories and killed off the weak ones. In fact, we've tried various versions of that scheme, from Sparta to Nazi Germany. People are generally no more programmed for child raising than they are for mating.

We may advance one hypothesis about early deprivation of touch. Very likely, it interferes with later ability to enjoy voluptuous sensuality. It may be that much of our inability to caress and hold each other these days comes from childhood insufficiency. The fact that so many people in this decade come to the doctor for assistance with taking pleasure in being touched bears quiet testimony to this tragedy.

Beyond simple touch, however, we must consider the patterns of personality and relationships which people develop after exposure to parental vagaries. In the real world, parents frequently create children who cannot trust and depend sufficiently to have happy and singular marriages. Parents may, themselves, have unfortunate combinations of the major personality traits. Some may have pattern disorders. Others may be psychotic, either regularly or at intervals. And even if both parents are perfectly charming, consistent, and loving, they hardly prepare a person for the odd lot of outsiders who will require being coped with. Most everyone has a particular way of helping a child to separate. Often this becomes an exclusion, making the child feel unwanted, unworthy, somehow less than an entire being. This is the currency of anger at separation which breeds difficulty in forming a positive sexual ego.

Touch bonding comes first, frequently inadequate, nervous, and conflicted, but still a primal bond. Attachment—the recognition of parent figures—comes next. Simultaneously, also, children become aware of their parents' rejection and separation behavior. Thus a personality pattern is evoked which forms the matrix for future relationships involving touch, attachment, and separation. For example, authoritarian, aggressive, punitive parents can begin a child's life in the usual way: by feeding, holding, hugging, stroking, and diapering. The child then recognizes its parent—feels attached. But soon that important figure is hurting, preventing, ordering, punishing. The resultant may take a number of directions. A child may grow up to feel unworthy of having a sexual partner, undeserving of touch and pleasure. Such parents may also produce someone who cannot enjoy sex unless humiliated in much the same way that he or she received parental attention. Another possible result is the creation of an equally aggressive mimic, who mistakes giving punishment for giving love and can only have sex if there is some subjugation to it.

What stimulates bears an intimate connection to the transactions of childhood. The way a parent handles emotional attachment and separation will affect what turns a person on or off in later life. Supreme sexual exaltation through loving marital dependence can hardly be a consequence of having been subtly or overtly frightened, neglected, punished, berated, ignored, or otherwise abused.

Researchers tell us that children suffering separation from their mothers first protest angrily, then cry in despair, and finally become emotionally detached. When mother returns, they behave indifferently. They do not risk a return to the old closeness. Clearly, when parents have sufficiently abused their children's sensibilities, wittingly or not, a permanent derangement or detachment of feeling will take place. Nor will the children easily be able to invest themselves in others. Sexuality will be most free in those situations which do not call for emotional attachment. If the damage to sexual ego is great enough, sexual excitement under any social circumstance may be impossible. We only feel sexual when we are anxiety free. Feeling close may provoke too much unconscious fear of being deserted.

After being shaped in the parental crucible, our characters may tend toward attachment to others, detachment from others, or some ambivalent mixture which we must resolve. People who prefer to be solidly bonded to others usually crave to protect or to be protected. They like to depend, to feel as if someone is there as the Bible describes, to lift them when they fall down. "Two are better than one."

The craving to dominate or submit also promotes attachment. Some people only feel the intensity of their sexual power when they are firmly, indisputably in charge, even causing their vassal to suffer the indignities of their rule. Others respond with their best orgasms when submitting to fair or even to unfair government. Safety lies in union, in belonging, pleasant or not. Those who like to depend, or those who are seriously concerned with having or giving true power, take to monogamy as their most exciting sexual life-style. Whether the key ingredient is the thrill of total possession or the fear of loss, it seems to be enough to stir both sexual heat and sexual loyalty. Such people tend to have character traits which are primarily dependent, aggressive, or obsessive-compulsive. Certain people with paranoid tendencies may be monogamists, too, distrusting everyone but their spouse.

At the other end of the spectrum are the people whose upbringing has taught them either the virtues or the necessity of detachment. When this is ego syntonic, or experienced as a positive quality, the person takes pride in "not needing" anyone. To feel possessiveness, or jealousy, is experienced as an infantile absurdity which every adult must outgrow as soon as possible, or be considered hopelessly juvenile. When the sexual ego is built on such a foundation, monogamy can hardly be the answer. To be able to go from one person to another without feeling torn and mutilated is the aim, one which has cost much pain in the progress out of the nest. Lovers may come and go. Being able to have a different one each night can be seen as a culmination, an achievement. Jealousy, dependence, and attachment seem the barbarities of a civilization in its infancy.

People whose sexuality is entirely detached from any bonding behavior—and there are surprisingly large numbers in this category—do best, obviously, in mobile sexual situations. However, society has not yet accepted them as being quite normal. Most keep their feeling, or lack of it, quite hidden. Some pretend to make bonds with others and embark on foolish marital fiascos. A few turn to prostitution. Many engage in "liberated" sexuality. They have even tried to proselytize the joys of having "purely" sexual recreation though disease has become an increasing deterrent. Even so, they continue their sexual play. Many have become scientists in the field of sex research. Their detachment is peculiarly suited to the effort.

Beyond detachment are withdrawal, distrust, and, finally, absence of interest. In these states, people often stay away from sexual relations altogether because the implications are too painful. Pathology replaces defense, and the sexual ego is crippled by severe paranoia or forms of schizophrenia.

Personality traits which appear most suited to the life of emotional detachment are the narcissistic and the schizoid. These people manage sex without affection very well. Since compulsiveness can assume many forms, certain obsessives are also able to experience their most intense sexual moments when they do not particularly care about anyone. Perhaps these very intelligent people are the ones who, thoughout history, have been telling us that sex is a separately functioning system. In any event, they are all rather poor candidates for monogamy, nowadays, though they often suffered it in the past.

Relationship patterns that mix attachment and detachment are the most complex and difficult. They cause infinite conflict. They are the subject of almost every piece of literature ever written directly or indirectly about sexual practices. They exist when a person divides his or her dependence and sexuality between two or more different people. To be more precise, a mixed pattern generally exists when a married person engages in either open or secret hanky-panky with one or more third parties.

Most commonly, devotees of the mixed pattern enjoy a marriage or some other living arrangement which approximates a marriage. This satisfies the need for attachment and security, and also offers moderate sexual pleasure. Outside of this relationship, there may be a singular lover or mistress who provides sexual ectasy. There may be a series of "romantic" infatuations which cause a good deal of high excitement at intervals. There may be indiscriminate and detached sexuality. Or there may be a little bit of everything.

Why is this pattern so popular? It used to be the basis for the male double standard, but recently women have been adopting it with equal, if not greater, zeal. How does it develop? Since it is so widespread a *modus vivendi*, should it not be formalized more explicitly? Is "open marriage" a solution?

The fact is that separation begins quietly and ineluctably soon after marriage. Most of us, in whom the capacity for attachment has been reduced by gentle degrees, if not by brute force, respond to this separation according to the personalities we have long since developed. Our response determines the future of the marriage, affectionally and sexually.

The separations that begin after marriage are subtle compared to being left at school for the first time or leaving home for college. Jobs require that people stay apart for most of the day. They usually begin when the honeymoon—that brief recapitulation of prekindergarten days—is over. Some work involves more prolonged absence: selling, acting, lecturing, flying to business conferences, traveling to the moon. While people must earn, and few would choose to remain together all day every day, a change of the marital ambience has begun to occur.

When children are born, the separation is even more concealed: after all, a child is the visible symptom of a close relationship. But there is a shift of attention away from each other and toward the newly arrived person. The rift increases. In-law intrusion may exacerbate the schism. In the early years of marriage both work and the incessant demands of young children place a huge burden of emotional isolation on both partners. Yet they seem more unified than ever, by parenthood, responsibilities, problems of survival. They are often hardly aware of being apart.

At this critical juncture, certain married people begin to lose sexual interest in each other. They are mystified and confused by lessening of feeling. Some take refuge in the old adages: the honeymoon is over. Others consider the contributions of more convoluted thinkers—perhaps they are suffering the Oedipus complex. Their mate has become a parent, and they are unconsciously repressing the incest taboo or the fear of retaliation which reduces the attraction. Each marital partner is being rejected in a thousand ways and even when there is no overt conflict. It feels, indeed, the way rejection by and separation from parents felt. The response—often attraction to another person—is the product of a great many years of prior training in moving away from old attachments.

The types of people most likely to experience sexual stirring as a response to separation run a wide gamut. Most obvious are the histrionics who must retain their emotional "base" while they experience varying degrees of excitement for others. Almost any small parting will make them desperately lonely. Often histrionics are women, but more and more men are dramatizing themselves these days.

Passive-aggressive people are less obvious and probably more numerous. Angered by their separation, they retaliate in secret fulfillment of their needs. Ordinarily, they don't know what they are doing. They are the last to observe that they are meting out payment for their anguish by committing stealthy, uncivil, and very exciting deeds.

Obsessives, of course, fit into all categories. They tend to become extramaritally infatuated. A third person occupies so much of their thought and fantasy that they need not experience or confront the pain of their marital distance. They live in a dream of meeting and embracing, of considering what they will say, wear, think, do, of perpetual thought about all the details of future satisfaction. The present, with all its discomforts and frustrations, need not exist at all. They can keep it up for a lifetime, and often do. The rest of the classic types are the more detached people, who have married in response to societal pressure, or under the brief spell of an illusion that they could become dependent. If they are narcissistic and exhibitionistic, their partners will know about their activities and either condone them or not. Being attached only to themselves, they usually couldn't care less what their married roommate thinks. The schizoid adventurer may be so detached that he or she hardly knows what is happening. Somehow or other they always find themselves in bed with a new person, without preconceived intention or active plan. It simple feels good, and there is no desire either to harm or to love. When detachment turns to fear, the schizoid stays home, but most of those who are out on the street engage in sex without the least connection to any emotional reality.

Should partners share their extramarital lives with each other in "open" marriage? Of course, if both are detached sorts of people for whom the union is a path to wider experience. People who do not comprehend jealousy, possessiveness, and all the rest of the attachment feelings are especially suited. Whether expansive discovery of many people is morally superior to cultivating exclusive closeness with one person can hardly be an issue.

If one person, however, is a strict monogamist, the other, who wants to share his or her secret loves, had best wear a breastplate, bring along a lawyer, and make a reservation at the nearest psychiatric institution.

Since the uses of extramarital sex are so various—retaliation, denial, satisfaction of immature needs for constant love and admiration—"telling" each other most often does not enhance "communication." It generally starts open warfare. A compulsive wife, at home with three small children and the scar from her Caesarean section, will hardly find it titillating to know that her husband fell to the charms of a pink-nippled young secretary. A dedicated husband, working round the clock to support his utopia, his suburban home, his beach house, his ski house, the maid, and his four children at private school, will not ruminate with great delight about his wife's affair with the ski instructor. "Open" marriage is for those who can handle it—the detached, the independent, the recreation seekers. Sometimes it is helpful to those who do not yet understand their sexuality. "Closed" marriage, with its clandestine complexities, is also only for those who can handle it. Of course, it might be simpler if we all knew a little more about staying close, about being perfectly monogamous, but the world does not seem to be moving in that direction. Touch bonding, attachment, and separation, then, very likely form the nucleus for personality traits in general, and sexual personality in particular. Do we trust that another person will receive and return what we give? Do we suspect that they will ignore, abuse, take without thanks or reciprocity, discard, or ridicule our offerings? If we anticipate rejection of any kind, how will we defend against it? The mechanisms of defense cluster to create those typical ways of handling problems and approaching new situations which form the rudiments of character.

To be sexually paranoid is, in part, to believe that another person will harm one in some way by erotic contact. At some early time, it is likely that the touch of a major parental figure was extraordinarily unpleasant—nervous, rough, inconsistent—that attachment was never satisfactorily accomplished, and that separation was not well defined.

In severely dependent personalities, touch bonding and attachment have been too close, too intense. Often people cannot even break the bonds enough to move on, but remain a child in the home. Sometimes they do make a transference and later they form sexual dependencies of such force that all else in life is meaningless. Conversely, severe dependence often develops in people whose bonds were quite unsatisfactory but who, responding to some other salutory experience that gave them a glimpse of security, find in their mates a substitute for early love. These are the adults most vulnerable to the collapse of sexual ego when a partner is unfaithful.

Whether sexual paranoia, dependence, withdrawal, exuberance, exhibitionism, or any other trait emerges appears very much related, in clinical practice and retrospectively, to the nature of primary parental contact. Later societal and developmental experiences can alter the initial response, but the formative imprint remains the same.

Sex feels best when there is some connection, no matter how remote, indirect, or paradoxical, with the most powerful early ties. If lullabies, holding, and rocking were the best of babyhood, then it is likely that an adult will find music, even "rock" music, an erotic accompaniment to motions associated with copulation. If a child has been held, and read verse, one could anticipate some stimulation from romantic poetry. Since pornography, however, is not a usual parental means of amusing children, its relationship to sexual excitement has to be paradoxical. Nursery sounds and feelings are difficult to equate to black garter belts, bare bottoms, and boots. However, enjoying pornography, prostitution, and all the rest of the sexuality that is still classified as sinful appears to relate quite concisely to the vicissitudes of attachment and separation. The lady in boots, as sophisticated people now know, may represent an equivalent of stern maternal discipline, a paradoxical form of love.

As for those who equate sexual ecstasy with religious sentiment, it is an old habit to turn to heaven when one cannot find a sustaining love on earth. Indeed, some say that is what belief is all about.

The answers to questions about sexual pleasure, however, are frequently more complex than these abbreviated generalizations. A rounded view of the subject demands inspection of the deterrents as well as the stimulants. In the chapters that follow, I will examine the sexual egos of people who possess each of the major personality traits, as well as the effects on sexuality of neurotic mood trends like depression. Though I do not propose specific resolutions to doubts and difficulties, I offer these chapters to help clarify individual dilemmas and to suggest directions that an aware human being may take toward sexual fulfillment.

Part II

PERSONALITY TRAITS AND SEXUAL BEHAVIOR

3

Dependency:
Sexual Reliance

Nothing could be more obvious than that we must depend on one another for survival. It has been suggested, indeed, that the human race is like a vast colony of ants or a formation of birds in flight. We walk, fly, swim, and ride around this globe, doing for ourselves and one another like a single organism with billions of parts. Sometimes, when disease occurs, we kill off parcels of ourselves: in wars, atrocity chambers, ideological disputes. Basically, however, at least thus far, we have agreed to keep the majority of our world self alive. To do this we must trust, rely, cooperate.

Healthy dependence is clearly the key to ultimate human survival. In the world, as between two people, it is remarkably difficult to achieve. For the most part, we all have a vulnerability to at least one of the pathological features of dependency. To be dependently ill is to avoid responsibility and decision making, to be unable to tolerate criticism, to fear being alone, to be incapable of self-assertion, and to need reassurance at all times. However, whether we are so feeble-willed as to require care in a public institution, or only tempted now and then to give our better selves to the rule of others, it seems axiomatic that dependence, healthy or pathological, promotes sexual union. It does not necessarily create or improve sexual pleasure. Dependent relations can be devoid of ecstasy. Yet the need to rely on or submit to someone else frequently finds expression in sexual intercourse.

Four major forms of dependence appear to arouse copulation behavior in humans. On the positive side, social dependence, or the terror of being alone, sends people rushing headlong into marriage or to the nearest bar for a night's company. Economic dependence and sexual gymnastics have a high correlation. A parental type of dependence, the expectation that someone else will give helpful orders, care, instruction, and advancement, stimulates considerable erotic sensation.

On the negative side, pain dependence—the craving to receive hurt, either physical or emotional—seems to be one of the most powerful aphrodisiacs of all time. This is often related to the sadism with which many parents expressed their concern. Children accustomed to having their bodies or sensibilities abused tend to preserve their punishments in later life by forming relationships which imitate early models. Security has become associated with pain.

Both receiving gratification of dependent needs and giving it can be immensely arousing. Those who derive satisfaction from supporting, parenting, or inflicting pain on people who would be better off without these attentions generally demonstrate that form of dependency which underlies aggressive character traits.

Social dependence can lead to promiscuity, monogamy, or selective sexuality. Psychiatrists have concentrated major efforts on curing promiscuous women of the need to say "yes" to sexual proposals simply because they were afraid to be alone or needed to be held. This insecurity used to be most prevalent among women who would defeat their material ambitions by being too easily led into bed. If men could have them for sex, they would not want them for love. While it might do nothing for sexual pleasure, mental health meant being staunch enough to resist encroachment by a fulsome penis in the service of more deliberate goals.

In an era when standards were different, this was indeed the way to greater emotional autonomy.

Women can still become promiscuous by having sexual relations out of loneliness. So can men. We continue to recognize the process more in women than in men, perhaps because women are more ashamed of it. They become depressed about it, even though most men no longer are so foolish as to discard a fine bedmate for her moral impurities. Men tend to take pride in numbers, no matter what their motivation for achieving a high score. Women continue to receive societal approval for intelligent selection from a limited experience. Very likely, from time to time, most of us have had sex or are tempted to have it out of simple loneliness. Our gregarious need drives us with a strength that is quite out of proportion to any rational requirement. Only when having sex for company becomes a compulsion that destroys other goals and purposes is it an action that requires professional intervention.

Social dependence can lead to sexual monogamy in both the best and the worst sense. At its best, two people trust and rely on each other for a satisfaction that strengthens them against all of life's accidents and disasters. Though too few attain this ideal, it certainly seems worth our finest efforts.

At monogamy's worst, couples can remain in lifeless pacts for mechanical release, or none at all, merely because they are afraid to chance the isolation of being apart, the awful moments when they must be alone in the search for a better love. Dependence on the reliable presence of another person can be strong enough to destroy all possibility of human happiness. It is both our greatest danger, if the marriage is bad, and our greatest source of courage, if the marriage is good.

Sexual selectivity, of course, seems the most hopeful consequence of our social need for sex. Making a choice of one partner or many, based on intimate understanding and a desire for mutual welfare, we may come to reasonable terms with a morality that is suited to today's freedom. Old-world cynics may scoff at the notion that men will ever give up the drive for conquest, or that women will ever be free of a need to be abused. New-world liberationists will insist that the desire for sex, no matter what its motive, is reason enough to have it. Perhaps there is a better way.

Economic dependence, or the promise of it, has an all-time reputation for inspiring sexual union. On the grander scale, the jeweled crowns of Majesty, Excellence, Emperor, and Great Khan have traditionally excited women. Wealth has the power to stimulate vaginal lubrication in many women who will admit to it, and in many more who will not. Wealth also incites male erections, although confessing this erotogenic effect is very bad form. In any event, in past centuries, kingdoms united through sexual emissaries, great lands merged, dowers bound merchant families, possessions were considered due cause for sexual bewitchment. No one objected to the inflammatory nature of riches until recently when, with democracy, hunting gold from any place but the hills of California became not only a religious sin but also an antiegalitarian activity. People long ago gave up their fear of divine retribution for acquisitiveness, even for avarice, but fear of human punishment, as meted out to those in the tumbrils of the French Revolution, has somewhat reduced the lust for empire.

If money stirs equal fortunes to mate for the power and security of it all, the amorous longings created in the hearts of the poor are so great as not to be spoken. Nor does the possessor of the gold have to be pompously rich. He or she need only have more or earn more than the seeker to create dependence. A salesgirl can have as mighty an attraction to the store manager as any moderately prosperous widow to her wise and well-heeled investment counselor. Women's wealth, however, is most effective as a quiet fortune, a trust, a bank account, a portfolio. To elicit ardor, male "face" must usually be maintained. The woman who obviously earns more than her potential lovers may experience some difficulty in finding suitors, since men tend to become depressed when it is plain to the world that they are not financially superior. However, in our era of economic stress, this old mystique appears to be changing.

While it may seem a self-evident platitude that riches and sexual excitement are often related, people in search of their own unique aphrodisiacs seem either to have forgotten the adages or to have denied them completely.

Women who come for therapy of their recently developed "low libido" often mention, in passing, that their husbands have lost their jobs, or an equivalent fortune. Men lose interest when, incidentally, their wives' investments have plummeted.

Nor need the wealth belong necessarily to a partner to devastate by its absence. It is well known that financial loss causes depression. Sex therapists have found depression, either overt or covert, to be a leading cause of impotence in men and low libido in women. Therefore, it is of critical importance to assess the relationship between economic dependence and sexuality and to give it the due status it merits as a motivating force in viable sexual unions.

Women have no penile barometer to measure the relationship between finances and libido, but we can be sure that they, too, become depressed by their own losses, if their personalities find security in having means. Security, and particularly financial security, does allow sexual excitement to develop. Safety promises freedom from anxiety, and sex is always best in anxiety-free situations. Beyond safety, riches promise vacation idylls, sensuous clothes, luxurious foods—all the trappings and circumstances of sexual pleasure. Except for young love, or illicit love, which can both flourish vigorously in a tenement, the more seasoned variety seems to do better on a moonlit yacht in the Mediterranean. Or at least a Caribbean cruise.

Even when economic dependence does not arouse passion to any solar heat, it often encourages performance of the sexual act. Afraid to lose their life-support systems, women will consent to sex whether they enjoy it or not. So will a great many men. As the world well knows, there may be little difference between a prostitute or a gigolo and a well-furred wife, a bejeweled mistress, or a man whose English tailor owes his livelihood to the lady. The world knows a bit less about the couples who cleave together because one partner's job provides a food allowance that might otherwise need to be supplied by a welfare system that is difficult to tap these days.

Dating patterns and their relationship to economics have also undergone some recently confusing changes. The old dilemma concerned whether or not a woman should feel guilty about not having sex when a man treated her well. If she felt excited by his largesse, the guilt was made more painful by the message in her loins. Sometimes the conflict drove women to avoidance and sexual repression. More often, they simply gave in to the old devil sin, took the presents, and didn't much enjoy the sex.

Today, with women paying their own way, the old trouble crops up less frequently. The new trouble is the difficulty many women find in becoming aroused unless they feel securely dependent. They also often tend to resent men whom they support half or all of the way, no matter now much they intellectually wish to feel otherwise. Men also are often at pains to become aroused unless they provide. Though the new system makes it easier for dependent people to decide not to have sex, it may only be because the old stimulation is missing. Though that may be just as well, in preparation for a future when everyone shoulders an equal share of the burden, we have not yet found a love potion to replace the antique brew of talents and shekels that made Mammon so sexy.

Human reliance on greater powers assumes many forms. Whether the power is supernatural, institutional, or personal, investigators of the psyche suggest that the original model for dependence is the parent-child relationship.

Being nourished by our parents teaches us to expect care and sustenance from people of higher status, or even from awesome religious colossi. The consequence of such trust may be high spiritual exaltation, pleasant security, or servile misery. Whatever the governance or the conditions, sexual arousal seems to be a frequent companion of the relationship between the ruler and the ruled. It can be exciting both to dominate and to obey.

The connection between sex and religion, while not inevitable, has certainly been observed. From the active worship of Eros and Aphrodite to the ultimate asceticism of a nun taking the vows of marriage, sexual union as a reality or a symbol enhances the attraction of the divine.

Men of power have long known their aphrodisiac effect on certain women. A stocky, bespectacled gentleman like Henry Kissinger would seem to lack the distinguishing physical appointments of Robert Redford. Nonetheless, he seemed to enjoy his reign as a national sex symbol. Previous to his marriage, his name was identified with some of the most ravishing women of our time, both physically and intellectually. He defined it himself by stating, "Power is the ultimate aphrodisiac."

As they rise in society, women are discovering their erotic queenship. A successful professional woman confessed to me, after several sessions, that she was involved with a series of young men: blond-haired, blue-eyed Ivy Leaguers. "Precisely the type who had ignored me in college," she said, "but now find my power irresistible. They fetch for me, and they wait on me, and accept my sexual ministrations as a gift." Unlike the man of power, this woman was troubled enough by her prowess to report it to a psychiatrist rather than to the press.

While a dependent relationship is at its sexual zenith, however, phychiatrists are rarely called for consultation. When a woman wants instruction, support, or advancement from a mentor and finds her genitals involved in the quest, she does not usually seek help if sexual gratification accompanies other receipts. It is a common experience among female students who are attracted to teachers that when the father figure looms in regular classroom sessions the attraction is strong enough to provide flattering and exciting sex. The teacher exists more as a symbol than a reality. Once the semester is over, the enchantments often diminish. It is not nearly so satisfactory to be courted by a lover who suddenly appears as he was all along, perhaps aged, perhaps bitter, and even trapped in a modest profession.

The old formulae, happily or not for the new sexual ideology, appear to work for many people who want to understand more only when the excitement disappears or when they have been frustrated, disappointed, or deceived. Psychiatry begins by pointing out that they have expected magical fulfillment of infantile wishes, as indeed they have.

When the power dies, too often the sex goes with it. A female patient, encouraged by her physician husband, went to medical school. When she had been a housewife, she had basked in his reflected glory. As a student, she responded with sexual gratitude to his tutelage. However, once established as an attending member at a prestigious hospital, she complained that the sexual magic was gone. "I find myself attracted to other men," she said. "I feel rotten about it. He helped me achieve independence, and now when I no longer need him, I find I'm no longer attracted to him, either."

Unfortunately, dependent gratitude is often much more of an aphrodisiac than independent thanks. This is, indeed, a sore and often tragic point in the dynamics of human sexual relationship. We would like to believe that love between equals is the richest love of all, but so often the intricacies of personality deny this ideal. It is one of the risks we take when we dare to grow and change.

One of the most common misappropriations of the words "sexual boredom" is also frequently due to a shift in dependency relationships. "My wife helped me set up my business. She worked with me, kept the house, and was everything I wanted in bed, too. I could never have made it without her. I needed her for fifteen years, but now I find her boring. My secretary doesn't have half her character, but she's the one I want to sleep with."

What an otherwise intelligent and thoughtful person attributes to the romantic cliché of physical attraction is, in reality, the attraction of another, more powerful dependency relationship. The man no longer needs his wife because it is his secretary upon whom he relies for both his office needs and the bracing satisfaction of feeling young again. Dependency is power, whether it is exercised deliberately or intuitively.

It is only a small step from the secure excitement of being ruled to the masochism of finding sexual pleasure in pain. Recapturing bliss by submission to indignity extends dependency to a final limit. Safety lies in hurtful contact with someone who represents a parental figure. In some way, all the masochistic behavior I have clinically observed appears related to a perverted expression of parental attention.

In bed, dependency more often leads to erotic extinction than to an eternal flame of passion. Sex may begin with such fervor that even touching fingertips will spread a total body message. The initial phase can carry a high spirit of anticipation, an illusion that the sorcery of character, pocketbook, or hierarchal position, will alleviate all woes. When troubles resume anyway, sex seems an impostor.

By contrast to the excitement of some dependencies, others are too frightening to particular people to stimulate passion. Submissive fear overwhelms the coital act and prevents the growth of pleasure. Dependent men are heavily susceptible to impotence; helpless women often can hardly become excited, much less attain satisfaction. As they are afraid to assert themselves in life, so they are afraid in bed.

They cannot say what they want: they might offend or reverse the roles of dominance. They cannot do what they want: unexpected action might provoke intolerable criticism. Indeed, the illness may go so far in bed as to preclude all self-knowledge. Subservient people may not even feel permitted to understand their needs or to do anything about them. Making decisions about when, where, and how to have sex are too much responsibility, too great an assertion of a self that hardly exists. To be aroused is to desire, and to desire is beyond the capacity of someone who can only passively obey.

In the beginning of such relationships, there may be considerable sexual activity, in fear of loss. Without gratification, after a time, the effort may become pointless. If the marriage begins to feel secure enough, sexual activity may entirely disappear. If the dependent person realizes he or she has been duped, been too willing to ascribe to others qualities they do not possess, all pretense to reciprocity through sex may be abandoned.

Dependence, then, is at once a keen stimulant to sexual appetite and its most potent depressant. Since it neither can nor should be eradicated from our disposition, the answer seems to lie in that sensitive balance between reliance and self-government which is essential to sexual liberty.

4

Histrionic Display:
Sexual Theater

"All the world's a stage," Shakespeare declared, but did not add that the cast of characters always bills the histrionic personality in huge letters. The rest of us are merely bit players, stagehands, and mechanics, whether or not we know it or like it. Not love or work but drama is the essence of life to our self-selected stars. How much attention can they get for their performance? Can they also manipulate plays within plays? How many roles can they handle at once?

They address the best of their talent to the scenarios of love. When in full dress, and performing well, they can convince each person upon whom they radiate their charm that he or she is the most important, most valuable human being on earth. If they direct their energy to husband or wife, for that moment the gullible spouse is king of the universe or queen of the Nile. Meanwhile, a series of lovers may believe themselves to be the very incarnations of all the world's joy, the only spirits of true pleasure to inhabit an otherwise morbid globe. Nor could the histrionic live without friends—the only real affections being camaraderie and loyalty. But children are the highest peak experience; no relationship on earth is so fulfilling. A psychotherapist, of course, is the very personification of love's divinity. The only price exacted from others for the privilege of being considered so wonderful is that they have few troubles of their own, talk sparingly, give endless time, and most of all, be moved to tears, laughter, fear, or anguish by the plight or wit of the grandest entertainer of them all.

Seduction is the primary art of the histrionic character. When that is successful, all goes well. However, it would take a master magician to seduce everybody all the time, without arousing jealousies, disbelief, competition for center stage, and other unpleasant emotions. The game plan has to fail, and usually it does so rather early. Sometimes, it never works at all.

To compensate, the histrionic turns to less artful but more direct maneuvers for attention. He or she makes it clear that nothing anyone can give will ever be enough. Love, time, sympathy, affection, presents, rewards—all are limited, lacking zest, spontaneity, and really warm feeling. Furthermore, no one else suffers so much in the tragedy of life, which has chosen to inflict singular devastations upon this one poor soul. Tears of outrage at the cruel world alternate with helpless smiles of Christian resignation as the martyrdom proceeds. Every obstacle is an Everest, any triumph a miracle against insuperable odds. Temper tantrums are spaced between periods of despair and glorious rays of hope. Life with a histrionic, whether he or she has only a few of the traits or develops into a totally disordered personality, is never dull.

The distinguishing traits are, therefore, an insatiable and dramatic quest for attention, great demands on others' resources, and an emotional intensity out of all proportion to the stimulus.

More women than men make drama out of life, since it has traditionally been men's role to respond with cool behavior in crisis. A man who shouts "Oh, my God," and bursts into tears on getting a flat tire might be towed away instead of the car. There are, however, male heterosexual histrionics. Heavily identified with the "feminine," they nevertheless make love to women, usually "masculine" types. Most male histrionics find homosexuality more appealing.

In the past, dramatic, demanding, and highly emotional women were loosely and pejoratively classified as "hysterical." Considerable confusion existed about the term because it refers, in its most well-defined psychiatric sense, to a neurotic condition in which a psychophysiological difficulty, such as fear of sexuality, is represented by a bodily sign such as paralysis or anesthesia.

This condition, hysterical "conversion" of a fear into a bodily symptom, was largely a woman's disorder; hysteria was almost an exclusively feminine category. The name itself derived from the Greek word for womb. In ancient times, women's emotional difficulties were presumed to stem from the wanderings of this "erratic" and mindless organ through the bodies of those who didn't have sense enough to commmand it securely in place.

In those first loose designations of the highly emotional woman as "hysterical," it was also presumed that her excesses resulted from inhibited sexuality. No matter how sexually seductive she might appear, the wise psychiatrist knew she had severe sexual problems. Today, the newly classified "histrionic" may or may not have sexual inhibition. Most often she does, but sometimes she is quite sexually active and responsive. What distinguishes her from her sociopathic sister is that she does not deliberately use her sexuality for permanent gain. Even if she has acquired an advantage through use of her body charm, she is more apt to discard it impulsively than to add it to her collection.

Recognizing a histrionic female is far easier than detecting her male counterpart. Her appearance is usually the first clue. She is likely to bleach her hair. Twenty years ago, her breasts rose above a décolletage that was deliberately a trifle too scant, or they protruded in forthright announcement under a sweater. Today, the nipples and fullness below are frequently displayed beneath some clinging fabric, if not revealed under a long, loose neckline. If less can be worn, she wears it. Bright colors are her favorites: a profusion of pinks, reds, and yellows attract like posters for a carnival or a parade. Yet in spite of the florid surface, one can't mistake her for a prostitute, or even dismiss her as vulgar. Beneath the dazzle, she moves and talks with an indefinable pathos that approaches dignity. She's hard to puzzle out.

The woman seems to be gay; she flatters, admires, amazes. She laughs a great deal and often seems to be arriving from a cocktail party at ten in the morning—that is, if she's not having an early morning cry while telling you, with equal gusto, about life's abuses. The abuses follow a routinely similar pattern. All complain most of the emotional distance of their mates. Their men are cold, orderly, too involved in business; they never remember the little things, never bring flowers. There is no communication in the marriage—their husbands never say anything interesting, never express a feeling.

Sexually, the most frequent complaint of histrionic wives is that their husbands are either poor lovers or impotent. This is hardly surprising, since the women demand so much that it is clearly impossible ever to satisfy them. If the physical techniques are adequate, they feel the men do not verbalize enough, do not say "I love you" with sufficient passion and frequency. However, rarely do they feel their men's caresses are any more effective than the automated pats of mechanical hands. "He has no subtlety, no finesse. It's like going to bed with a computer. Three minutes of rubbing and kissing, one minute on the clitoris, and then he gets in and pumps away until he comes. As soon as it's over, he goes and washes himself. What am I, contaminated?"

While it is true that most histrionic women do tend to marry compulsive men, one usually finds their complaints ill-founded, although they seem so convincing. Most often, the men who have not become impotent have given up trying to please. They have settled for a routine that they feel should meet their wives' demands. Should they continue to try to please, something would always be wrong, and they would lose what little virility they retain.

With all the fireworks, one would think that the women, themselves, were sexual dynamos, but that is rarely the case. Most of the time they are able to become aroused, but many cannot take sexual initiative or attain orgasm. There seems to be a common fear that should they become sexually competent, their seductiveness might then lead them into facing real situations which they cannot handle. They want to maintain the attention of being stimulated, followed by due respect for their moans of frustration when they do not climax. They could not bear the loss of focus on their misery should they allow that they have been sated.

At their seductive best, some histrionics live highly eventful lives full of staged passions and petty deceptions. They may move from one role to the next, suffering brief infatuations and quick tragic endings. Volatile and charming, often dependent on a single steady "anchor" for their lives, a mate who enjoys their show, they can sometimes muddle their way through the years without causing excessive damage. A few battered lives, perhaps, but no tragic disasters.

However, the need for attention is usually too great to be fulfilled by relatively innocuous arrangements. After impotizing her man, a histrionic woman will often further dramatize her fiasco by taking one or more lovers. Of course, she cannot keep the extramarital relationship secret: to do so might mean being satisfied with less attention than she could get from a real imbroglio. Besides, a quiet affair might demand more durable emotions. The battles between offended husbands and exposed lovers begin, and in the midst of the mêlée, our heroine drinks too much, threatens suicide, finds a psychiatrist. It is difficult to distinguish her wrist-cutting gestures from serious suicidal intentions, and one does not often take the chance. She may find her way to a mental hospital, with twenty-four-hour-a-day attention.

At a level intermediate between the more integrated thespian and the hard-core personality disorder is the temptress who cannot become sexually intimate at all. Although it seems her most unlikely inconvenience, sexuality forms her greatest barrier against the world. Generally afraid of or repulsed by intercourse, she has given a bad name to the institution of coquetry. The promised pleasures metamorphose at the bedside to revulsion and hostility. "I just can't. I don't like it. Please don't make me—I feel sick when I even think about it."

A frequent and often much envied member of our species, the coquette exists at all economic and social levels. Has she been always with us? Was there a troubled Eve who dressed herself in gaudy leaves and lured Adam to further disappointment? Or is she unknown to other sexually unrepressive societies?

The histrionic classification describes a significant percentage of American women. They may be fancy-free and potentially dangerous, provocative but sexually guarded, or full-blown examples of all that is raucously tearful in sisterhood. Their problem has many more ramifications than simple sexual inhibition or craving for attention. While parents who gave all the wrong reinforcements may certainly be at fault, a study of power relations and the intricate scheme by which subjugated women keep their self-esteem alive is equally to the point. Emotional intensity is a force which can be used to dominate and direct. The ability to attract by strongly visual means is another obvious source of strength. Dependence can topple an oak, if the weight hangs heavy enough.

Male histrionics, while relatively rare, are probably more prevalent than is commonly believed. The essential disguise is that their traits have a greater chance of being egosyntonic, reinforcing their sense of capability. Even in our present sexually free decade, a woman who seduces a chain of hearts may still feel promiscuously foolish. The man who engages in repeatedly infatuated attempts to be loved but can never be satiated is still regarded as more of a hero than a wastrel. Short-lived emotions are so common as to be a matter of male pride. To be able to feel deeply committed to one woman on one night, and a day later to be roused by and have sex with another, simply because proximity is exciting, is regarded as an ability rather than an example of poor self-control. Show-business provides such men with an opportunity to display their prowess and be praised. They rarely need to fall back on tears and tantrums to get more than their share of attention. Since it is also not particularly difficult for a man, unburdened by child care, to have time to earn a living, there is less likelihood of his resorting to infantile maneuvers to retain a strong dependence on his mate's protection. Seductive men are generally not regarded as automatically stunted intelligences at sea in a more practical world. They seek and get a lot of loving because women find them perpetually bewitching. They are the gentle Don Juans, who only hurt those who are credulous enough to believe in their devotions.

When a male histrionic has an attack of impotence, however, he may lose his charm and become every bit as demanding, temperamental, and desperately childish as his female counterpart. Now he has nothing to use for collecting approval. Admiration rather than power of any other kind provides the currency of relationship for the male histrionic. If he cannot relate through pleasing others with his lovableness, and particularly with his charismatic genital organ, he will insist on the limelight for his black vapors.

Since identification with the "feminine" is often so much a part of this disposition, it is not surprising that so many histrionic men turn to homosexuality, particularly to

that aspect of the condition which features openly effeminate tendencies. Great euphoria attends finding a new
lover; a transient hailstorm of despair erupts on loss of an
old one. If not enough men are attracted consistently, the
sense of self is leveled. The resultant anxiety and pain of
loneliness, of being without attention, are often too intense
to withstand even for a night. Indeed, one of the difficulties
which must beset any therapist trying to determine
whether these patients are troubled by their homosexuality
is to distinguish between a personality problem and a dilemma concerning appropriate gender choice in a partner.
Since such men are usually quite certain that they could not
be happy with a woman as a mate, one must conclude that
their major burden (like that of so many histrionic women)
is characterological.

What is the allure of histrionic temperaments? Why
are so many people spellbound by their fatuous or fatigu-
ing performances? Seductive, demanding, tempting, either
shallow or overemotional, they seem to consume far too
much time and provide far too little reward for us to take
so much interest.

The enigmatic fascination of life's actor-manipulator
lies in an uncanny ability to make sensitive and perceptive
observations about others. When the audience is lost,
bored, enervated, or frustrated by repetitive bids for un-
divided notice, the histrionic will suddenly become an intensely personal and astute observer of a victim's character.
Mind reading seems almost a gift. Even those without
distinguished intelligence seem to have an intuitive insight
into the ways of engaging other people. A quick foray into
the listener's favorite subject, a helpful comment on how
best to manage a problem, a telling remark on some characterological inadequacy, praise in some unaccustomed
area—the real stars know how to transfix and immobilize
their quarry for the next round. They will perceive our
hidden anger at them, our guarded coldness to the world,

our special talents, our vast unrecognized spiritual integrity. In sex, they will observe the nuances of our fantasy, the moments when we are most vulnerable to wickedness, the moods of fragile sadness when we long for perfect union. For most of us, locked into our individual compulsions and fears, the histrionics are a treat and a threat. Bewildering us with their seeming concern, attentiveness, flattery, they are equally capable of turning on us with rage and devastating dramatic anger. Once we are captured, our souls in their hand, they can begin the leechery again. They flirt and kiss and complain of our inner deadness. Anything for attention. Anything for the love they could never reliably get in their infancy, for the love which their desperate trickery can never achieve.

5

Narcissism:
Sexual Egocentricity

People who love themselves too much have been a constant source of fascination to those of us whose self-love is a blend of self-confidence, doubt, and fallibility. We strive toward evolving our best selves. Will we live long and happy lives if we never look at our image in the water, or will we die, like Narcissus, if we love our reflection too much? As we quest, we consider religious morality, which bade us to be modest and humble. We also read the popular texts which counsel us to become formidable opponents and champions. Instructions for winning the game of life often seem to resemble the definition of a narcissistic character disorder. Through the centuries, we have questioned how much self-love is appropriate to the structure of human character. Although we have by no means arrived at a definitive answer to that riddle, we now also ask about the relationship of narcissism to sexual fulfillment. Does self-love promote or hinder sexual response?

The psychiatric definition of narcissism goes much further than that picture of the lovely young man who, lost in naive contemplation of his beauty, takes our imagination back to the still, clear waters of ancient Greece. He does not need the world's attention to enhance his image. In psychiatry, narcissism may be a stage of development, a condition, a character trait, or a character disorder. In this section, I shall address only that limited aspect of narcissism in which self-love is not truly love of self but rather the creation of a grandiose image. The pain of damaged narcissism accompanies many other emotional difficulties; its treatment is often the very core of therapy, especially sex therapy. However, lack of self-esteem is usually accompanied by some other encompassing defense, like obsessional or hysterical behavior. For simplicity, I shall limit this discussion to the brightest and most obvious side of the coin of impaired narcissism, the "egotist."

Hypothetically, pure narcissists believe themselves endowed with the best of everything. They never admit failure, doubt, or defeat. They consider themselves brighter, better-looking, and more competent than all the odd vermin who inhabit the world and have the audacity to identify themselves as human. Often demonstrating their superiority by the distinction with which they upholster their bodies, they allow us to look at and admire them.

They sustain an astonishingly cheerful, optimistic, and vigorous outlook. They encourage us to idealize their virtues and dispositions, at the same time making sure we understand our position as inferiors. Some day, if we pay close attention to their actions and behavior, we may approach their perfection, but probably not in this world.

Total narcissists are evil. That is fascinating, too. They don't care a fig for the well-being of others. The worse off the rest of the world, the more wholesome they feel. They may actively exploit whoever happens to be useful along the way. They fib and boast and tell fantastic tales, usually without realizing that they are actively prevaricating, not merely telling white lies. Accused of wrongdoing, they have impeccable reasons, which conveniently define the unimportant offense.

They rarely come to see a psychiatrist, much less one who specializes in sex therapy. Nothing is ever wrong with them. If they do visit a professional helper, it is usually only because that is what the best people do. If they should eventually learn to admit a weakness or two, it is in the spirit of being better and stronger than others because they are capable of admitting a carefully selected problem. ("It's hard to handle so much success." "Why do so many men love me?")

Most often, in my clinical experience, narcissists, or those with limited narcissistic traits, are male. Society still encourages men to be strong and women to be weak, men to be faultless and women to take blame, men to provide and women to gain the paradoxical power of dependence. Enough narcissistic men occupy positions of considerable societal power for us hardly to notice them, unless they commit outrageous political atrocities. When a woman is openly narcissistic, however, she stands out of the crowd as a horrendous anomaly, sometimes gaining power, more often losing it soon after it is achieved; like a quail in a field of wrens, she is an easy target.

Of course, there is no such person as a "pure" narcissist, just as no one is thoroughly schizoid, paranoid, dependent, or anything else. Again, we need some narcissism, just as we need to be a bit paranoid, in order to survive. We need to love ourselves and to know that others are not invariably on our side. However, too much of a good thing can be a disease, like dining nightly on chocolate ice cream, or being an alcoholic.

Generally, the wives of narcissistic men come to me and want to know how they can improve their own sexual responsiveness. Since their husbands cannot possibly be at fault (their men have clearly said so), they must bear the burden of inadequacy. If they cannot have orgasms or sexual pleasure in the thirty seconds it takes their mates to ejaculate, something is askew in their own responsive system. Not excited by their husbands' rapid progress from climbing into bed to intercourse in the missionary position, they wonder what is wrong with their own arousal. After all, being together for a dozen years or more should lead to quicker reactions.

If and when such women can persuade their partners to enter therapy, it is only by the ruse of needing to be helped themselves. If a man's narcissism has not entirely destroyed his humanity, he may be convinced that his august presence may, by itself, assist matters.

Though I have encountered many male sexual narcissists, who revere their organs as they might worship a golden embodiment of divinity, this sexual syndrome in women again seems to be rare. Attractive men rarely commit suicide because the world recognizes their sexual vigor. Females, however, have a reputation for doing themselves in because their physical attributes, no matter how impressive to others, are not enough to warrant self-esteem. The "sex symbol" who actually commits suicide is usually a woman.

Though women have the reputation for self-love because they are said to spend more time and money on appearances, they are rarely in love with their sexual selves. Clothing and cosmetics are designed to conceal "flaws" and attract attention, but not to make an incontrovertible statement about superiority. More of an appeal than a command, the trappings of traditional female self-indulgence are a stance of weakness. The woman who has abandoned make-up and gleaming, multifaceted baubles may have more self-love than her overdecorated sister—and, in these days when the artful achievement of the "natural look" has become for some a fetish, she may not. Men who expect devotion, though they wear shapeless clothes, smoke rancid cigars, and wash their hair infrequently, have a far higher quotient of vanity.

Male narcissists love their bodies more than their clothes. They stroke their penises with absolute affection and pride. They "love their cocks." If erect, they extend their handsome appendage to be kissed and fondled, as though doing their partner a great favor. If not erect, they may regard a partner with some disdain and contempt for her inability to raise the thing. To the man who loves himself too much, problems are always someone else's fault.

Many of the female narcissists who do exist seem to believe that their limited abilities are the final word in erotic bliss. One that I encountered believed that her clitorally induced orgasm was the supreme feminine achievement. Deep vaginal penetration nauseated her. She considered it ignorant of men to thrust intensely. Because she only occasionally had an orgasm on intercourse, she considered being routinely orgasmic a subscription to dull routine. Because she had only one orgasm when she did achieve climax, she believed that multiply-orgasmic women were nymphomaniacs. I suppose we all subscribe to beliefs which corroborate our personal experience, but we admit that, after all, we might be wrong. No such possibility exists for the narcissist.

Self-exaltation, then, rarely inhibits sexuality, but it does stunt sexual growth. When limits cannot be expanded because pride interferes, the result is deadening. If this does not disturb the person who has decided that he or she is perfect, it may deeply damage anyone who chances to live with such a paragon.

Narcissists, however, rarely remain with the same partner for long. They don't usually depart by themselves; they are more often abandoned. The ones I have known have a high divorce rate. Spouses come for psychiatric help and need immense support in escaping their life bondage, a vassalage that has often enhanced their own self-esteem by identification, and destroyed it by the same mechanism. Sometimes suicide seems the only way out of the dilemma. When left alone, the narcissist quickly collects a new coterie to use for self-aggrandizement. There was something pathologically wrong with whoever intruded melancholy on his or her right to enjoy the heyday of the senses.

Being in bed with a male narcissist can be an experience in sexual and emotional masturbation. Men praise themselves monotonously for the size of their organs, proficiency, longevity, and special skills at eliciting orgasm. They do not even ask questions. It is not "Look at me, am I not the most wondrous of men?" but rather "Be privileged to behold me, I am the miracle."

Women tend to express their narcissism less overtly. Their self-involvement emerges as concern only for whether or not they are pleased and satisfied, without a thought to their partner's pleasure. It is all for them, in bed as in life. They put their men through paces, earning, bearing gifts, rubbing interminably at the place which delivers orgasm, without thought of reciprocation.

Initially, these maneuvers often provoke intense uncertainty, which can lead to high excitement. A woman may believe that she has won the sexual sweepstakes. A man, given the faintest nod of approval from his self-absorbed partner, may feel highly honored. Ultimately, however, women withdraw and men give up. If they don't turn to others for reassurance of their existence, they either lose interest or become impotent.

Narcissistic traits, like dependent ones, encourage sexuality unless they are so extreme as to ruin it. A moderate amount of narcissism is very attractive, sexually, to most people. We like human beings who keep themselves clean, smell good, dress well. Many of us feel safe, and therefore sexually excitable, in the presence of those who seem to know what they are doing, have things under control. Narcissism as true self-love inspires much admiration, identification, and imitation. When self-love becomes a lifelong infatuation, however, we may try to profit from the model, but be forced to leave when we are totally and irrevocably left out or despised.

Masturbation has been considered (among other things) as the height of narcissism. Most of us have struggled, if briefly, with the concept that autoeroticism is an unhealthy perversion of more generous sexual instincts. We should not be content to satisfy ourselves. That self-gratification is fundamentally antisocial and antisexual has been one of the strongest tenets of religious thought.

One could imagine, therefore, that narcissists engaged in vast amounts of self-stimulation in front of three-way mirrors, with an additional view from the ceiling. This does not seem to be the case. On the contrary, narcissists regard it as something of an embarrassment, a social and sexual failure, to have to stimulate themselves while alone. As one intensely self-admiring patient said to me, "I don't see why I should do it to myself when I can get a girl to do it for me. They love it." He, incidentally, only came for a consultation because his wife, my regular patient, wanted my opinion of what was wrong with her for feeling jealous of his amorous exploits, emotionally neglected in bed, and sexually humiliated by his promiscuity. I had to help her slowly to abandon her penchant for masochism both in tolerating such an infantile peacock and in blaming herself for his disorder. He, of course, refused any offer of assistance, stating that sex was a personal matter. He was willing to help his wife, but there was nothing wrong with him. Since vainglory results from a serious lack of self-esteem, which must be provided by the homage of others, narcissists basically find themselves unexciting. They do not seek help for this problem.

The riddle of Narcissus, seldom defined and rarely recognized, is that the aspiration of psychiatric and humanistic impulse is to create an individual who essentially knows himself (Socrates) and is satisfied. But, as in all personality development, the balance is precarious. The distinction between self-acceptance and self-indulgence is definitive.

6

Compulsiveness:
Sexual Obsession

The compulsive is a person driven to perform irrational actions. Compulsive people are also often obsessional, haunted and preoccupied by one thought, plan, idea, or feeling. The condition sounds like a dread disease, as though a singularly committed microbe put its repetitive stamp on the brain. Nevertheless, moderately compulsive personalities have given much to the world. Without them, science could not grow, businesses would fail, artists would get bored, and religion would die for lack of conviction.

The only trouble with being compulsive is that the habit often screens whatever else is happening in one's personal life, not to mention the world. Some compulsives are hard put, for example, to know that it's Tuesday and it's raining. They may be more concerned with studying the neurophysiology of giant squid axons, practicing an economy of truth, painting a modern version of Ecce Homo, or improving their tennis.

In sex, the obsessional aspect of the disorder predominates, acting in an intemperate, even unconscionable variety of ways. Just as syphilis is called, in medicine, the "great imitator" because it manifests symptoms so much like those of other diseases, so the obsessional relationship to sexuality could be called the mighty mimic, the immense impersonator. Almost every condition of human affection can be an obsession, mistaken by its owner for the genuine article. So difficult is it, in fact, to distinguish the false persuasion from the bare truth, that many of us spend years in psychoanalysis, weighing matters, free-associating, besieging our unconscious in order to find out—to discover—that it's Wednesday, and it's sunny, and leaves dapple in the sea wind, and some passions might, after all, be real.

Obsessives may negate sexuality or consider it responsible for all human and nonhuman behavior. They may treat it as life's most careless and most intense pleasure, or as its most exacting responsibility. Sex may be heaven unending, or hell for all seasons. It is the life principle. It is the death principle. In short, whatever it is, the believer brooks no dispute, and that's how we know it's an obsession.

Most unenlightening among those who would define sex precisely for us are the new sexual "scientists," who claim it is the simplest biological experience, like urinating, breathing, eating a hot dog, or jerking your foreleg when your kneecap's tapped. Considering the seismic clamor about sex for the last ten thousand years, that seems a bit too obsessively simple.

The obsessional person looks through a well-defined peephole at reality. If psychopaths can never give, if schizoids pursue interior visions and paranoids are endlessly abused, obsessionals are sempiternally concerned with improving matters. Tomorrow must be better. When everything is in order, when the obsessionals have cleaned, tidied, and white-gloved the springs of life, when they have cajoled, pressured, clouted, and pulverized others into believing as they do, and it all boils down to a manageable system, things do have to look up.

Other people are a particularly irritating block to obtaining the greatest good for self and country. They often have to be herded firmly into their little places unless, of course, one chooses to ignore them, or destroy them.

With devotion and discipline, faith and work, true belief in the cause, however, all could cooperate to make the world a finer place for the obsessive's impossible dream to come true.

Nor is there any end to self-improvement. Though the road to perfection is not precisely a superhighway, being fraught with minor obstacles and detours like boredom, fatigue, anxiety, illness, and death, these can be overcome.

All the facets of life stand in need of polishing and sharpening to better endure immortality. Skills must be practiced; all the details observed. The constant corrosion of uncleanliness must be scourged. One has to become more hygienic, more precise, more adept at everything. And heaven forbid any detail of art, craft, or housekeeping be left to someone else.

Sometimes, totality being clearly out of the question, the obsessive narrows the field and concentrates on something that seems more likely to be within grasp. A perfect home, orderly children, an obedient wife, the cure for cancer, the purification of one's soul, may all be fit and singular goals. The obsessive devotedly applies all energies to one ideal. The result, some people say, is what makes the world go round. Others, less convinced of man's omnipotence, judge that it could continue to rotate effectively without such purposeful intervention.

The obsessive devotedly applies all energies to one ideal. The goal is paramount whether he or she is espousing it as a cause or just as obsessively ignoring it in the belief that it cannot be controlled; it may be best hurried out of sight or adapted to a life pattern along with eating and exercising.

Some obsessionals work at perfecting their sex lives. They are intimately and fiercely concerned with the appearance and activities of their genitals in minutest detail, rather like researchers working with an electron microscope. A few even convert this interest into science.

* * *

Male sexual obsessionals regard every flicker of their penis, every rillet of sexual feeling, as an event rivaling matters of state in importance. They are the Prousts of the pudenda. They make mental notes, and sometimes written ones, about the exact angle of erection, degree of hardness, and duration of excitement for every sexual event.

This habit of remembering, measuring, and evaluating can at first seem a celebration of man's ability to renew his vigor, a confirmation of youth, a delight in the frequent phallus. Behind the superficial glee, however, lies the obsessional fear—the need to check, to triple check, to make sure. This preoccupation is reminiscent of the man who returns several times to make sure his house door is locked. Something morbid is going to happen. An act of forgetting, a carelessness, may lead to cataclysm. The stoutness and viability of the organ need regular surveillance. As long as the penis continues to respond to its owner's surveys, all is well. However, life provides our antihero with its usual Scylla and Charybdis, the angry dogheads at their wrists growling in anticipation. The twin dangers, women and aging, both threaten to bite off the godhead.

Clocking and timing performance with each woman, not to mention subtle investigations of penile width and length, become part of each coital act. Occasionally this is overt; usually it is disguised under cover of speechless passion. (Nearly ten minutes. Thrusting 40 percent of the time. Percentage could be a bit higher. Near climax twice. Near loss of control first time. Full hardness for about six minutes. Then softened to prevent orgasm. Second erection extremely long and full. Base of penis a full hand's circumference. Caused slight pain to partner. Good orgasm on thrusting, five strong contractions, three weaker ones, etc.)

The big danger is, of course, that the contestant will not win every event. At some point in the infinity of sexual acts, one will fail. The robot-athlete will go limp, be recalcitrant, go human. The cause might be any straw of circumstance: a stressful day, too much to drink, a partner's irritable remark. The result is emotional holocaust.

The obsessional begins to seal his fate with the wax of prophecy. He feels imperfect, humbled, impotized. The single, devastating trauma presages a lifetime of sexual caducity. Women may be kind for a while, tolerate their empty vaginas, then slowly depart like visitors at a hospital. Others, less understanding, may seek Megaeran retribution for the insult to their pride.

Harassment by the compulsive fear accelerates. There must be a way to control the tool, to make it work. Like a muscle, it seems only a physiological device, temporarily strained. How to restore it?

Erections, like happiness, have an ancient secret. The harder a person tries to achieve the elusive goal, the farther away it is. The frantic search for erection (and happiness) can lead to total loss of both, like chasing matter to the jaws of the black hole in space, where it disintegrates, mysteriously and cosmically perverse.

Frustration may set off a depression with impotence in the obsessive personality. The greater the experience of failure, the deeper the depression. With increased depression, sexual sensitivity diminishes, until interest and ability may be further damaged. A trivial event in the life of an obsessional can set off serious perceptual and emotional disorder.

At the other end of the obsessional spectrum are the somber men who attempt to ignore the importance of sex and sexual performance. Not able to enjoy it, they dismiss it, sometimes consciously, sometimes not. Today's educational system, still modeled on a university structure conceived in the Middle Ages, continues to produce "scholars" who emphasize a life of the mind over the pleasures of the body, as though they were different phenomena. These people have a wide assortment of defenses against sexuality. It may be that something is askew in their whole sensory arousal scheme. Some do not seem to be affected by pheromones or to notice the provocative sexual activity surrounding them. Others can be led into sexuality and even exhibit sexual responses culminating in erection, intercourse, and ejaculation, but the participation is largely reflexive. Their thoughts are elsewhere: on some unsolved mathematical puzzle, a philosophic argument of global importance, the next step in an experiment. Caught *in flagrante delicto,* they would probably be at some pains to realize that they weren't, for example, playing chess. In consequence, many suffer from premature ejaculation, a disorder which often reflects lack of awareness and sensory perception. The orgasm comes and passes. There is no slow layering of passion, no pulsing white pleasure, no transcendental moment. Recovery and quick cleanup are the order of the moment.

Male obsessionals may go well beyond ordinary neglect of sexuality. They may turn it into religious mandate. To describe the self-torture and ritual debasement of the human body, as practiced by men obedient to a higher will, is a study in masochism that could rival a history of China in weight and scope. Obsessionally denying sex, these men were singularly concerned with it. The history of religion in certain of its antisexual teachings is a story of tenacious, psychic aberration that can almost be compared to the world's record of periodic massacre, considering the destructive effect on life.

Women, too, may be preoccupied with anything from professional and business life, to consciousness raising, to domestic responsibilities. In the domestic sphere, female compulsiveness reigns unchallenged. These women often have a façade resembling their male counterparts, but expressed slightly differently. Just as some male obsessionals, on the surface, give no hint of the race for omnipotence and perfection going on inside, but rather seem relaxed and unexcitable, so the woman conceals her albatross. She beckons with a promise of restfulness. Evoking memories of new notebooks, sharpened pencils, freshly scrubbed classrooms, she promises reward for all work carefully done. She invites our fantasies of sheets whitened in the sun and softly ironed, flowers on the table, spotless glass and silver. She transports us to a polite, dustless world where roses grow untrampled at the far corners of the tennis court.

She seems so bland, quiet, charming; so effortlessly efficient, so well ordered. The unfortunate price is that, in bed, she may mainly be concerned with the folding of blankets, precise ventilation, and tomorrow's menu.

Everything finally arranged to ultimate perfection, she may lie down next to her waiting partner, stretch tentatively, and start to worry. The anxiety that hangs on the bedposts aborts most attempts at sexual relating.

Many women do not camouflage their obsessions with housework and ritual so politely. We recognize the obvious compulsive, the more open variety of valkyrie, far more readily than her civilized sister. She never really looks clean, yet hygiene concerns her constantly. Rollers twist her hair into a plastic palace covered with the same daily square of Japanese chiffon while she services the household gods. Only on formal occasions, like weddings, does one get to see her entire head. She wears a "housedress," a garment frequently cut so as to reveal the armpit and its owner's apocrine abilities. She eats and cleans, sweats, and gets fat. She uses a lot of Lysol in the bathroom. When her husband joins her in bed at night, the hair rollers present an insurmountable barrier against comfortable relations, not to consider her dissatisfaction with the way he has disposed of his dirty socks, his undershorts, his competitors, and his money. He often goes rapidly to sleep in self-defense.

Between the gentlewoman and the sanitary beast is the efficiency expert. Allotting a certain prescribed time for all her activities, she often neglects to include coitus in her household duties. It doesn't occur because it isn't scheduled. If intercourse does shoulder its way into the time-table, this obsessional generally places it after the eleven o'clock news. When everything important is over, sexual relations may take place. If an erection doesn't appear during the allotted time, she considers the sexual agenda discharged.

Adding children to the lives of such women frequently places their sex lives in danger of extinction. Predictable, inanimate domestic objects can occupy all their waking moments; put live, dirty, wriggling children into the picture, and the need for control may overwhelm all sexuality. The bedroom door must be left open in case the baby cries. If the door is open, the other children can come in. If children can wander in, sex is out. That's how it is when things go well. Should the children become ill, do poorly at school, develop behavior problems of any kind—twin beds, if not separate rooms, take care of the sex monster by starving it.

Feeling oppressed and helotized by their property and their progeny, each type of woman—among at least a dozen more varieties of household compulsives—has in common with the others a concept of sex as an act of submission and of orgasm as a loss of control.

Always grappling to order and subdue their human and nonhuman environment, they cannot summon the defiance to attack that which seems, a priori, unconquerable. Best, therefore, to avoid sex. Reduce its importance to a few thrusts received for the perpetuation of man and drop the subject forthwith.

While no absolute rule can be laid for the type of sexual dysfunction expected in these women, anorgasmia on intercourse occurs most commonly. They tend to have little difficulty masturbating to orgasm privately; in seclusion one can control the time and timing of orgasm. No one else is present; therefore no one else can assume control.

The remainder of these women may have difficulty reaching any climax at all.

The patterns of obsessive defense against sexuality (and often against aggression as well) are so rich, complex, and various as to make one feel like a tourist at an Oriental carpet bazaar. The Sarouks, Kirmans, and Bukharas are easy enough, but how to identify all the rest?

The woman who tailors her body and clothing to a state of newly purchased perfection intrigues by paradox. These women groom each day as though readying themselves for their final appearance supine at the front of the chapel. The purpose of all this immaculacy is as mysterious as the soul of its creator. Certainly it is not to attract a man, take off the clothes, and get mussed up. One has to conclude that for some it's the same repetitive, magical protest against decay and death that inspires most obsessional behavior. And sex, somehow resembling death, must be treated as the adversary. The abandonment and anesthesia of high excitement suggest a fatal disintegration. These women are afraid. Frenchwomen refer to orgasm as *le petit mort,* the little death. Many American women fear it as the genuine article.

Women who unconsciously negate sybarite longings don't beleaguer their husbands and children only. Some become career women, and as such they also may invade the business and professional world, where they do a splendid job. With an uncommon need to lead, pressure, and control, they are often thought of by their male colleagues as possessing the scrotal contents known as balls, sometimes with admiration, more often with derision. Suffice to suggest that some women enter the commercial rounds in order to avoid any connubial servility at all. They must remain impenetrable, on top, and in command of their passions. One need not become a nun any longer to exorcise sex. A job in advertising, with lots of weekend homework, will do the same thing.

Women obsessed with sex, itself, are the most difficult of all to characterize. Though Aphrodite was the goddess of love and sex, and real knowledge about the field has always been ascribed to women, the female sexual obsessional is elusive.

The woman who analyzes her every sexual sensation and fears failure, unlike the overconcerned man, is relatively rare. We have not long emerged from that antediluvian time when women were hardly allowed to be aware of sexuality, much less to enjoy it. The need for a woman to perform with exact attention to detail has not developed, perhaps, because precise medical investigation has only recently begun. In any event, women rarely insert rulers to measure the length of their vaginas or use them exteriorly to calculate the size of their clitorises and vaginal orifices the way men study the inches of their penis. And most women are unaware of their cervixes, nor could they contribute an opinion about whether or not they possess a Grafenberg spot. Diameter, shape of opening, sensitivity to touch—all are ignored or bypassed.

Vaginal sensation, a particularly threatening subject, slides past unnoticed, the quest for it suppressed. Women learn with surprise that they are able to experience the sensation of pressure, to detect the presence of an object, but virtually cannot appreciate touch on the vagina mucosa. This is entirely normal, yet many women have considered themselves frigid because they could not discriminate touch vaginally. Rather than admit such psychic and physical disaster, they ignored it.

However, all the sex-related material on the market has some impact. The "how-to-do-it" orientation, the books written for therapists, the manuals crafted by professional writers from the hand-me-down concepts of sex therapists who make Leo Buscaglia seem like a pessimist—have begun to produce a new crop of female obsessionals. They are concerned with such matters as how soon they lubricate, how fast they can reach orgasm, how long they can stay "high," how many orgasms they can have in succession.

Many of these new female statistical experts have begun to feel anxious if they don't have orgasm on every occasion; a few now feel inadequate if they don't have multiple orgasms. Considering the enormous popularity of sex in the media, however, the number of adversely affected women still seems small. Perhaps it is a sign prognostic of how far we have yet to go in the cause of female consciousness that only the hippest of newly educated females and the most hep older collegiate generation (frequently scientists) have turned their obsessional propensities toward the mechanics of sex.

7

Passive Aggression: Sexual Strategy

Many of us announce, by way of negotiating life's orbit, that we are not only difficult to please but also impossible to live with. We may post signs warning of our eccentricities: "Beware, I own too much, drink too much, quarrel too much, or am intemperate in my self-denial." We offer up our frailties as food for gossip, and like birds attracted to the luxury of a feeding stand, people come to our cottages to peck away in cozy familiarity.

Passive-aggressive personalities contrarily try to conceal the wickedness that would help us to love them. They whitewash their motives and behavior with such patient expense, such meticulous care, that they convince us of their unselfish probity whether we are suspicious or not, and whether or not they are malevolent.

Philosophers have been debating the problem of good and evil for millenniums now. Are we born good, only to be corrupted by the writing on the *tabula rasa*? Are we born evil, with the taste of the apple transmitted in the womb? Are we in need of constant supervision by the reigning deity? Are there no good and evil at all, but only the laws of nature: survival and conquest versus destruction and loss? Are there no laws of aggression in nature, but only transformations of energy? The passive-aggressive's response to these important if unanswerable questions is that he or she was born good, is obedient to the controlling deity, and survives without harming others. If he or she should commit evil or create havoc in the fight for survival, it is unconscious, unplanned, and certainly inadmissible. Others may now and again tend to notice it, particularly mates, friends, colleagues, and psychiatrists, but the passive-aggressive stands, like an impervious Buddha, with head in heaven and feet on the ground. When the trial ends, everyone will see the goodness.

To accomplish great discomfort in others by doing nothing overt at all is the master game, the singular achievement, the silent victory. Ignorance, forgetfulness, withdrawal, silence, lack of emotional display, and lack of opinion form the major arsenals. If the passive-aggressive does not learn the rules which will protect others, he or she can hardly be accused of ignoring or breaking them. . . . A forgetting is in no way intended to hurt the feelings of the person who waits in vain for whatever salvation the meeting promised. . . . If anger threatens, best to withdraw rather that fight. . . . Emotionalism always leads to an irrational conclusion. . . . Opinions invariably lead to argument. . . . And the unprotected, the forgotten, the aggrieved, the disturbed, and the hatefully opinionated are left to clamor at emptiness. No one has actively done anything; there is no one they can accuse of hurting them at all.

Sexually, the most dangerous passive-aggressive games involve the use or nonuse of birth control devices. Forgetting them, not liking them, suffering them, using them improperly: all kinds of pain can be inflicted on others without taking any share of real responsibility. If a woman is passive-aggressive enough, she may get the opportunity to kill the beginnings of a human being without committing a crime. If a man is sufficiently uninvolved, he can have pain inflicted on his partner and he can see his unborn child destroyed as well.

At the level of coital intimacy, passive-aggressives may suffer from any of the sexual disorders, although there may be some correlation between this personality disorder

and premature ejaculation. Logic suggests that a man, by
not being able to control his ejaculate, might be depriving a
woman of the pleasures of coitus, frustrating and punishing her, without actively performing any injury upon her
body. One could view this as the ultimate passive-aggressive
ploy.

However, there is usually real discord between people
who find that their bed has become an unconscious battleground. The man who is behaving passive-aggressively
more often than not has something to be significantly disturbed about. Angered by his wife, he may begin to ejaculate earlier and earlier. It is not a deliberately rapid release,
but rather an involuntary emission in response to anxiety.
The anger causes the prematurity. Although the man does
not choose to be dysfunctional to frustrate his wife, it may
seem that way.

The passive-aggressive trait not only may cause disorder, but also emerges in the way a person handles the
problem. If a man ejaculates more rapidly than he wants
to, and also makes no effort to understand that his partner
needs additional tenderness, needs his hands and his
mouth to satisfy her, then he is behaving passive-aggressively. The relationship often deteriorates gradually, as
opposed to coming apart in any more active way. Slowly, the
woman's bitterness grows, forming a webbed cage that prevents his coming in and baffles her reaching out. They stop
talking about sex; they stop talking very much about anything. They may even stop looking at one another. Touching becomes impossible. Unless the woman enjoys the
sadism of berating a man who will not fight directly back,
there is no drawbar to keep the union coupled.

If a woman cannot have orgasms on intercourse, but
makes her partner feel inadequate by saying nothing in a
wounded way, she is passive-aggressive. This relationship,
too, can fail. If she is constantly displeased, wordlessly
critical of him, hurt, he often retires from trying. Perfectly

capable men frequently allow not only their personal but also their business lives to wither under pressure of this incessant gelding. And the woman who takes no responsibility for supporting her own sexuality, but continues to heap her weight on her husband, will inevitably turn the marriage into a lingering, swayback death.

The trait permeates every aspect of a relationship, from the time of meeting (when the passive-aggressive waits for the other to make the first move), to the time of parting, when the passive-aggressive engineers it so that the other person will break the bonds and say good-bye.

If there is no sexual disorder at the outset of such a union, a problem will certainly develop in time. Most often, the crepuscular "low-libido syndrome" settles early on the pair. Without a sexual difficulty to start matters badly, one or the other member will find some other way to ruin their lives. On the male side, isolation and distance are often sought. Oddly enough, and hard to conceive, the most ferocious weapon for inglenook battle is the newspaper. Preferably large and imposing enough to conceal an entire seated body, with Gothic type pronouncing its sacred venerability, the newspaper presents the sturdiest shield against communication yet invented. Other gambits include the computer, television, home repairs, friends, and anyone or anything which will prevent participation in the verbal vagaries of domesticity.

This rejection, often across the board, with no irritable word spoken, is one of the most common and confusing circumstances in American marriage. The retaliation, a hostile absence of sexual interest, may be disguised as headache, gynecological ache, bellyache, or some modern version of nervous vapors. No one ever gets angry or has the least idea of what is going on.

Wives who serve as maids-of-all-work are generally knowledgeable, alert, and talkative enough about their homes; their passive aggressivity usually expresses itself by denying the importance of any activity beyond the fireside. Politics, national issues, the intricacies of a husband's work—all these are outside their ken. Even professional and working women may choose to be subnormal in their comprehension of these matters if they see themselves as servants in any capacity. Forgetting the hostility that made them lose interest in the first place, they allow great gaps of knowledge and opinion to separate them permanently from contact, not only with their husbands, but with the active world.

What emerges is the polite enmity characteristic of so many marital anastomoses, the underground loathing which confuses so many children by its benevolent exterior. Unable to talk, to touch, to argue, to brace the relationship firmly against the conjugal footboard, the only communal behaviors left are eating, praying, and complaining about taxes. Often enough, in these halcyon days of sex therapy, such people, believing themselves gentle, loving, peaceful, and representative of all the civilized virtues, come to me for help with the problem of no longer being "turned on" by each other, no longer being "in love." They want me to catalyze the recapture of their sexual eagerness. They don't want "psychology" because clearly they have no "mental problems" and are otherwise perfectly happy.

Whenever I see two mannerly but sexually deprived people facing each other in utter ignorance and absence of spirit, I suspect they need far more than a quick course of "touchy-feely" to reaffirm their humanity. It is a long and often painful path that begins with the confrontation of self and leads to destinations of relationship which promise no more harmony and peace than truth of self will allow.

8

The Paranoid Approach: Sexual Espionage

Paranoia as an aspect of schizophrenic illness involves delusions of grandeur and of persecution, often accompanied by hallucinations. Psychotic paranoid patients may, for example, believe that spy rings operate to observe their lives, and will soon close in to take their life-support systems away. They have delusions of grandeur, either directly, believing themselves to be specific important people, or indirectly, believing themselves important enough to be of concern to spy rings or other agencies of persecution. Paranoids may hallucinate images of their enemies or voices warning them of conspiracy.

People with a predominantly paranoid approach to life (as compared to psychotics) believe that their gifts, skills, talents, or possessions are immensely valuable, and that others are always contriving to hurt them or take them away.

These people are hugely fearful of being abused. The sense of their own value is inflated because they are convinced it is worthwhile for others to spend considerable time and effort figuring out how to harm them, how to deprive them of their rightful belongings and stations. The paranoid personality is very cautious. He or she does not readily enter new deals or make rapid decisions. The fear that others will take advantage, disapprove, or abandon often paralyzes action. Life-styles tend to be monotonous and constricted, to keep from facing new perils. The world is full of nasty, oppressive enemies.

I do not intend to discuss the sexuality of those who are psychotically ill. Nor am I describing people involved in paranoid reactions or paranoid states. But there are enough "miniparanoids" in the world to comprise at least 30 percent of mankind. They would not, even by many psychiatrists, at first glance be thought of as at all disturbed. Indeed, a small dosage of paranoia is necessary to make our way through the vagaries of chance, competition, and exploitation. But these miniparanoids, although not neurotic, have more than average paranoia. Yet they defend so well, hide so much, as to be quite passable—even delightful—in society. Often they reveal themselves most dramatically in the intimate relation.

Sexual paranoia may include the belief not only that sexual feelings are harmful, but also that intimate relations will cause physical or emotional damage. Men or women with a severe paranoid tendency are susceptible to the range of sexual disorders. When imaginary dramatizations of pain, anguish, or suspicion intrude upon the impulse to sexual expression, physiology responds and performance fails. Paranoids also tend to exaggerate the failures of their partners: "He is being deliberately impotent in order to frustrate me." "She can't climax because she hates me."

Paranoids are thinly armed against the antiquated legends which forbid sexual satisfaction. They listen and believe that masturbation deforms its practitioners and exposes him or her to public ridicule. While most of us regard ancient shibboleths with scientific skepticism, the paranoid finds confirmation for his or her own distrust of the sexual condition when advised that sexual relations deplete energy or, in *Dr. Strangelove's* lexicon, exhaust our precious bodily fluids.

However, the vagaries of the world are such that the suspicions of the paranoid are not always without basis in reality. Among the most imposing inhibitors of the paranoid's sexual drive are two genuine considerations: venereal disease and unwanted pregnancy. Indeed, the man or woman who totally disregards these possibilities often pays a severe price for a cavalier indulgence. For all our medical sophistication, syphilis and venereal disease do exist and can be epidemic. Other sexually transmitted infections, like herpes, have assumed new proportions. Acquired immune deficiency syndrome (AIDS) is the nightmare of the eighties, worse than any previous illness suspected of travelling with the sexual impulse. The male or female who resists Dionysiac abandonment for fear of a venereal souvenir is no more paranoid than the prescient adolescent who distrusts the reliability of withdrawal as a birth-control device.

Traditionally women have the more valid right to be suspicious of the consequences of sexual entertainments. Females bear the babies. And in that ancient time when it was considered appropriate for a male to deal casually, if at all, with his legal or illegal offspring, a woman knew that an episodic dalliance could leave her with a living legacy.

Cultural paranoia passes slowly. Even today, when it is to be hoped that increased awareness has brought responsibility for children into closer parity between men and women, statistics indicate we are far from cured of the fatherless family. Little wonder so many women continue to suffer the paranoid legacy of their sisters and regard a man's sexual advances as potentially exploitative.

Male suspicions are less intense. Our culture does not hold that a woman abuses a man by sleeping with him. A man would be considered passing strange if he burst into tears because a young woman seduced him.

Beyond cultural influences, paranoids develop their own physical terrors of sex. A man may fear that his partner's secretions will harm him, that she is dirty and will soil him with her mucus or her menses. He may fear castration, with the attendant fantasy that teeth inside the vagina will bite off his penis.

Paranoid women fear being torn and bludgeoned by a penis regarded more as a battering ram than a wand of delight. They may experience a man's ejaculate as a slimy waste, not to be deposited in or on them except as an insult. Even the rough play that lovers indulge in their excitement—biting, sucking, scratching—can become, in the paranoid imagination, a precursor of rape or murder.

Oral sex and even an external anal caress can be particularly difficult for paranoids. A man may conceive of a woman's mouth as an organ of aggression; a woman may think of kissing a man's penis as a humiliation. The buttocks and anus are either sources of defilement or, paradoxically, sexually inviolable.

Paranoids fear psychological abuse even more than physical damage. Men and women whose personalities are dominated by paranoid tendencies are distrustful of their partners. They suffer acute fears of committing their feelings to someone else. They are afraid because they don't want to be "hurt." Women tend to be more open about these misgivings; men are inclined to be more guarded in acknowledging the reasons for resisting commitment.

The paranoid man's fears are frequently heightened at the moment of direct sexual confrontation. The sexual wiring of the paranoid man is so contrived that the more abundant the temptation, the more dramatically he may recoil from what he perceives to be the bait of a trap.

The paranoid is convinced that for a moment of pleasure he will be made to pay with a lifetime of obligation. Never mind that the lady has assured him of the casualness of her concern—the true paranoid knows better. People never confess their motives until the catch is won. Sex is a vast conspiracy, a contrivance to rob him of his freedom and encourage a dependence and need which only by the most diligent discipline may he learn to live without. Paranoid women may have similar reactions to engagement with their lovers. It is possible that a woman, too, may see a happy sexual encounter as an instrument to entrap her. But it is more common for the woman paranoid to suspect the male of the opposite motive. "He just wanted to use me." "If I allowed myself to make love to him, he'd never want to see me again."

In sexual relations, where paranoia is not so great as to preclude touch altogether, partners evince their fear of being hurt by not telling each other what they want. This is particularly true of women, who imagine the most dreadful ridicule and rejection will follow a statement of their needs. A paranoid woman will suffer the coarsest sexual onslaught or the crudest attempt at stimulation, conceive of herself as totally victimized by the sex act, yet never utter a word to educate the selfish behemoth in her toils. He is a depriving sadist who can read her thoughts, understand the nuances of her desire, and yet persist in his ineffectual gyrations in order to damage her further. If she tells him, it will only infuriate him and make matters worse.

When a man is too paranoid to tell a woman what he likes, he usually becomes impotent. He also suffers this disorder when he projects that she is critical of his efforts or dissatisfied.

Revelation of sexual fantasy is one of the most powerful sources of fear of rejection and retaliation. Afraid of jealousy or loss, men and women often do not share their mental lives, thus impoverishing their pleasure and communication. Paranoia may not only paralyze the body; it may also imprison the mind.

Finally, incidents of sexual malfunction may be viewed with infinite suspicion and distrust. A paranoid woman will conclude that an impotent lover or a premature ejaculator is deliberately depriving her of sexual fulfillment. A man may view his partner's delayed or absent orgasm as a certain indication that she harbors deep-rooted resentment against him. Yet impotence or failure to have orgasm may have nothing to do with the relationship between two specific people. Personal history may be the problem.

Both men and women suffer what may be their most intense apprehensions in those bedtime moments when harbingers of ecstasy are supposed to be choraling in the vestry. For some, whether they succeed in making love or not, the aftermath of union resembles the desolation of the battleground.

9

Schizoid Withdrawal: Sexual Avoidance

Psychiatrists classify all the mystery out of life. In shrinkdom, people no longer think themselves possessed by gods or devils; they are either manic or depressed. A man is not visited by the ghosts of his evil passions: he is paranoid. A person is not blessedly and miraculously happy; he or she is hypomanic. And so it is with those most fragile of human representatives of heaven, the schizoids.* Popularly, we feel that they are "out of it." Sometimes we wonder if they are saints, or, if not saints, at least brushed by a paradisal dust which has rendered them even-tempered, solitary, and good. They often appear to be in the spell of some mystic reverie which we dare not interrupt lest it shatter and its owner be shattered, too, or frightened off. We always speak to them carefully. Confronted with the rudeness of truth or direct feeling, they may not quite know what to do. In psychiatric jargon, the schizoid is withdrawn, tends to autistic thinking, is excessively sensitive in interpersonal relations, and has difficulty with the expression of ordinary hostile feelings. But jargon doesn't capture spirit.

---

* Scholars today may differentiate between an "avoidant" personality disorder and a "schizoid" problem. Avoidant people are thought to want warm relations but to be unable to obtain them because they fear related anxieties. Schizoids are thought to be too distant even to want warmth. The distinctions are so fine that I have used the old inclusive term for simplicity.

Schizoids, or people with some schizoid traits, comprise a high percentage of the world's "intellectuals" and "artists." After all, what is an "intellectual" or an "artist" but someone who prefers, for the most, to withdraw from ordinary commerce and spin fantasies into stories, theories, and pictures. They are the silent, thoughtful people who observe more than participate, the ones who always appear mildly pained and distant. Schizoids may also be the quiet aloof workers in the office, or the inscrutable laborers who have to be "left alone." If criticized or confronted, they will suddenly quit work rather than defend themselves or fight back. Immensely sensitive, they may also be hugely gifted. More often than not, their gifts disintegrate under the cudgels of criticism that stronger if less talented minds survive.

So easily deflated, schizoids are barely equipped for making friends, much less making love. In human society, forming sexual attachments is hardly a procedure designed to be without stress. Considering life's wayward circumstances, a pleasant union at a salutary time is difficult enough to achieve, much less a perpetual idyllic harmony. If two people can love without any payment on the rack or the cross it is almost a natural wonder. The road to sexual felicity can be a bit rowdy.

Thus, the schizoid person preserves emotional solitude, venturing out largely in structured situations and unstructured dreams. Real contact with others is a constant bombardment. Life spent alone is manageable; with others an inner pandemonium goes on beneath what seems to be an imperturbable façade.

Schizoids seem, on the surface, and to an uncritical eye, to have all their emotions arranged neatly out of sight. Often appearing much younger than chronology dictates, their faces may be as empty of care and strain as of warm feeling. Yet beneath that curiously young and blank look, the most intense human melodramas may go on, beyond being infatuated or in love.

When the schizoid person wants to form attachments, the pain of possible rejection is so simultaneous that he or she may feel as paralyzed as a locomotive pushing full strength against impenetrable steel. Best to stay away from love, or even liking. Instead, an imaginary attachment can take place, a perpetual fantasy whose intensity may build until it dominates all conscious moments. This fantasy is beyond infatuation or being in love because desperate longing can never be admitted. Other infatuated people tell their friends, their families, and before long communicate it to the precious person, in vivo. Not so the schizoid. So much is expected, desired, wanted—to reveal the immensity of the need is to begin to admit an insanity. The secret is embarrassing, inadmissible, profoundly terrifying.

Often the threatening situation is avoided altogether. Such feeling for another human being belongs to a different dimension of reality, like high tragedy or the grim tortures of fairy tales. If the schizoid does not submit to the fate of an empty life, he or she compromises by conducting extraordinarily insubstantial unions.

People who suffer this much in relating to others must do something to discharge their sexuality. The solution usually lies in masturbation. In some it may become a daily habit lasting for hours. Staying at home as much as possible, they may masturbate endlessly, often in front of a television set, which is the limit of comfortable human contact. Others cannot bear even this, and arouse themselves in quiet rooms behind locked doors. However accomplished, this is the kind of masturbation our elders were so afraid of. They forbade the habit, thinking that any practice of it would lead to such preoccupation. Masturbation does not lead to mental illness, but aberrant mental processes may lead to excessive self-stimulation.

Braver schizoid people, not quite so ill or so near being truly schizophrenic, will hazard the risk of touching skin with another human being. They will go, in the comfort of anonymity, to the "massage" parlors and "health" clubs. Some urbanites can manage the "sex" club. Many men rely on these as their sole avenue of sexual fulfillment.

Female schizoids have no such sexual conveniences. Even if "houses" existed for feminine satisfaction, most American women would find it discomfiting even to consider the possibility, much less ring the doorbell. Such an excursion would be an odyssey for the hardiest of womankind not engaged in the trade itself; our timid adventuresses couldn't begin to conceive it.

What is left for the woman who might be able to tolerate physical but not emotional contact? In urban areas, singles bars and other meeting places provide some outlet for the few who dare them. More often, apprehension wins. Sexual relations may be shelved for a lifetime. The gentle old spinster who lived by herself, never spoke harshly to anyone, and rarely ventured beyond the local market, was probably quite schizoid.

At the next level of psychosexual valor, the schizoid may jump the hurdle and form attachments without any physical reinforcement and often not even much verbal exchange. Again we find some cultural differences between men and women. Men are more readily able to make a "split," to separate the unreachable ideal from the available body. In fact, many men consider this dichotomy entirely normal. One of my earliest patients, a very frail spirit, could have sex easily and sensually with a fat and accommodating neighbor, "a real Bronx type," who managed, somehow, to have coitus while her hair was up in stiff rollers. However, he could barely talk to his ideal, a fair clean-cut secretary whom he had admired for many years from his position as office clerk. Had he succeeded in getting her into a seductive situation, he would have been impotent. He was, of course, overwhelmed by fantasies about his ideal. The more vivid, the less likely to come true. He saw nothing bizarre about this split, however. Everyone he knew said there were two kinds of women.

Women are rarely able to separate body and spirit in such a pragmatic fashion. Little in our culture condones this practice. For a woman to have an animalistic lover while not being able to respond to the man she idealizes seems a psychosexual aberration. Worrying about it may prevent her from getting as much as she might out of the simple contacts that she is psychically able to manage.

Contact with another human being on a complex plane—a contingency of thoughts and plans, of feelings, ideals, and spirit—is usually too rich a brew for the abstemious schizoid. Such closeness seems more than a heavy burden. It feels like a monstrous liability. Under its weight the schizoid ego may be devastated.

Caught between longing and frustration, desire and terror, the schizoid begins to build a dream the way a child, reprimanded by his elders, sets off to the edge of the ocean to build a castle higher than any real house on land could reach.

The dream-love lives at reality's edge, close enough for the mind to conjure, too far away for the body to touch; near enough to stimulate all the glands and senses, too high and too distant ever to capture. Like a kite floating on string that cannot be shortened, the schizoid dream hovers persistently, never to be reeled in, always capable of crashing.

There is an important difference between the schizoid dream and those fantasies, even obsessions, that we all create eagerly from time to time. The schizoid's object is generally someone who is, in fact, quite attainable. The imaginary liaison is not with some improbable potentate or cinematic symbol of romance, nor even with a member of a different social or economic class. The kite, the castle, the marvelous fantast, can be the girl who serves hamburgers at McDonald's, the library clerk, the lifeguard, the shoe salesman. Just as there are enormous numbers of paranoid people who live with visions pursuing them, so the schizoids may spend their days in pursuit of a vision.

As might be expected, schizoid people tend to be timid in bed or near it. A kiss on the lips may seem a strong commitment. Soon quarrels could arise over almost anything: what time do we meet, where do we go, what do we do, who takes the lead? Never to begin affection avoids all clash of wills later.

If kissing starts, what next? To be taught the acts of love may be an unbearable humiliation. Showing ignorance and the need for being taught, setting up a situation in which one can fail, are huge risks to an already devastated ego. Avoiding education seems the safer wisdom.

Intercourse, itself, can represent an intense bond leading only to the pain of severance. What is a more intimate security than two bodies fitting together and exchanging life? To appreciate the potential adhesiveness of such passion is to avoid it. Schizoids destroy themselves by protecting themselves too much.

10

Aggression: Sexual Conquest

As with perhaps no other identification of personality types, the antisocial projects the riddle of good and evil. Indeed, in the most rational and ordered of worlds, those among us who destroy human life and property, who flout our codes and ignore our civilization, should suffer serious impediments in loving. It would seem fitting that personal sexual pleasures be denied those with a penchant for inflicting pain on others.

Our myths, unlike our moralities, would have it otherwise. There is a tendency to regard the outlaw as a flamboyant lover. The "hood," prototype of the American gangster, has become a symbol of male virility and machismo throughout the world. The most extreme examples of antisocial behavior—even perpetrators of violent crime—are frequently seen as either extraordinary lovers or people whose emotions are so distorted that they are incapable of experiencing the sexual satisfaction available to less violent beings. Like most observations of the human condition, neither polarity is entirely true.

Since criminals have not been my friends, and are rarely my patients, I can only venture a cautious speculation on their sex lives: people in the enormous business of crime probably do little more fornication than all the rest of us. Our view of the antisocial personality as sex machine

93

may be like the concept of black man as stud or Oriental woman as geisha. Some are, most aren't. Just as some henchmen are dependent on the boss, or afraid to hold jobs because they feel inadequate to work, so it must be that nonconformists run a wide gamut of sexual behavior. The few I have encountered as patients—men who have used guns, or trafficked in fraud—have demonstrated very firmly entrenched sexual dysfunction.

To equate hypersexuality with sin seems to me a primitive notion. The definitive study of criminal sexuality remains to be done.

The odd paradox is that people who use sex for conquest, to hurt and disappoint others, or to gain a middleclass kingdom, are often not the obviously bellicose, shouting, demanding human beings we usually identify as aggressive. The sexually driven man may thrust his point firmly home. He is an ingenious persuader, sometimes trading on silence and crudeness, sometimes unctuous in his pursuit, but he rarely loses his temper. The seductively voracious female hardly ever displays her talons. Her victim only knows she has been there by the invisible scars she leaves. Men who explode with rage at trifles, women who present as punitive, loudmouthed shrews, rarely, if ever, use sex as a weapon. They can't. Although S-M and the joy of suffering have achieved recent popularity, very few people have orgasms on verbal or physical abuse. Acrimony is not a common aphrodisiac. Obviously unpleasant people do not collect sufficient admirers to discard them at will. When fortunate, they may find a single passive recipient for their fusillades. More often, they engage an equally illtempered partner. While learning to express anger may often release orgasm in the timid, we cannot conclude that angry people are sexier. The uncouth do not possess a master key to sexual Elysium.

The aggressive citizen who manipulates the borderline between acts of self-assertion and acts of brutality is a far more common visitor to the sex therapist's office. Indeed, mild cases of antisocial personality may enhance economic or political success. We are fascinated not so much by total misfits as by people who disobey the rules of propriety and are rewarded handsomely for their greed, avarice, and insensitivity.

Most often male, these people frequently take "figure-head" wives, women who seem content to identify with their husband's political or corporate success, who are coiffed and padded with the plump solidarity of pin-cushions, and who do not recognize that they are the cover for a heavily adulterated kettle of fish. Usually their suspicions are raised by an attack of vaginal infection or venereal disease, which they could not reasonably have acquired from the immaculate plumbing to which they are accustomed. Sometimes they learn more directly: their husbands may be publicly named as correspondents in divorce cases, beaten up, or involved in drunken brawls. Such aggressive men must not only conquer their sexual prey but also must ultimately hurt and humiliate their wives.

For some of these men—the ones who tend to become heroes on whatever scale—sex is only an aspect of the competitive game which they have been rigidly raised to play. Parents have unabashedly expected them to achieve, in sports, business, politics. They are molded to become competitors in every aspect of life, like thoroughbred horses.

Rivalry between siblings is encouraged. There is no shame in defeating, even crushing another human being, as long as the play is within some rule or societal standard. The need to have a vigorous extramarital sex life is, in part, a sport with society: to be a pillar of the community while at the same time holding a winning hand in defiance of its most sacred written rules. Perhaps the strongest dynamic involves unconscious hatred of the parents who raised them to be so fierce and loveless. They retaliate against mother, in particular, by humiliating her through her representation in the wife. Everyone is an opponent to the grandeur of the chief.

That these men cannot be tender lovers who find bliss in sharing kisses and love songs must be self-evident. What arouses them is only the achievement of success. Sometimes the intensity with which they pursue a female goalpost can be misinterpreted as love: the woman who receives gifts, flowers, and other devotions may respond with an affection that has nothing to do with reality. For no one else is the adage, "He only wants me for my body," so true. Whether conquerors are sexually competent or not can only occupy our conjecture. Presumably they are, else the pursuits in which they so frequently engage would hardly be pleasurable. However, the penchant for victory can be the most potent adversary of sexual triumph: men who feel they must order their penises to perform on command are the most vulnerable to sexual debacle. Thus it is that so many seekers after the erotic gold medal go tumbling headlong down the slope of the giant slalom. Women are preserved thereby from being merely a series of flags passed on the hill. Nature has helped women, and provided a mechanism for societal stabilization, by endowing men with performance anxiety. The best way for a man to avoid a bad trip that might produce impotence is to stay home in a safe bed.

While often expressed by acquisition of many partners, sexual aggression can also be practiced on a single captive female. A woman may be made to feel thoroughly inadequate by a variety of maneuvers. It is important that these tactics be distinguished from similar withholding actions that might result from performance anxiety.

For example, a man determined to dominate his wife and destroy her sexual ego might never respond to her sexual overtures but only insist on her response to his, no matter how busy or preoccupied she is with other things. One patient, determined to obtain a female slave, only kissed and fondled his wife when she was asleep, doing dishes, or bending over the laundry. He had no history of impotence and could respond to her requests if he chose to, but he actively enjoyed her discomfort when he repeatedly accused her of not being "spontaneous." Another gambit this patient used was to compliment his wife when she looked dowdy and to demolish her when she dressed up for parties or formal occasions. "You look better in your housecoat," he was fond of saying. When she was sexually active and responsive, he would tell her she was trying to castrate him with her passion: when she lay still, he accused her of being cold. All this was defined in a private session as a program to "bring her into line." Of course, he had deeply rooted fears of his own inadequacy, as most sexually aggressive men do, but they were so far from the surface as to be unavailable to rapid therapeutic techniques. Just as the aggressive man who delights in multiple conquest often denies his motives and merely thinks of himself as a sexual athlete, so the domestic destroyer simply thinks of himself as preserving the proper order of things.

Aggressive sexuality means having sexual relations solely as a form of conquest. It implies destroying another person's sexual ego in order to obtain dominance. The forms it takes include having and unilaterally discarding or degrading many partners, relating destructively to one person, or playing partners against one another. At less common and more pathologic levels, it includes rape and sadism.

People who indulge sexual aggressivity need not be overtly criminal. Often, they are arrogant, deceptive, and manipulative. The one mildly redeeming characteristic they share, however, is separation of their economic motives from their sexual intentions. They are not interested in lucrative spoils from sexual encounters. That perversion belongs to another, more dependent class of sexually aggressive people who may more truly be labeled sociopaths.

Pure sexual aggressivity is rare in women, though today it is becoming less of an oddity. To make sexual conquest is not merely to have sex, but to elicit the desire

for more permanent attachment, which is then abused. In
the past, men held the cards for conquest because women
sought to hold onto men for economic reasons. Women also
tended to wish to cling to their sexual partners for emotional security and out of fear of becoming promiscuous.
Self-esteem, for women, was largely gained from the ability
to sustain a singular, committed relationship. Fifty years
ago, therefore, women had few weapons for being sexually
aggressive. Men more often had the economic advantage.
Their sexual ego did not depend on a singular relationship. The only tool most women had was creation of an
emotional dependence, but once such vassalage was won
there was not much point in throwing it away.

Today, able to support themselves and also beginning
to find sexual self-esteem in numbers and variety rather
than through commitment, women are more apt to discard
and even impotize their partners. Indeed, given equivalent
self-esteen at the starting gate, it is far easier for a woman
to destroy a man's sexual self-confidence than it is for a
man to destroy a woman's. A woman can restore confidence
based on numerical encounters merely by increasing her
solicitation and invitation. A man must, of course, perform.
When a woman has told him that his penis is too small, his
timing poor, and his foreplay awkward, he may well have
difficulty sustaining an erection in the next sexual situation. Curiously enough, women are far better equipped
and more naturally able to be sexually aggressive than men
are.

Motives for sexual aggression among women range
from fear of intimacy to active retaliation against a parent
or a societal code which has badly injured their sexual
selves. While almost any combination of early and later life
events may cause it, the motive of social approbation (except by radically militant feminists) is conspicuously absent.

Sexual aggression against a husband has often been,
in the past, a woman's defense against coming to terms with
her own sexual inadequacies. If a woman's husband cannot

perform, then she need not be expected to enjoy sex or have orgasms. Today, with more women finding enhanced self-esteem through numbers, women will often impotize their husbands so that they can be "legitimately" free to have lovers. This is a more direct approach to the problem than men have used: traditionally, men have desexualized their wives by making resentful servants out of them, and then, unsatisfied with the lack of eroticism in their marriages, have had a good excuse to foray abroad. Women can do the job quicker and better, if less subtly.

Other aggressive personalities who rarely come into conflict with authority excel at manipulating. Never openly arrogant, indeed frequently appearing friendly, warm, open, and self-demeaning, these people develop skill in the high art of eliciting trust at first sight. Psychiatrists sometimes label them "sociopaths," although no legal action can be taken against them. They are not only interested in abusing other people's emotions, but want everything else they can legitimately get.

Everyone loves a sociopath—except for friends, family, and lovers. Perhaps it would be more accurate to say that most people start out by being attracted to sociopaths, and end up flagellating themselves for the weakness of their generosity.

People with sociopathic personalities appear to suffer no guilt for the multitude of petty and moderately serious wrongs they do to others. The most expert sociopathic personality can elicit enormous amounts of whatever his contact owns or feels, without ever violating a single law.

Most sociopaths are as charming as they are intuitively devious. They smile warmly to all; if there is a chance of increasing their receipts, they may entertain, comically or tragically, with consummate theatrical skill. The price of the ticket is high, however, and keeps going up. Sociopaths will take your food, clothing, and guest rooms; they will borrow your money on a permanent no-interest loan; they

will crawl through any emotional chink in your love relationships and rob you of your children's respect, your lover,
your mate. If they could, they would strip you naked of all
your worldly and spiritual possessions, leave you standing
like a scarecrow in a field, and kiss you sympathetically
good-bye, with appropriate sadness for your fallen estate.

I use the plural "they" so as not to distinguish between
masculine and feminine. However, male sociopaths are
thought to be far more numerous than females. The reason for this unfortunate bias in nomenclature is purely
cultural. It should be of interest to the movement for
female liberation. The dependence which constitutes sociopathy in a man, who is theoretically able to work and
provide, is considered perfectly normal in a woman, who is
theoretically unable to provide. Of course, when a woman
routinely sets about stealing lovers and husbands, she may
be considered nasty, crafty, and manipulative. If she leaves
a string of broken hearts, after emptying them of loving
gifts, she may be considered a cruel mistress. (Compared to
the sociopathic woman, a prostitute gives value received.)
Still, few psychiatrists call her a sociopath. Most would
mistakenly label her a hysteric, or a histrionic personality.
Any woman who puts on a good show without much to
back it up is identified as histrionic by a high percentage of
doctors, even though the sociopathy may be outrageous.

Male sociopaths are usually very active and effective
sexually, often to a much higher than normal degree. That
is one of the secrets of their fascination. Under circumstances that would ordinarily shrivel the cockiest penis,
they function with sublime indifference. The precarious-
ness of their position seems to give added zest to the
performance.

Male sociopathic gambits may include all the varieties
of Don Juanism in which the hero must seduce the heroine
and then leave her for the next damsel. The sociopath also
frequently tries to depart with as much of the lady's trea-

sure, apart from her sexual valuables, as he can legitimately garner. The conventional Don Juan, the sexual aggressive, however, is satisfied with emotional sadism alone, an unconscious sadism, because he does injury to another which he does not see as such. He simply experiences discomfort and must move on. This is the pure psychopathy of feeling: an extraordinary effort to obtain a transient power and acceptance, which is then abandoned. No one is richer, but a fraud has been accomplished on the giver, who has been damaged and may have difficulty trusting again.

Female sociopathy is a relatively new entry in psychiatry. The history of the world up to the time of mid-century America gave women the opportunity to be histrionic or criminal but rarely sociopathic.

Except under unusual circumstances, when a woman was heir to power or fortune, she made her way in the world by means of the men she attracted. It was acceptable, given this societal order, for a woman to employ her charms, her wit, and her body to secure all she could from a man. But the contemporary woman, who may not always have competitive parity with men, does have access to the means for self-survival with dignity. Therefore, when she employs her wiles to exhaust a man's assets and then deserts him, it is a lack of character which we may identify as sociopathic.

Like male sociopaths, the females often function sexually very well. Their ploys may generate an excitement that is quite stimulating, especially when they are operating successfully. Since a victorious maneuver often involves first giving and then denying sex to the victim, such ladies generally have a few lovers to whom they turn for satisfaction and to complain about their current marital hardships. It's an active life.

The sexual strategies that these women most often use, whether consciously or not, are designed to reduce the

swash and machismo of their plunder. The simplest deceptions work like bear traps on a friendly large monkey. One
of the easiest is to deny ever being satisfied, no matter how
excellent a lover the man is. Some mysterious quality is
missing; the relationship is never exhilarating enough. Or
something is wrong with his touch. Or, best of all, it's
possible to have orgasms on oral or manual stimulation, but
not on intercourse. This last has to be stated with the right
amount of contempt. The implication must be that other
men have been able to do it better. Conducted properly,
these tactics can make a psychologically vulnerable man
feel so inadequate that he gratefully surrenders his fortune, his principles, and his heart.

11

The Affective Factors: Sexual Mood Trends

Among the many varieties of people who grow in the world, there is one very rare and curious type. Psychiatrists label their unique personality "hypomanic." Others call such people "very happy," "spontaneous," "enthusiastic," "childlike." The hypomanics are so exceptional as to be quite unforgivable. Perhaps that is why analysts do not believe their joy. Underneath it all, they must be suffering. Their euphoria is a defense against a world which more often bestows tragedy than bliss on its inhabitants.

They smile on awakening and, if male, feel pleased with the erection that inevitably accompanies their entrance into the new day, just as it accompanied their arrival from mother's womb into the new world. Female hypomanics waken, stroke their own breasts and bodies luxuriously, and if there is a male at their side, almost invariably make some affectionate or erotic contact. If not, they may (God forgive them) hum a tune, or play at hand shadows with the sun. Their days begin and end with warmth and cheer—and they have happy lunchtimes, too.

Sexual contact, for these people, may be restricted to one partner, in whose absence they contentedly mastur-bate, or spread among many. They seduce in a moment: to meet them is to have one's paranoia suddenly disarmed, to want to give security and joy. Yet they rarely take advantage knowingly. They are as unusually good as they are happy.

The hypomanic feels sexual through every crisis which might be stressful and debilitating to others. It would take an extremely toxic to fatal illness to reduce the drive. Indeed, the meticulous analyst notes a pressure behind the sexuality as beneath the joy. At the extreme of hypomania is the manic state, the active phase of manic-depressive illness, in which sexuality is violently aroused, and the sufferer wants to copulate almost continuously. However, it is rare for a hypomanic individual to cross the border into mania.

Because of their unreserved optimism, hypomanics respond minimally to disappointment, or defeat, or loss. They find some benefit in every catastrophe: death saves people from a worse fate; poverty is easier to negotiate than riches. They never collapse under an emotional burden. If a love affair is unsuccessful, they soon anticipate the next lively experience. If a project goes badly, they readily turn to another. They do not know the depression, anxiety, and other discomforts which most people feel for a long time after personal or professional debacle.

Most discouraging of all, for those of us who are not so fortunate and who have envy, they tend to make love with vigor, skill, and ingenuity. Thoroughly enjoying themselves, rarely bored, they tend to monogamy, but can as well adjust to multiplicity.

It would be interesting to explore the comparative backgrounds of these people to try to find out what combination of disasters has made them so impervious to ordinary woes. Perhaps psychiatrists who have encountered more of these people than I have can offer a valid theory. So much research is done on what causes schizophrenia; time could as profitably be spent on the origins of hypomania. The insoluble problem might be trying to find enough of them to put together for a study. I have never met a total hypomanic, but only people who use euphoria as a major defense and live lives that cause others to avoid them at those intimate moments when pain shared could create the most meaningful happiness. On reflection, even with this hypothetical personality type, sexual difficulties can arise. The spouse of the hypomanic individual may not share his or her élan at all times, and may become sexually withdrawn or otherwise disturbed because sex, as comfort, can never be achieved if there is nothing one needs comfort against. The "happy" person lives alone in his or her ebullience. That may be one of the subtler tragedies of life.

The mood trend most transparently related to a change in sexual energy is depression. Yet it is some measure of how alienated we are from our feelings and our bodies that so many men complain of impotence, so many women of sexual indifference, and so few realize that they are suffering from this strained emotional state. While not the only cause of sexual vicissitudes, depression certainly contributes the devil's portion.

What is depression? Psychiatrists and other students have begun to write books about it with the same intensity as poets. If the forties and fifties were the age of anxiety, the sixties through eighties are the decades of depression. We turn to the media each morning and night for our daily dose of pain, to paralyze us even more than we are crippled by the smallness of our lives. We read Plath, Berryman, Mailer, Oates, Roth, Rhys, and all the others whose rage lies confined betwen hard covers. We see in art our grotesque immobility. We contemplate that our universe will soon run out of supplies; we slow our birthrate. We have lost the hope of a new empyrean salvation.

The spirit of our times is enough to hobble at least a majority of penises and to stiffen an equal proportion of vaginas. The sexually responsive remainder must all surely be hypomanics or psychopaths. By some singular miracle, however, universal depression has not afflicted the genitals of mankind. Male flaccidity and female numbness are usu-

ally limited to people with very personal cause for malfunction.

Although an increase in sexual drive is a common
defensive maneuver against depression, it is not a tactic
available to everyone. And as often as it works, for a time, it
also loses effectiveness when the deeper problem continues
unresolved.

Depression can be subclinical: not evident as anything
more than a pessimistic way of life, a personality tendency,
an unpleasant emotional state. In the ordinary course of
life, such people worry away time, sleep poorly, work irreg-
ularly. The world moves for them in a somber haze. Even
small events can convince them that all will soon be darkness and it is not worth trying to keep up the light.

When depression shows more clearly, it may be called
"neurotic," although this term has lost some favor with the
new clinicians. Such neurosis is an excessive response to
loss or failure. A particular event may cause more than
ordinary cessation of interest in life. Further along the scale
is a "psychotic depression," in which a person, without
necessarily being affected by any specific event, becomes
completely paralyzed and unable to think or function at all.
It may be a purely chemical phenomenon. No matter what
the severity of the depression—subclinical, mild, neurotic,
or psychotic—sexuality almost always suffers.

The sexual problems that most often accompany depression are loss of libido and impotence. Both the person
whose life-style tends to be depressive and the person who
is suffering a clinical depression are prone to absence of
sexual interest and capacity.

Sexual problems caused by depression are very different from those which can be alleviated in a few weeks of sex
therapy. They arrive as slowly or as quickly as the depression becomes manifest; a gradual or sudden loss of libido
takes place. No surge of desire, no passion to touch or be
touched, no joy precedes any unions. The man or woman
who eagerly fantasizes sex and then at the crucial moment

either cannot perform or respond has a different problem. Depression may be an insidious process. Interest and passion are either constantly at low ebb or become gradually reduced. Erections, rather than being lost, tend not to rise at all. Women become vaginally dry, unresponsive. They turn away from sex and prefer to go to sleep.

The person whose life-style is depressed needs help in removing psychological burdens. Most often these are related to difficulties with handling aggression or self-assertiveness. When a person has become accustomed to taking blame for too many of life's disasters, never being angry at others, he or she may carry about an unfair share of the world's guilt. When a person cannot speak for what he or she wants, having far less than one deserves can be depressing. Sex and *joie de vivre* must suffer.

The human being subject to a clinical neurotic depression, a sudden or slowly developing attack of painful hopelessness, needs support and possibly medication. The depression may have been caused by something quite unrelated to the person's sex life: a failure, a humiliation, a realization that one has touched an intellectual or physical limit. Although a heavy part of the response is sexual, the return of sexuality is generally secondary to a return of interest in life and activity. Psychotic depressions are treated by medication or electric shock. Sexuality generally returns when the episode is over.

I have written of depression as producing a loss or lessening of sexuality. What about the converse—loss of sexuality leading to depression?

Sexual loss threatens the depressive personality most. While the majority of us are not regularly depressive, we do frequently have emotionally dyspeptic moments, when it seems clear that no human of any worthwhile stature will find our generative equipment worth fussing about ever again. The depressive personality, however, lives with a constant sense of present and impending decay. When a real deterioration occurs, an impairment of any body part, a scar, an angioma, a fracture, the depressive, conceiving the entire body as a sexual organ, steps a ring lower in the purgatorial descent and suffers, suffers. A pimple may be the erythematous flag of cancer; each new wrinkle another spadeful out of the gravesite. Hypochondriasis results in severe cases, often less from real fear of death than from terror of the loneliness that lessening of sexuality can bring or, even worse, fear of the loneliness that lessening of attractiveness can bring while sexuality is still intact.

Another source of depression in those prone to it may be an episode in which sexual activity failed to occur when expected. A man may anticipate having a splendid liaison, find himself flaccid, and become depressed about this incomprehensible event. Such impotence does not necessarily lead to depression, but in the person whose life proceeds from one gloomy forecast to the next, the incident may seem to presage a final desolation.

So it is with any of the real tragedies that may come to our intimate selves: loss of sight, hearing, or any sense, or of any body part. We lose an aspect of our sexuality. Older analytic thought has suggested that such losses "represent" castration; in fact, they are castrating in that the chances for attracting a partner go down with each impairment. Who will want us, blind, deaf, lame and bald, wrinkled, pale, paralyzed, or with a slow, incurable illness, whether or not our sex organs function? Depressing, indeed.

Between the hypomanic and the depressive personality there is an intermediate variety: the cyclothymic. These people are alternately rather hypomanic or depressed, often for long periods—months at a time—without any correlation of their mood to outside events. They are not happy for a period of time because life has gone well, or sad because of grievous circumstance. Their mood seems independent of life events.

Very much like the cyclothymics, except that their mood varies from day to day or hour to hour, are people with "labile" personalities. "Up" one moment and "down" the next, their sexuality varies directly with their moods. So it is also with cyclothymics, except that their moods last so much longer.

This changeability would not be a problem in itself if sex did not usually involve two people, at least. Not only the shifting sexual needs, but also the pendulum of other cravings, may drive a partner up the nearest wall for height, distance, and perspective.

Part III

PSYCHOSEXUAL
DISORDERS

12

Disorders of Desire

An unhappy truth of the conjugal world is that men and women have many more sexual disorders than were suspected by scientists only a few years ago. Naming and defining has become a new preoccupation. In this men have had the advantage, naming their infirmities with accuracy and according to obvious realities. The greater part of the male reproductive system is superficially visible, remarkable for its clear signals. Penis and scrotum are exposed. Conditions of the male erotic apparatus, hung front and center on the torso, have been carefully delineated. Whether the penis fills, or ejaculation arrives early or late, or erectile ability differs from one partner to another—all have been meticulously examined. Not so with women.

In the late 1970s, a "task force" of the American Psychiatric Association went to work to clarify and simplify. They reduced what was already known to easy categories defined in intelligible English. They permanently discarded "frigidity," that old medical catchall so misused in the past. The APA also rejected that male embarrassment, "impotence."

Women are no longer simply piping hot or refrigerated, nor are men powerless. Instead they suffer "inhibited sexual desire," "inhibited sexual excitement," and "inhibited orgasm." These terms do away with the old pejoratives, frigidity and impotence, as well as with the

113

tongue-twisting though pioneering nomenclature of Masters and Johnson, who gave us "primary and secondary orgasmic dysfunction."

The realm of inhibited sexual desire is complex and controversial. It would seem to me that, for simplicity, the term "inhibition of desire" should refer to that condition in which a person has never experienced desire. The person may be actively averse to having sex, may feel the whole subject is offensive, if not abhorrent. Or, he or she may simply be indifferent, may never wish to have sex. (Following my original definition of this state as "aversion," Masters and Johnson now call it "primary aversion.") The idea might best be understood by analogy to people who don't comprehend the joys of opera. They may hate it and stay carefully away, or they may indulge a mate in the ritual without understanding what on earth is so interesting, beautiful, or exciting about people singing incomprehensible songs on a stage.

That would seem enough territory for the term "inhibition of desire" to cover, but some propose that it include any problem that reduces a person's willingness to have sex with a specific partner, even if they have had no previous problems.

The problem of desire disorder may therefore be seen as either virtually global to sexual difficulty or relatively rare, depending on the definition of desire. In a strict sense, if desire is simply the intellectual wish to have good sex, the disorder is relatively nonexistent. Most people want good sex, whatever they conceive that to be. And if they don't want good sex with an important partner, they usually want to be positive about it, want to want it. To continue the opera analogy, it is as if they don't like it—or don't like a particular opera—but they really want to like it. They have a sincere desire to appreciate it, which is not inhibited. My own preference, therefore, is to limit my discussion of the term "inhibition of desire" to those relatively rare conditions in which people do not wish to have sex at all, and have never wished to have it, without any overt conflict about their lack of interest.

With that limitation, however, we would be left with the category "inhibition of excitement" to cover the vast multitudes of cases of sexual lethargy that come to a sex therapist. That is not sufficient. These people bring problems that most often relate both to their willingness to have sex and to the excitement they experience in anticipation of and during the sexual act. They have combined problems of desire and excitement, for which no formal term exists as yet in the American Psychiatric Association's diagnostic literature. Problems that reduce a person's willingness to have sex (desire) often also reduce responsiveness to sexual activity (excitement). The manual recognizes this, but as yet no encompassing term exists. As an inclusive term, therefore, "inhibition of arousal" seems appropriate.

Cases of this combined problem now come more often to the analytically oriented sex therapist (or psychiatrist specializing in psychosexual disorders) than they do to the behaviorally oriented sex therapist. The same professional who may help a premature ejaculator merely by prescribing the "stop-start" exercises does not usually have the skills in psychiatry or marital psychotherapy necessary to deal with inhibition of arousal where nothing is functionally wrong. Given felicitous circumstances, the person can function well enough to have an orgasm, remain erect, or have lengthy intercourse. It has become necessary to deal with the sexual problem that might once have been considered an obvious consequence of a person's marital or connubial rift—and left undiscussed. This dilemma is now not only included in the therapy but can afford a focus for exploring the entire structure of a personality, a marriage, or a relationship.

Beyond indifference and aversion, then, we find extraordinarily widespread difficulties with inhibition of arousal—with combined problems of desire and excitement—that cause sexual avoidance and ambivalence.

While this inhibition of arousal may be a response to a specific sexual dysfunction, most often it reflects personality difficulties or interpersonal conflicts. It is more a disorder of motivation and response than a functional inadequacy. In a sense, it is the newest, the most comprehensive problem in psychosexual therapy, a problem that has always existed, yet has not been named or treated precisely.

AVERSION

Aversion surprises the erotic scholar by its relative scarcity, even in women. Of course, a psychiatrist may see a skewed sample because those who are truly averse to sex would probably not consult an expert in the field of assisting sexual union. Nevertheless, it would seem that there are few who cannot feel even the slight skin warmth, the capillary widening that presages active desire. Hardly any men despise all sex as weakness. Few women despise it as an archaism. This is remarkable because, after all, the old morality warned both men and women, and especially women, of the serious risk to marriage and mental health should they enjoy premarital or extramarital sex. For women, the new morality of liberation involved a few believers in a form of female *hubris,* an orgy of man hating. Men were generally unnecessary. Several hyperactive studs could repopulate the world by artificial insemination. The male sex was ecologically extinct. With both the old and the new sanctions operating, one would expect to see more emotional padlocks on the vagina, more of an armed guard against sexual submission. Yet with all the propaganda to the effect that the penis is a vestigial appendage, necessary neither for procreation nor for pleasure, the number of sexual recluses remains remarkably small.

Sexual aversion reigns largely among severely disturbed people. Paranoid schizophrenia, conversion hysteria, and depression are the major mental illnesses that it accompanies.

The paranoid schizophrenic may see any sexual approach as an attempt at injury. Some view any attempt at touching or feeling as preliminary to murder or castration, but are able to keep their delusions and their hallucinations to themselves as they go about their daily work. As long as they are successful in avoiding contact, they continue to function.

Classical hysterics (who are quite different from histrionic personalities) display their antagonism to sexuality with a "conversion symptom." The sufferer, most often a woman, becomes literally anesthetized or paralyzed, although there is no neurological basis for the deficit. The physical fraud can be detected by a canny neurologist; the emotional problem is no fraud at all. A deeply rooted fear or repugnance to sexual intimacy immobilizes or desensitizes the person's body.

Depression, the most lethal sexual executioner, kills the impulse toward all that is fervently human. Self, joy, tenderness, and lust disappear. The severely depressed individual sits, plucks at clothing lint, refuses food, does not care.

Denial of the alarming sexual impulse may, in other emotionally disturbed people, result in an obsessional quest to erase sex altogether. Some, in their effort to eradicate their bodies, develop anorexia nervosa, a disease in which they slowly starve themselves, often to death. Anorexia is becoming more frequent today, in spite of all the literature that tells us to enjoy. I have seen it in both men and women. Without fat, without flesh, women's breasts cannot reach their natural fullness, nor the buttocks become those posterior equivalents of breasts, two mounds behind, that entice men from any angle. Men without fat wither alarmingly. Their muscles disappear; their skin sags; they lose masculine vigor. Many anorexics, wishing to be free of all that binds them to physical reality, see fat as an evil.

They transpose their fears of sexuality and fertility into disgust with any flesh existing between skin and bones. They deny themselves the gratifications of every body passage: of the mouth, the vagina, and even the anus.

With equally stubborn persistence, many severely compulsive anorexics, especially women, give themselves to work as passionately as others renounce themselves to starvation or to God. The office replaces the convent or the monastery. Thinking always of the next task, inventing jobs, worrying about work not done well enough, can absorb a lifetime, trim desire to a dead stubble, close the body with unremitting and unfelt anger against life and love. To be aroused is to miss a moment's contemplation of work, to suspend aggrandizement and even endanger self-preservation. To be sexual is to fail.

Fear of sex may also be a phobia, like a terror of flying, or crossing the street, or standing in a high place. The alarming symptoms are very much the same: palpitations, breathlessness, a constriction in the chest, a cold sweat, and the overall apprehension of doom. Some authorities feel that a fear of sex is not a true phobia because it does not represent some other fear, in the way that a horror of knives may represent a defense against aggression. However, sexual panic can indeed represent something else: an avoidance of the pain of intimacy, desertion, rejection, and all the hurt that the danger of closeness implies.

Aversion to sexuality continues, unfortunately, to exist. We have not yet eradicated mental illness, nor have we any sure proposal to thaw the arctic chambers of human love.

INDIFFERENCE

Another disorder of desire is lack of interest in sex. There may be no active fear or repulsion, but rather a simple absence of concern. Affection feels good, but it never becomes sexual excitement. A genital caress might as well be a brush against an elbow. Pornography is as interesting as a travelogue about flat Midwestern farmland. Love is a pleasant sort of caring. Most of the cases of this disorder are brought to therapy by their mates since the indifferent partners, themselves, are not sufficiently concerned to seek help.

Women who have major hidden aggression against men may feel indifferent to sex. Compulsives, passive-aggressives, and paranoid women are the most frequent types, their "sexlessness" being symptomatic of an anger that they repress or deny.

Many dependent women marry men who become surrogate fathers or brothers. These men sometimes help them to achieve scholastically or professionally. In these sad chronicles, the parental or sibling incest taboo, or the rivalries, often reinforce inhibitions too strong for the women to break. They may never be able to feel sexual toward their husbands, although they may suddenly be aroused in later life by a different man.

Early discouragement of sexual expression by a girl's family has often been correlated to later absence of interest. There are, indeed, families in which female children are not only prevented from expressing their normal curiosities about themselves and others at an early age, but also restricted from sexual contact later. If such girls receive physical affection, chances are that adulthood will bring only an excitement disorder. But if the family manner is cold, without the closeness of hugs and kisses, and there is no evidence that the parents have sexual relations, a disorder of desire becomes more likely. It takes great deprivation to extinguish desire, however, and families which passionately deny or decry sex seem, in my experience, to have immense additional psychopathology. This, rather than any specific antisexual injunction, is likely to be the culprit.

* * *

Male indifference to sex most often reflects the same concealed anger as that which we see in women. Depression may or may not be obvious. Impotence is often a symptom, but even that may be ignored. Men use the same defenses that women do, relying mainly on overcommitment to work, to household hobbies or sports—especially passive spectator sports—to anything that may absorb their time and keep them away from erotic involvement.

Men are unconsciously angry at women for the same reasons that women hold invisible anger toward them. It is important to recognize that when the symptom of anger is sexual indifference, the cause is usually related to significant influences in the person's past rather than to present disagreements. Only some aspect of over- or underconcern for a child could lay the groundwork for such a loss of libido.

Familial patterns that may herald male indifference generally include some exaggeration of any normal scale of interaction. If mother is too peaceful, too bellicose, too overprotective, too uninterested, or if father is too dominant, too insensitive, too uninvolved, too overinvolved, women may suffer by comparison or contrast. In clinical practice, the most common situation I see relates to men whose parents were jointly too peaceful and too uninvolved. When a woman becomes normally upset or argumentative, the man interprets it as all-out aggression and withdraws. Such men generally become confused, passively depressed, and sexually indifferent.

One needs to distinguish between lack of sexual interest and loss of it. Men lacking sexual interest from the start are rare: I have talked with many women who have never experienced any sexual stirring, but I rarely encounter any physically normal men who have never experienced sensuality or any craving for fulfillment. Loss of sexual interest can occur in both sexes, however. It can be a phobic response to trauma as well as a personality response to a partner. People may simply become frightened of sex in much the same way that they can develop fear or distaste for anything else. What you are afraid of, you avoid, or pay as little attention as possible.

On a psychological basis that is also physical, men whose parenting was uniquely unaffectionate may also lose interest in sex once the aphrodisiac effects of novelty and conquest have worn off. They simply do not understand affection or how it can lead to sexuality. In even more difficult instances, such men may not even comprehend the erotic impulse because of their early deprivation. Women may marry them in the hope of bringing them out of their physical isolation. Often it is a hopeless and thankless task. Some fundamental neurological connection has been damaged.

13

Disorders of Arousal

AVOIDANCE AND AMBIVALENCE

People's major personality traits determine whether they will ultimately welcome sex in their lives as a significant contributor to happiness or dismiss it as essentially useless. Most healthy people, no matter what their character, engage in and enjoy sexual courtship and the early years of mating. In the time-honored tradition of mammalian life, when two people want to mate they set aside aggression and come together in a most unusual harmony of intention. One seems to know what the other wants to do almost before the other can think it. A new euphoria attends life's simplicities; if the emotion is not love, it is often mistaken for that high estate.

Precisely how long this period of relative peace between the sexes is maintained has not been studied, but the standard phrase about the end of the honeymoon speaks to an overwhelming number of people. An early mating period terminates. People either move on to new partners for another mating infatuation or they remain with each other. How long the honeymoon lasts—a few hours or a few years—is an individual matter. After courtship, which has its perils for some but is relatively easy for most, there is the maintenance of the bond. This is quite difficult for almost everyone.

When people stay together it almost invariably involves a release of aggression after the courtship phase is over. Old defenses, old armaments against the disasters of life are reconstructed. Premarital personalities take form again, sometimes with increased negative vigor because now the defenses must be stronger in order to deal with a partner constantly there.

Couples grow hostile. They move apart. The loss of sexual interest signals the end of that intense, impetuous period we remember well enough to repeat again and again in reality or fantasy through all the phases of life.

So it is that people come to a sex therapist with the complaint of lack of sexual desire or excitement. They may be stringently avoiding a sexuality that was formerly pleasant, or they may be ambivalent about wanting to participate in the act that once seemed to invest their entire life with meaning. Sometimes they may feel kindly toward their spouse. They may admit him or her to the old pleasures. At other times, sexual delight seems gone forever. A husband is too clumsy, too ineffectual, too noisy, too addicted to spectator sports. A wife is too silent and long-suffering, too fat these days, too miserly with herself. Character traits have begun to emerge in their negative as well as their positive guises. The realities of sexual dysfunction or sexual dyskinesia may become apparent.* Sexuality retreats. People either avoid each other in bed or merge fitfully in unions that belong more to recollection or to others than to the human being on the other pillow, the person with familiar features whose strangeness is becoming known.

For a moment, in the fierce trust of first love, a passive man may overcome his tendency to huddle within himself. He may seek out a woman and tell her his soul. He may stir

---

*Sexual dyskinesia is a term used in this book for the first time. It is meant to refer to lovers who are ineducably clumsy, in the same fashion that people with dyslexia cannot see words or coordinate correctly. Indeed, sexual dyskinesia may be a variant of dyslexia. One might call it more simply "sexual learning disability." Many people, both men and women, complain that their mates cannot learn the simple techniques of sexual communication, no matter how often instructions are repeated. If neither stupidity, ill will, nor inhibition can be indicted, there must be some organic explanation for the defect.

himself to gifts and generosities of which his dominating father would certainly disapprove and to which his mother might respond with thrifty depredation. His new-found mate, accustomed to receiving everything she wants from more indulgent parents, feels that the courtship treasures are her birthright. She is comfortable being thus celebrated and expects the homage to continue forever. After marriage, it stops when the bank account dwindles and the inlaws whisper to their son about the extravagantly spoiled spirit of his bride. Sexuality dwindles, too, along with the presents. The complaints of abandonment and deprivation begin as the marriage between a passive-aggressive man and his dependent, narcissistic, and mildly histrionic wife begins to take shape.

The stories that reveal this pattern of sexual diminution are various as life itself. They form the core of the case histories of both marital discord and the death of sex, be the partners married or not. What starts in splendor ends in tatters or, at best, moderately well preserved at the thrift shop.

Perhaps the most commonplace tragedy takes place between the person brought up to be affectionate and the one who is comfortable being physically distant because his or her childhood was barren of warmth. A man might have grown up in a loving family where kisses, hugs, and comforting strokes were a daily provision against the harsher realities; a woman might have matured as an orphan or a deserted child, perhaps in another country. Frequently women raised in England are proud of not needing the demonstrativeness of being touched, as are many Americans who grow up in families of English and Teutonic descent. Such couples often meet and marry on the veritable wings of an extraordinary erotic impulse: at some unconscious level she is aware of the affectionate resonance behind his sexuality; he is aware of all the repressed passion behind her lust. Eroticism alone, without a conscious affectional component, often has an intense meaning to people who have not spent their lives touching the members of their family. She reaches for him as she has never sought anyone; he is overwhelmed by and grateful for the magnitude of her desire.

As they live together, their customary life-styles return. She seems unaware or rejecting of his out-of-bed kisses, the hugs after breakfast, the hand holding during walks. She develops a habit of putting him off that persists into the bedroom because she has begun to see him as an invader of her private bodily territory. Indeed, his perpetual interest in her has become an invasion of her time and her mind. She develops her solitary skills and moves along in her career. More withdrawn than she might have been had she not found it necessary to battle her husband's closeness, she develops a reputation for being an excellent, if isolated, worker.

Sex dies between this woman, who has developed her orderly, obsessional, and perfectionistic traits, and her husband, who clings, depends, and seeks approval. They find that they can only enjoy sex with each other when they have been apart for a long time. After the quarrels about household matters and recreational preferences become more frequent, they begin to find that sex with others, people with whom personality clashes do not have time to develop, is the only solution to their lack of attraction to each other.

The libretto for the wounding of desire and the death of excitement can be created by imagining any configuration of personality traits emerging more strongly than ever after being released from the miraculous constraints that keep people enamoured of one another during the halcyon days of courtship mating. If an obsessional person denies his or her competitiveness in the course of selecting a mate, it will surely assert itself to damage sexuality later. If a paranoid personality fears the punishments that success will bring, a happily successful relationship cannot exist very long. If the narcissistic person cannot reach for inti-

macy or the schizoid fears it, ultimately they will return to
their corners and come out fighting. The trap is infinitely
human: we hope that mating will release us from the psychic structures that have imprisoned us. We may idealize
our new partners. Sooner or later, they become angry at us,
or we at them. Where resolution cannot satisfactorily be
made, the personality reverts to its pre-mating qualities.

Once anger has emerged from the Pandora's box of
premarital personality traits, a mate often responds with
fear and the desire to retaliate. A sexual dysfunction may
now come into being: impotence, premature ejaculation,
orgasmic inhibition. This happens because the aggrieved is
unwilling to say "no" to sex, but the unpleasant feelings
surrounding the relationship make sex unpleasant. Sexual
ambivalence leads to dysfunction. Sad to relate, the dysfunction often remains after the source of anguish has been
removed because performance anxiety replaces fear and
anger. Even though the discord is resolved and one partner
no longer fears or dislikes the other, he or she is afraid of
not being able to perform. The same effect—impotence,
premature ejaculation, orgasmic inhibition—can persist in
couples even when other difficulties have been satisfactorily
adjusted.

When sexual affection has been thus damaged, people
suffer an unwillingness to engage in a frustrating physical
relationship. There are a few occasional attempts to have
intercourse, but the joy of the impetus has been severely
depleted. Many settle for a life of sexless cuddling with a
long-term partner. They cannot resolve their performance
anxieties even though their love for each other has grown
over time. In such cases, brief sex therapy may be profoundly effective and longer-term psychosexual therapy
may not be required.

Curiously enough, many people whom I have treated
do not recognize their lack of arousal until it has become an
inability to perform the sexual act. Men, particularly, are

vitally concerned with the concept that they ought to be able to perform under all circumstances. Often they may not even be aware that they dislike their partners. Not until their erection tells them that matters are not as firmly positive as they should be do they know that something is wrong. Women tend to know that they are not sexually enthusiastic more intuitively than men do. They know that they are not aroused, yet they are capable of sexual performance. On the whole, therefore, women complain more openly. They understand that the reason they didn't lubricate or have an orgasm is that they were conflicted about having sex. Men often have to learn from their penises that they don't know what they want.

Single people, too, may lose the inclination to have sex even though they are not subject to the wear and tear of domesticity. Those people who prefer a series of noncommitted encounters may lose heart after someone becomes overattached and makes drama out of a casual night in bed. Or they may suffer an unexpectedly painful rejection that makes the next relationship, or the whole idea of sex, uncomfortable. Indeed, the whole spectrum of personality disorders that may emerge after a time in a committed relationship may prevent that very relationship from occurring. More seriously disturbed people—especially the schizoid and paranoid types, as well as those who have also been labeled "avoidant," may stay away from sex even though they feel some excitement. They may be able to combine desire and excitement in fantasy but not in action. Or they may be of two minds about the whole seemingly unwieldy machinery of romance, intimacy, attachment, successful bonding, procreation and all the emotional life work that accompanies the continuation of the species. Inhibition of arousal can occur at any time in the sexual life cycle to prevent courtship, make it difficult, or interfere with bonding.

* * *

Inhibition of arousal may, of course, result from any situation that creates strongly unpleasant responses. The key determinant may not be interpersonal. It may be quite simply logical. Fear of disease—particularly herpes and the acquired immune deficiency syndrome (AIDS)—has recently dampened a great deal of sexual responsiveness. People are not so eager to have clandestine or varietal sex for fear of what they will contract. Married partners are also limiting their participation with each other: women have become unenthusiastic about oral sex with mates whom they know to have oral herpes, even when those lesions are in remission. Men are becoming more reluctant to receive oral sex, too, as well as to participate in sex acts that are out of the ordinary, like anal sex. Couples for whom such behavior was routine are now reducing the scope of their pleasure. Although this is a normal variant of arousal inhibition, it is worth mentioning as a sign of our times. It is especially worth noting because there are those who are predisposed to overreact as well as those who are too cavalier. Finding the right balance is, as always, life's challenge.

One may address oneself to a hierarchy of fears that can be popularly understood, such as fear of intimacy, fear of romantic success, or fear of pleasure. One may approach the difficulty from the point of view of a predetermined personality structure that is fundamentally schizoid, avoidant, passive, or obsessive-compulsive. Whichever way one chooses to look at the dilemma, the quenching of sexual intention and the limiting of sexual action are the curious consequences of those situations in which we feel that we are not—or fear that we will not be—nurtured. The sexual act stimulates nurturant responses in animals as far down the evolutionary ladder as sheep; how much more complex is human response! We try, however blindly or awkwardly, to protect ourselves from an alien world. In this way, too, we indirectly guard our offspring.

EXCESSIVE SEXUAL AROUSAL

By far the most common cause of excessive sexual arousal in men and women is mild depression. Yet mildly depressed men who want more sex because they think less of themselves for some other reason rarely come to a therapist's office. They are more likely to be found in singles bars, or in bed with a new partner. Sexual stimulation in defense against life's discouragements is more often a male than a female behavior; promiscuity remains more socially acceptable in men than in women. Nevertheless, there are women, too, who find solace in indiscriminate sexuality. We do what makes us feel better, not necessarily that which achieves a rational relief from pain. A loss, a need to retaliate in a marital setting, often lead to a temporary abandonment of sexual limits. The need to display, conquer, tabulate results—all the ramifications of the various personality traits—may now emerge as regularly and openly among women as they have among men in the past.

Why people become depressed, what they do about it, and what they get from what they do vary with character. In response to mild depression, compulsives may chalk up a score. Narcissists may increase the number of their sexual admirers. Aggressives may need to know how much they are adored by the emotional havoc they can create. Histrionics pursue attention. All seek what they have come to accept as a symbol of love, no matter how distant it is from true feeling. These behaviors indicate psychosexual disorder when they are destructive to others or seriously interfere with life satisfaction and productive work.

Compensatory sexuality often results from mild depression. As dark spirits grow more intense, however, most people are unable to respond sexually at all. Loss of libido is frequently the most definitive early symptom of serious depression, along with loss of joy in life. Desire, the wish to have sex, disappears along with the excitement that is spe-

cific to the bodily moment. Erections subside, even in sleep.
In deep depression, desire and excitement are often absent; arousal is extinguished.

On the other side of depressive illness, psychotically
manic people, both male and female, often want to copulate continuously while they are in the "high" phase of their
manic-depressive illness. Perhaps women in this state provided the first impetus for that controversial label
"nymphomaniac," now fallen into disrepute.

Today, many sexual experts continue to believe that
any manifestation of the sex drive ought to be expressed.
Women, especially, have been repressed too long. No matter how many times a day a woman may want coitus, or how
long she wants to go on with any one act of intercourse, or
how many men she wants to have, she should feel free to
enjoy her unlimited potential.

The first "scientific" philosophy of sexuality held that
repressed libido caused anxiety. The sex drive could transform into a painful sensation that had no adequate cause in
a person's life circumstance. Once sexuality was expressed,
such irrational anxiety would disappear. Believers in this
old formulation run the danger of misinterpreting it to
mean that boundless sex is the final answer to all of life's
emotional discomfort.

A gentler approach to the relationship between sex
and anxiety is to see sexual touching and holding as one
way of relieving the survival anxiety that forms an essential
part of our nature. We have a periodic need to hold and to
be held. This gives us our basic sense of security. Some
women can differentiate this need from sexual arousal
associated with other stimulants; most cannot. Women who
need so much sexual contact that all else in life is secondary
suffer a primitive anxiety that can only be put to brief rest
during the sexual act. They are not aware of their infantile
craving to be constantly held.

Some of these women are multiorgasmic, requiring
twenty to thirty orgasms in a single sexual experience and

being willing to stop only when they have reached total physical exhaustion. One young woman, though she managed to hold a simple job, could not return home at night without a man. She suffered a sexual insatiability that led to endless and monotonous orgasms. Her anxieties about moving ahead at work, depending on her boss, performing adequately—were all channeled into a need for orgasmic release. Only when she was able to face these fears and begin to overcome them did her sexual tension decrease. She no longer needed sex to erase both her fears of abandonment and of asserting herself.

Many women who need so much phsyical contact are not orgasmic at all. They are impelled by a perpetual fear of isolation and nonbeing that is as intense as any lonely baby's cry in the middle of the night. In their search for the most elemental bodily reassurance, they wind up in bed with men under every conceivable condition of indignity.

In the past, men were likely to label any lusty woman in search of sexual experience as a nymphomaniac, a woman uncontrollably in search of contact with her nympha, or labia minora. One of the happier consequences of the sexual revolution is that careless labeling is no longer practiced. But the immature and inadequate woman, who needs a large arm around her all the time, still spends a great deal of time in many bedrooms. I do not believe we should call her a nymphomaniac. Often, she is not even aroused.

While conditions do exist where women seek more sex than might be considered healthy or normal, perhaps the simple designation of "excessive sexual arousal" or "excessive sexual activity" describes the problem better than the old Greek euphemism.

And though it hardly seems a painful condition to those who are unafflicted, some men experience too much arousal. A small group suffer from "satyriasis," or insatiable venereal desire usually associated with old age. These men do not come to sex therapists. They are more often to be found in homes for the aged or contained in the family bedroom. Perhaps some do not have excessive wishes at all but merely have no way of releasing their sexuality. One rich old man, not altogether mentally competent, was nevertheless able to arrange to have a professional come to his home to relieve him of what he considered the indignity of masturbation, as well as misguided lust toward his nursing attendants. When satyriasis does exist, it is probably related as much to organically disturbed mental processes as to any personality difficulty; while Greek names have charm, and satyriasis is less pejorative than nymphomania, as a medical diagnosis, "excessive sexual arousal" probably states an unbiased case better. Even so, since excessive arousal does not appear in the diagnostic manual of the American Psychiatric Association for either men or women, the condition is most likely to be observed only in a patient's nursing notes.

Male Maladies

DISORDERS OF EXCITEMENT

Erections may fail at any time in a man's sex life, or under any circumstances. He can lose his ability to penetrate before he has ever been successful in doing so. He may fail after a long and good sexual relationship. He can lose his erection with one partner but not with another. Physically, the explanation of all impotence is remarkably simple. Becoming and remaining erect physiologically resembles digesting a good meal, sleeping soundly, or having an especially splendid bowel evacuation. These bucolic functions are mediated by the parasympathetic nervous system. When all is well, when comfort and contentment are mixed with exactly the right amount of pleasurable anticipation, neurons send out acetylcholine to signal the penile blood vessels to dilate, to relax. Blood rushes in, to lodge and pass through the great spongy and cavernous bodies of the organ's shaft. Gates, in the form of pressures and valves, have opened. The marvelous hydraulics of erection transform a limp appendage into a large and purposeful instrument. It only works, however, when the master feels no fear.

Fear makes the mouth dry, the heart beat faster, the palms sweat. On microscopic beads of adrenaline, the emotion carries to all the gently, steadily rippling organs inside the body and shocks them into stillness. Blood vessels constrict, the stomach pales, the regular undulations of glistening colonic labyrinths cease. And out of the hundreds of thousands of tiny pocket spaces in the penile network, the ichor drains, to join all the fluids streaming to a battlefront. When we have fear, we need muscle for flight or fight. The blood leaves the penis (never an organ of man-to-man combat) and supplies the engines of war and retreat. Since achieving intercourse by means of a bloody biceps or a stoked gastrocnemius would hardly be acceptable, were it possible, the intimate relation loses its *modus operandi.*

When impotence is not caused by drugs, organic factors, psychosis, inexperience, ignorance, or unusual circumstance, the demons are characterological. Male sexual performance and personality type are frequently related, just as clothing, choice of furnishings, and choice of occupation are individual and contingent. People are not "hot and cold," "good or bad lovers," "sexy or uptight." Everyman's sexuality is as uniquely his as a fingerprint. Indeed, every sexual relationship has its own tone, meaning, consequence. There is no common denominator of gourmet joy or ideal procedure. Nor is there any one cause or cure for impotence.

Upbringing contributes to the creation of an impotent man, no matter whether his failure occurs at his first try or later on in a random encounter after a life of sexual prowess. The governing principle is: what kind of man do certain parents create?

Many combinations may produce, for example, the aggressive man who is peculiarly susceptible to impotence. Most obvious is the father who acts as a role model; more subtle is the domineering, punitive mother who raises her son to be a bullying self-promoter in order to gain more approval than his weak, perhaps gentle father. Sons of ineffectual mothers, alcoholics, or psychotics—boys pressed too early into adult roles for which they are unprepared—often compensate with aggressivity. The lineage of the disorder is variable. The consequence is a man who lives by the concept—which could impotize an army—that he must demonstrate martial command at all times. Not only does he have to win all the time, but he has to fight all the time. Sex is the ultimate battle. The big women, wielders of knives and other kitchen weapons, must be subdued, worn down, beaten. In the courts, over the counters, in the office, at parties, and certainly in bed.

Sex often goes well for this type of man as he ravages the lush populations of single and married women. They are "cunts," easy or hard, good or lazy. They must be damaged first before they damage him. The odd thing is how many women, thinking these men are purposeful, competent, and secure, positively dote on them. The aggressives are today's darlings, often accepted as normal, particularly in American society.

Impotence, however, often lies in wait for the aggressive at the slightest reminder of his need to be cared for. Sex with a woman who demonstrates any kindly maternal impulse may, if he cannot hurt her quickly, make him flaccid. Arousal must be combined with some form of brutality—emotional or, in the more troubled, physical. Sex is chase, conquest, and either pillage or possession. It is not nursing or warming. These are experienced as uninteresting, if not disgusting.

Whatever threatens the total dominance of the aggressive causes impotence. Kindness, understanding, forgiveness, care, and tenderness are the surest weapons against his erection. Conversely, his partner's anger, fear, and terrified submission excite him, for against these he can win.

Men need not be stoutly aggressive, however, to be fearful of passively receiving. They may also need to be compulsively in control, or be paranoid about whatever they may get.

Just as the most common cause of female dysfunction is the inability to take an active role, so the most insistent cultural cause of male impotence is an inability to be comfortable with passivity. If it is a universal truth that anxiety can destroy sexual sturdiness, then anything which reduces the discomfort will increase the erection. When, to feel comfortable, a man may need to feel securely under the control or protection of someone else, he will only get an erection when he has that feeling. If he has conflict about this dependency need, he will not get an erection.

The dependent longing most closely associated with a direct desire for care is the desire to submit. More than simply being fed, paid for, given a present, admired, groomed, or dressed, a man may long to be taught, told what to do, corrected, advised, given specific orders and assignments, and above all approved and accepted. If a man wants this role, and is also pleased by it both in his domestic and sexual life, he is usually not impotent. If he is happy being "good" and has found a wife able to make him feel that way, he generally has no difficullty with his sexuality. Trouble comes to the man whose conflict involves longing to be treated like a burgeoning prince, a royal son tutored and praised, yet expecting himself to behave like seasoned majesty.

The conflict created by the desire for passive care may drive men to the fantasy of being coerced into a receptive role. In order to enjoy, they must first—or simultaneously—imagine being discipined, punished, or tortured. The instruments of such slavery include everything from verbal abuse to the torture rack. Very few people understand the needs which nourish these seemingly perverse and desperate sexual stimulants. To relieve the shame and guilt not only for having sex, but for wanting to receive it gratis, for wanting to lie back and take, for not wanting to assume responsibility, the man must fantasy himself brutalized, forced, punished, even extinguished. Only when he smarts for it does he deserve his pleasure; only when he is tied and bound can he accept the inertia he would otherwise criticize so severely.

Therefore, many men can become impotent through their fear of being passive. Beyond this, they may also

become impotent because they feel uncivilized about needing self-punitive fantasies in order to enjoy sex. In trying to
suppress the awful wish, they destroy whatever possibility
they have for sexual pleasure.

On the near side of this most difficult world, men who
live by the dictates of mastery must be shackled into pleasure. On the far side, and less frequent, are the men who
are excited by aggressive thoughts about women but who
feel that these are reprehensible. The joy of mastery is not
allowed. They feel that, should they make demands of a
woman, she would either collapse, suffer, or scoffingly
abandon them. Like the impotent man who fears being
passive, the man afraid of leadership has fantasies which
progress from the innocuous to the outrageous. He may
find it erotic to think of making a request of a woman, yet
lose his erection on actually asking her to move her elbow
out of the way as they make love. Sexual feeling may only
emerge if a man imagines telling a woman to perform
various menial services for him, perhaps against her will.
Proceeding up the scale of violence, he may conceive of her
in bondage, a slave on whom he may perform as he pleases.
Often other men are conjured up to join the drama, men
who do more physical abuse to her than he permits himself
even in fantasy.

A notch up this hierarchy of humiliations brings us to
overtly violent fantasy: men who need to hurt, slap, whip,
and draw blood to allow sexuality to emerge. Simple self-
assertion won't do. Men who cannot say what they want of a
woman must dream themselves ten times more powerful, a
thousand times more violent than they are. They enlist a
bulldozer to dig up a patch of violets, and then become
impotized by guilt over their imaginings.

People, then, have contradictory attitudes toward the
"opposite" sides of their nature. Activity-passivity, power-
submission, gregariousness-solitude, brutality-sensitivity—
high hallelujah or dumb resignation—these and all the

other antonymous ways of being may coexist within a person. Impotence is the curse when a man accepts only one visage of himself. If he despises one of his antitheses, instead of respecting and trying to integrate it, he cannot act coherently.

Fear of homosexual impulses is related more to impotence than to any of the other male dysfunctions. The man who cannot accept his passive longings frequently associates them with femininity. Ignoring a decade of active feminism, many remain ashamed of any trace of androgyny in their vision of themselves. The art of sexual fantasy is to enjoy being both man and woman, not only experiencing one's own feelings but identifying with those of one's partner. For some, awareness of duality is a disaster. A man envisions himself the woman, with breasts and vagina, and realizes that he enjoys the man's thrust in an imagined coupling. He stops, repelled by what he identifies as a homosexual consciousness. His panic causes impotence.

Fear of passivity is most common in compulsive, aggressive, and paranoid personalities. Fear of activity is found largely in dependents, schizoids, histrionics, and passive-aggressives.

Beyond these fundamental tendencies, certain personality types are susceptible to impotence for other reasons. Paranoia, for example, encompasses a very special network of immobilizing fears which become revealed most dramatically in the intimate relation.

Some men's paranoia is triggered by their partner's lack of response; others recoil at fervid sexual expression. Whole delusional systems have been written into psychoanalysis regarding the female hatred of the male and its consequence in her lack of orgasm. (In reality, hostility to men is probably the least likely cause of a woman's absent orgasm on intercourse. The most common are ignorance of technique and guilt about sexuality.) But the suspicious man interprets the touch of such a nonresponsive woman as a brush with the witchcraft of medieval demonology. And witches must be burned at the stake.

The absence of a penis-induced trembling in the vaginal walls is ignominy enough. Should a woman suggest being helped by a mechanical appliance, a vibrator, the worst has come to pass; the mechanized world will destroy him, his power, his meaning, his sex. A robot armada waits to move on his integrity and demolish it.

If a woman feels disinclined, for any reason, to have intercourse with a mistrustful man, he concludes that she wants to hurt him or demolish the relationship. She may have been tired, anxious, or even simply more interested in something else at the moment, but he feels as though his inner self rather than his immediate sexuality has been rejected.

Any error in time arrangement, a delay that keeps him waiting, an inconvenience, is interpreted as a conscious, planned, deliberate rejection. No matter how good the reason, how bad the traffic, how important the needs of the boss-mother-child-friend who delayed him, his position in second place is equated with bottom of the barrel.

On the other hand, when a passionate woman makes love to a paranoid, he may feel encroached upon by her energetic demands. Being loved translates as being used to satisfy someone else's needs. Should the woman who luxuriates in her lover's body be not only expressive but multiorgasmic, doomsday has arrived. She will crush and defeat him with the rolling walls of her vagina, bring him to emission, then demand he rise again, and again, and again.

The suspicious man is convinced, when an active woman admires his penis, that she envies it. Certainly she would want the organ excised for her own dark purposes. It is, after all, the most valuable thing he owns.

High on this roster of mortification is the schizoid personality. More than simply fearing active behavior, these people fear human contact. The warmth of affection, which most of us seek like food and shelter, seems to be a source of pain to the most seriously afflicted. It is not a pain which will destroy, as the paranoid feels it, but rather a severe discomfort to be avoided. The schizoid man often avoids sex by accepting and tolerating a partner who has severe sexual problems. Feeling inadequate to solve such problems and needing help to be sexually self-confident on his own, he may accept impotence as an answer which threatens no solution to any dilemmas. If he cannot respond sexually to a partner who is too fearful to be aroused, the problem need never be confronted or solved.

When schizoid avoidance is combined with some obsessional traits, the result is often idealization. To have an obsession without taking any action, to ruminate in a state of withdrawal, to feel acute panic in the actual presence of the beloved—all require this combination of characteristics. And the more idealized a partner, the less well a sexual relationship is bound to go. The man who feels unequal to conducting even a simple conversation will hardly be able to function as a self-assured lover.

The old schizoid idealist frequently became impotent in the presence of the madonna of his dreams. She was the sexual innocent, pure of malice, delicate, lovely, and far too perfect to respond to his clumsy affections. The new impotence of the schizoid man involves idealizing the experienced woman, who both intimidates and tantalizes him. He fantasizes an immense sexual experience with her. Satisfaction will arrive with the peal of carillons and cheers from the tumultuous crowds. With so much noise and such an audience, it is small wonder that erections curl up and hide.

Not only is the new "liberated" woman a direct sexual threat, based on her fantasied erotic proficiency, she is also an intellectual peril. Schizoid men tend to think they are understood, that others comprehend their nature without their having to express very much. If ordinary people understand most everything about them, very intelligent ones will be able to read the core of their being. They will see everything, the good and evil, the complexities of thought, every reflux of passion. Of course, the schizoid doesn't feel comfortable with this much attention and understanding, since by comparison he feels so empty. There is so little inside. A very common schizoid feeling is of interior emptiness, sealed off, unfillable. Having nothing, able to give nothing, feeling—at the crucial moment—stupid and inept, he may regularly court fiasco until eventually he gives up the company of thoughtful women and finds a "lower" order of joy with an uneducable woman, an infantile personality, or a prostitute. Schizoid characters tend to function well sexually alone or with people who do not arouse the least competitive or dependent strivings.

Impotence often comes to compulsives as a surprise. The most common compulsive is the man who constructs rituals for toilet, work, dining, entertainment, and the range of human activity including sex. He must copulate at a certain hour, and a given number of times a week. He may parcel time for each act of forepleasure: like a masseur, he may circle each nipple a fixed number of times and then proceed through a litany of what he believes to be arousal procedures. He may incorporate a cleanliness ritual into the arousal drill by keeping basin and soap handy for pre- and postcoital ablutions. He can compass all of life and most of his preparation for death into a pattern.

The compulsive generally loses his erection "for no apparent reason." In fact, his rituals have disguised his anger at his wife, his irritation with his children, his sense of defeat that day in business, or his sadness over the death of his dog. Compulsives often do not perceive what they feel about what goes on around them, what affects them. They think they ought to be able to function sexually no matter what else is happening.

Compulsives can use their disorder both to deny their anxiety or to build it into an overwhelming obsession. The victim of erectile loss can begin to worry about never having an erection again (instead of contemplating why he is angry at his wife, irritated by his children, or upset with his dog). His sexuality can become the prime focus of his world. His mood, his sense of success, his life—can pivot on his penis. If only the thing would go up and stay up. That would be the key to all happiness. Without erections, life can seem a perpetual mortification. Love, home, children, loyalty, friends, business, country—all are chimerical fantasies compared to the absent hardness.

A defense against this madness is to obsess about something else—religion, business, and war are some of the common substitutes. Impotent obsessionals, especially bright ones, compensate. They may choose only to be alive to affairs of power: conquering and directing man's spirit, his purse, his pugnacity. They battle in place of bedding down effectively. But no amount of secular or spiritual power can cause a return to virility. It is, in the end as at the beginning, a personal state of mind.

ORGASMIC AND EJACULATORY DISORDERS

Premature Ejaculation

In spite of every missionary effort to devalue sex as a source of pride and grandeur, men continue, in their heathen way, to equate strength, success, joy, and rectitude with a potent and durable sex organ.

Premature ejaculation has been considered a major American sexual tragedy. Society and societal custom govern sexual standards. (In parts of Ireland, couples have intercourse as rapidly as possible, privately and clothed.) The American male ideal has been to last an hour or more with any female subject, "eight to eighty, blind, crippled or crazy." The discrepancy between this heroic ideal and any sensitive man's capacity is a great tribute to the common sense of nature.

If the informal social structure has made harsh demands upon the male's sexual performance, organized medicine has been even more stringent. Premature ejaculation was pronounced a serious form of impotence. Never mind that, for reproductive purposes, rapidity is really far more efficient than penile gymnastics. The American man, if premature, was medically impotent, powerless, without the masculine majesty of a durable reproductive machine. He possessed nothing but a quick little pricket.

One of the older cures prescribed by mandarins of medicine was to drive a cautery up the urethra, through the penis, to burn out a portion. The formation of scar tissue prevented forceful emergence of the ejaculate. This treatment was rather like choking a man with asthma to eliminate breathing trouble. Bizarre and sadistic as this treatment may seem, it was a traditional prescription, and traditions pass slowly in organized medicine.

Social customs and medical attitudes were devastating to the premature ejaculator of the first half of the twentieth century. They charged the hapless fellow with being a creature governed by obscene vengeance, his unconscious volcanic with repressed hostility against his mother, and therefore against women. By discharging his semen accidentally on a woman's body, he could desecrate and defile her. By ejaculating too soon, he could frustrate her. Thus he demonstrated the late effects of childhood injustice.

By contrast with the agony and mayhem of the past, which also included burning at the stake for women who "caused" men to have sexual disorders, today's diagnosis seem mildly innocuous. We now regard most premature ejaculators as having a sexual awareness problem. Ejaculating rapidly in response to a perfectly normal physiological drive, they simply cannot delay their adequate and highly gratifying reflexes. They may even be sexual superstars, instantly excitable, conveniently fulfilled. Now that most prematurity is technically so easy to cure, controlling it has become a requisite for socially acceptable behavior, like

learning to hold water. Society makes the rules, and it is a
truth universally acknowledged that physical control requires restraint until arrival at the water closet or slit
trench, bedroom or thatched hut. We have come to agree
that while it might be a pleasure to urinate, defecate, masturbate, fornicate, and ejaculate at whim, to be socially
acceptable is to be house trained, toilet trained, and sex
trained.

My experience indicates that there are two kinds of
premature ejaculation, primary and secondary. The most
common primary type results from an inability to be aware
of how and when to stop sexual excitement so as not to
ejaculate, a perceptual failure. This disorder is usually
present from the first sexual experience throughout later
life.

Less commonly, the disorder begins after a man has
had perfectly good control for years. This secondary prematurity usually occurs when he becomes anxious or fearful during sex. The sympathetic nervous stimulation brings
on an unwanted ejaculation in much the same way that a
boy might have a small and unpleasant orgasm when criticized by a teacher or before a demanding athletic performance. It can happen transiently or become a fixed disorder,
requiring therapeutic intervention. It may be situational,
occurring with one person and not with others. This form
of prematurity often becomes impotence.

In prematurity induced by anxiety the crisis is related
to a characterological preoccupation triggering the ejaculation. What makes one man fearful and another impervious
through life? Where anxiety causes prematurity, the same
personality factors that produce impotence are generally in
evidence and may result in erectile difficulty if the fear
becomes more pronounced.

As in impotence, prematurity is not peculiar to a
social, racial, or occupational order. The firmly limbed
steelworker is as likely to emit upon his lady's thigh as the

college professor to dribble love drops in his pleatless cor-
duroys. Nor is prematurity a dilemma unique to young or
old, introvert or extravert.

If some men's prematurity is a coordination problem,
like learning to button a coat or tie a shoelace, the significant question becomes what effect this has on a man's life
and relationships. When psychological problems—unconscious emotional difficulties—do not cause the physical
disorder, the disorder itself may cause some disastrous psychological effects.

Prematurity can influence a man's social and sexual
pleasure from an early age. Young boys often fear dating,
much less touching girls because they might be embarrassed by an ejaculatory surge. They delay their heterosexual life, starting to date after the great wave of adolescent
sexuality has passed and the pressure to ejaculate is reduced. These young men, suffering on the rack of their
unrequited fantasies, often do not dare to touch or kiss
until later, in their twenties. Their fantasy so outraces their
reality that the first sexual experience may be a powerful
disappointment. Intercourse may never become a pleasure.

If, in addition, the young man has a schizoid anxiety
about human contact, he may never relate adequately to
women or he may become able to function only with prostitutes. While other women may reject him for his rapidity,
prostitutes are satisfied, even delighted to have a quick
customer. The schizoid man may longingly dream of love
and marriage while copulating with a whore. It is a paradox which often produces inexorable pain.

If schizoids tend to retreat from their prematurity,
obsessionals often ignore it altogether. Some men focus
entirely on their work, both in bed and out. A commitment
to learning, to cerebral experience, are frequent preoccupations among obsessional premature ejaculators. There
is always a new problem to contemplate while making love,

an abstraction to be solved, a task to be worried. Sexuality is incidental to the greater concerns in life; the sensual experience is like getting a haircut or listening to background music while locked into more imposing riddles. Some men are able to focus so little on their sexuality that they truly do not comprehend that they come too quickly. Yet they are capable of the most intricate mental activity and it is not beyond them to construct elaborate systems to run institutions, governments, or the world.

Generally speaking, wives of obsessional men who ejaculate prematurely usually live in a state of constant emotional and sexual frustration. What was once a challenge—to get his attention and inspire his courtship—becomes a daily obstacle course. "Getting through" to him involves repetition, angry outbursts, tears, demonstrations of helplessness. She sweats, cries, curses, slams doors; he wonders what all the fuss is about and why he married such an emotionally unstable person.

The premature ejaculator whose personality survives on dependence becomes locked into perhaps the most difficult situation of all. Some marriages are based on one person's weakness and another's need to take care. At the plateau of such a union, the woman wields dictatorial power. If a wife is not by nature more voluble, demanding, and aggressive than her husband, she becomes that way in response to his need. She is his savior and he is the quintessential monogamist, totally afraid to test himself with other women. She has a sure grip on his inadequate manhood. She adopts the queen bee role: he is her worker, her drone, her colony. He brings her money and gives her service. He does what she directs whenever she tells him to do it. He is passive, humble, and cowed. He would be dependent even without the sexual malaise, but the consciousness of his prematurity imprisons him totally. He would not dare the search for a woman who might make him feel more whole.

When husbands are sufficiently docile, the marriage produces that atmosphere of repression and obedience characteristic of a totalitarian state. But unlike the state which imposes slavery by force of arms, the domestic bind is entirely psychological—an invisible yoke of pervasive power. One person functions exclusively through the will of another. Few servitudes are more complete or more tightly bound except where survival is threatened. The lure of money, the promise of power, the hope of eternal joy are all unreal compared to the security of firm female supervision.

Not all such dependency ties are quite so passive. Sometimes stealthy rebellion burns in the groin of the dependent male. He retaliates by silence, withdrawal, detachment. He undermines his wife's authority with the children. He reduces her achievements by refusing to share her pride. He is not passive-dependent but passive-aggressive. The brevity of his sexual act can become associated with the pleasure of frustrating his wife's dominance. Not only a cause for dependence, the swift sexual release also transforms into a weapon of anger at such a subservient condition.

Nor are all quick ejaculators so passive. An aggressive man frequently responds to prematurity by demanding compensatory power. Rather than surrender to inadequacy by donating his soul to his partner so that she will tolerate his sexual mewling, he takes command.

At the first intimacy, a spoiler can make the woman feel the early emission is her fault. He tells her he has never been premature with anyone ever before. Something she does has caused the quick overflow of his passion. She is emotionally dishonest—"that's it!"—and his penis knows it. Or she's physically clumsy and does not inspire him to put on a good show. Or, to produce a more pernicious pain, he may blame his prematurity on his exhaustion from the day before, implying a sexual marathon with a woman who really excited him.

Alternatively, in relationships that go on for a while, the aggressive takes the focus off his performance. He makes his partner feel so insecure about everything else that she barely notices their sex life. He reduces her to feelings of humility and failure by deploring her limited taste, dated style, impaired decisiveness, poor judgment; if that is not enough he criticizes her family. His overall superiority keeps her away from physical issues. It also doubles her satisfaction when she wins a point. Sexuality can hardly be noticed under such circumstances. If she does become aware that they make love, it is only with gratitude for the gift of human contact.

Married, the aggressive generally manages to keep his wife both immensely busy and always on the defensive. She must not, after all, discover what good intercourse really is. Women's liberation has unintentionally added a new dimension to the manipulative man's power. He ordains she be not only fertile and maternal, but also professional, and so fulfilled by the diversity of these roles that she has abundant joy and cheer to nourish him. And he, good fellow that he is, denies any competition or threat. He shares the domestic workload and the balance of the bank account. By no visible tally may he be computed a chauvinist. But he retains a pervasive though often invisible psychological advantage. And he uses it.

His advantage lies in preempting the power of awarding praise and blame. He governs his wife by his subtle dissatisfactions. He would not want her tied to the home as their friend Henry's wife (but, just the same, that was a glorious mousse Dorothea offered after the duck *à l'orange*). He says he is pleased and proud of her achievement in the strident world of free enterprise, but it is a loss that she, he, they find so little time to cultivate his latent love of chamber music. "That was remarkable the way Dorothea played Lully after the Cointreau. I had no idea seventeenth-century chamber music was composed for the baptism of the Dauphin. She certainly has civilized Henry."

Beyond making her feel domestically inept, he may also manage to make her question her altruism if she is not philanthropically or politically active. Political solutions in Asia are beyond her power, yet he ingeniously manages to make her feel frustration. Starvation in India was a household word when they were both children; nonetheless her jaded empathy makes her feel insensitive, callous. Whatever she says, the line of cheer eludes him. Alas, she sneaks off to the office and laments that she is not Julia Child, Golda Meir, and Edna St.Vincent Millay rolled into one. With such imposing failures, how can she question—indeed even remember—her husband's ineffectual ejaculatory splutterings of the night before.

Of course, husbands need not be so sophisticated to constantly demand more. A man can bludgeon his wife even from a base of disarming ignorance, shades of Archie Bunker. The imperative is to be center stage as the source of reward and self-esteem. The mechanics of sex can't beat that.

A woman's psychic inadequacy may go so far that she believes it is entirely her fault for not having orgasms on intercourse. Even if her husband's brief probe and poke hardly give her time to settle comfortably on her back, she may accuse herself of that now rare disease, frigidity. Since Freud's first invitation, women have been lining up for the analyst's couch when actually their husbands have practiced neither foreplay nor endurance sufficient to inspire a shiver of excitement.

Prematurity, then, may exist as a bodily state without a psychic cause. How a man responds to it will depend on his character. Prematurity may also be caused by the anxiety which underlies all defenses and makes them necessary ego functions. Distinguishing one condition from another may make all the difference in sensitive understanding and treatment of this disorder.

Inhibited Orgasm

In aspiring to love a woman by performing a total act of intercourse, some men are bound to the Ixionian wheel of excitement without orgasm. As the wheel revolves interminably, so they in their private hell, continue to thrust and try, and try again to release themselves. Yet only in privacy and isolation can they complete their pleasure.

The old definition in which men themselves classified retarded ejaculation as a form of impotence is not far from accurate. In severely fearful men, impotence—erectile failure—often develops to complicate matters even further.

A common denominator among these men seems often to be a fear or hatred of authority figures, caused sometimes by a tyrannical father, more often by a misguided mother. Many men who suffer orgasmic inhibition or retarded ejaculation never seek therapy because they take an active pleasure in depriving their mates of seminal balm. Others seek no help because they are rather pleased with their dysfunction. Women enjoy men who can last long enough to give them at least one orgasm, and preferably more. Such men fancy themselves superlovers, and do not wish to give up their high estate. Wives of retarded ejaculators, however, often are nervous and haggard, worn out by the constant demand and the continual frustration. Frequently they have become multiorgasmic with the steady pounding, but have lost interest in sex and orgasm.

When retarded ejaculators unconsciously hate women, they often have good reason for a conception of females as the living descendants of Heliogabalus's bull. An iron monster in which humans were burned at Roman parties, this sculpted torture device had an open mouth which emitted the screams of the dying. For some retarded ejaculators, the equivalent of being cooked inside the iron beast is to have an orgasm inside a woman. The most common witch at the cauldron is—once more—mother.

Mother is seductive, overprotective, cruelly dominant, or all three. Whatever she is, there is usually no subtle question about her character. She borders the pathological. One such mother fondled and kissed her boy-child's penis daily, after his bath, remarking with gustatory joy how delicious he tasted and how he would always belong to her. In order to escape her talons, the victim often found himself fantasizing murder during the sexual act, and at the same time trying to halt the fantasy. His mental accompaniment to intercourse was a bloody scene in which he had cut off his partner's legs and was to copulate with her bleeding corpse.

Another mother called her adult executive son four times a day to check up on his toilet habits and his food intake. His amatory scenario involved stretching his partner's vagina to a breaking point with a cannon-like penis. He held back his ejaculation with the fear of fantasizing that his emission would be a nuclear weapon that could blow up her uterus.

In life outside the bedroom, such men are often aggressive, psychopathic, or compulsive. Many tend to lose their tempers violently, being apt to use a fist or even a poker on the innocent provocateur. Of all the disorders, male orgasmic inhibition is the most likely to be a red flag for the presence of a severe power struggle in the relationship. Loss or absence of a reflex normally so easy to elicit in men is almost always accompanied by a deep and profound disturbance.

Not all men who cannot climax during intercourse are engaged, however, in a battle with mother as represented in their wives. Some schizoid-avoidant souls had early lives so deprived of warm mothering that they dare not trust the comfort of letting their semen free inside a woman. They are generally so accustomed to masturbating to orgasm that it feels better not to begin to depend for pleasure upon another person. Once release is experienced inside a woman, masturbation may become, forevermore, a lonely, painful experience recalling severe childhood agonies.

Nor need a man, himself, begin with intense inner conflict or deprivation to develop the disorder. A peaceable fellow may simply make the mistake of marrying a woman who is or becomes an arsenal of grievances all aimed at him. She may direct the artillery of her woes—her difficulties with sex, self-assertion, identity, monogamy—upon him so continually that his angry and helpless response may take many forms, including orgasmic failure, if not impotence.

Indeed, in the beginning of a sexual relationship, many delayed ejaculators start out by being premature. They develop such powerful musculature in an attempt to hold back their ejaculate that they succeed all too well and require training both in "letting go" and in delaying. The domestic conflagration flamed by a sensitive spouse around whether a man comes sooner or later may occasionally defy all patience. The condition may become permanently installed in his psyche as an expression of hostile withholding.

The obvious fear of impregnating a woman may also interfere with orgasm. This fear may derive from any number of characterological difficulties, such as unwillingness to create a child who will take away his wife's attention. Or some unusual trauma can cause it. One patient developed the problem because his wife repeatedly miscarried in their efforts to have a child. His response was simply protective against further physical distress for his wife and emotional pain for both. Sometimes a man's character, in the old-fashioned sense of caring and shielding against harm, can display its credentials in a sexual disorder.

Recently a possible physical cause of retarded ejaculation has come to medical attention: lower back problems involving one or more intervertebral disks. The difficulty may be related to nerve damage that decreases the ability of penile skin to experience touch. Ejaculation may be delayed because tactile stimulation is inadequate to create enough excitement. Men whose penises are anesthetized like this often need to resort to high levels of fantasy or to

have a novel and intense experience in order to ejaculate.
They frequently develop sexual lives that seem unusual to
those for whom the reflex is rapid. They may suffer considerable interpersonal conflict and despair because the loss
of feeling is so subtle that neither they nor their partners
can easily tell that something is missing. It may be difficult
to get a neurological evaluation of this condition, as well,
since the routine medical tools for quantifying sensitivity to
touch have not advanced beyond the primitive safety pin.
Research to develop an inexpensive touch-measuring device for physicians is urgently required.

Impaired Orgasm and Ejaculation

There are many men who do not feel as much as they
could during the climactic moment. Orgasm feels to them
very much like it does to premature ejaculators who have
limited pleasure because they are trying so desperately not
to ejaculate. While the rapid ejaculator may consciously try
to withhold orgasm because he wants erection to last
longer, the man with incomplete orgasm or orgasmic anesthesia may have an unconscious need to abort his orgasm.

Incomplete orgasm consists of a few minor contractions that feel more like a spill-off than a vigorous emission.
The muscles responsible for seminal expulsion do not contract adequately in the second half of the ejaculatory phase.

There are also men who ejaculate without feeling any
orgasmic pleasure at all. This phenomenon may be called
orgasmic anesthesia.

Fatigue or aging of the muscles elevating the scrotum
may cause a lessening of orgasmic force and a consequent
reduction of ejaculatory pleasure in many psychologically
undisturbed men. The people who may benefit from psychosexual therapy, however, are those who inhibit or repress awareness of sensation for psychological reasons
involving fear, hostility, or sexual guilt.

Differing personalities experience fear, guilt, and anger for diverse reasons. Any man can be traumatized if his

defensive system is threatened vigorously enough. Vulnerability to sexual dysfunction is much the same as susceptibility to any anxiety disorder. However, orgasmic inhibition seems to occur in men whose paranoia includes a preoccupation with control that may originate in early castration fear. The disorder can be a consequence of a lifelong fear of being both controlled and depleted.

Frequently the man's fear of ejaculating represents a fear of losing his penis to the woman. This fear is often further displaced to other symbolic objects. One man with the symptom of incomplete orgasm was afraid that his partner would discover his hidden bank account, and that he would then lose his welfare benefits. Another always experienced the fear before ejaculating that his partner might steal his precious photographic equipment if he allowed himself to become involved in pleasure and lost awareness of his surroundings. A third, who reported that at full erection his penis was only 3½ inches long, was quite consciously afraid that, in taking his ejaculate, the woman's vagina would cause the rest of his penis to disappear.

Relief from this sexual symptom can sometimes be effected through the use of a fantasy to take the sufferer's mind off his fear. A "gain" fantasy is often the most helpful: winning a sweepstakes and being handed the money by a beautiful, naked woman, or being given presents by a bevy of beauties. However, as mentioned in the previous section on inhibited ejaculation, many cases of this disorder previously thought to be psychological in origin are now considered very likely to be related to subtle nerve impairment. Although this idea is somewhat controversial, it seems the more sensible explanation when such a problem occurs in a man who enjoys affection and appreciates women. Certainly when all four difficulties are present—inhibited ejaculation, skin insensitivity, impaired orgasm, and orgasmic anesthesia on those occasions when orgasm does occur—a physical deficit would seem highly probable.

15

Female Maladies

SEXUAL EXCITEMENT DISORDERS

Inhibited Sexual Excitement

Sexual excitement disorder exists when there is a discrepancy between desire and ability. One woman may wish to become excited and not be able to do so at all; another woman may be easily stimulated by everything but vaginal penetration. Both have excitement disorders of different degree. In a man, an excitement disorder is clearly marked by the inopportune fall of his penis; in a woman, the signs are far more subtle and difficult to detect.

In most cases there is no clear demarcation between a desire disorder and an excitement disorder. Difficulties with desire almost always reflect on excitement, and vice versa. As previously discussed, I prefer the term "arousal" to include both. However, a physical phase does exist that corresponds to the concept of sexual excitement: the lubrication-swelling response of the female vagina.

Bearing in mind that the distinction between desire and excitement is academic and that they are often inseparable, I will nevertheless discuss female sexual excitement from the point of view of primary and secondary inhibition. Primary inhibition exists in a woman who has never experienced excitement even though she may want to. Its origins are difficult to trace because they lie so deep in the past. Secondary inhibition only occurs if excitement once existed but is now absent or destroyed. It may be traced to a conscious anger, for example, that "turned off" sexuality at some known time.

Primary Inhibition   The woman who eagerly desires sexual excitement but cannot feel it often reads sex manuals, sees sex movies, has intercourse with her husband or lover, yet never knows the faintest caress of pleasure. She studies and imitates sexual positions from pictures, hoping to learn sex the way she might learn mathematics. She may repeat the lewd words her lovers teach her, hoping to hear the sound of heaven through single-syllable channels. She may learn to play out her lovers' sexual fantasies in black garter belts, leather boots, or open-nipple bras. Men instruct her that the way to joy is through a hard-focus lens on cunt and cock, and she may learn to be remarkably proficient in the lore of the lust-bound.

Meanwhile, a history of parental deprivation or abandonment makes it miraculous for such a woman to have retained even a dream of delight. Severe chastisement for sexual urges, for affectionate longings, may have so mutilated her psychosexual apparatus that, as with the person who cannot enjoy meals or spend money without guilt, a normal route to satisfaction is entirely obstructed, eliminating sensation. The case histories are so variable that it would be impossible to describe the range of sexual trauma inflicted by parents, and taken very seriously by the sensitive.

Not all of the unexcited are so active. Indeed, most wait eternally for something to happen. They lie with their lovers and accept their passion, curiously all the while observing and wondering why this means more, or is supposed to feel better, than holding hands. Sex is like locking the parts of a jigsaw puzzle. There seems to be no real reason for doing it except to fit together.

Secondary Inhibition   Secondary inhibition differs from primary because it implies that erotic sensitivity previously existed in a sensual area but no longer does so. A woman once enjoyed the presence of a penis in her vagina, but now it is unexciting. A woman once liked to have her nipples massaged, but now the idea is uninteresting. Excitement is either suppressed or repressed, but not inhibited from the start.

Secondary inhibition is usually a part of an arousal disorder. Sometimes temporary but occasionally permanent, it is often a symptom of unresolved personality difficulties in a relationship. The usual complaint is that sex used to be exciting, but now is like a meal of boiled potatoes, barely nourishing and very dull. Only the most minimal sensations are felt during coitus, although once there was orgasm and joy. More a chore than a pleasure, many women accept this unpalatable ration as their lot in life. Everyone says that when the honeymoon is over, the long eclipse begins and so it seems. Sex is really a conjugal duty, if that, and the Victorians were right.

To catalogue all the probabilities that might lead to such a state of affairs would require a compendium of marital difficulties. Problems with child raising, in-laws, parents, partners, friends, jobs, business, school, pets, vermin, and mildew may all interfere with sex if a woman is vulnerable to anxiety. The tensions of life are the greatest erotic executioners.

After anxiety the most frequent source of sexual disinclination is hidden and unresolved anger. Passive-dependents conceal their feelings, compulsives deny them, passive-aggressives deliberately retaliate by indirection, particularly sexually. Schizoids retreat from any suggestion of bellicosity. Histrionics dissolve in an attractive plethora of emotion but never face their rage. The so-called "normal" woman may be a little bit of everything. Generally it is safe to say that she is not assertive enough. She is a sitting duck for diminution of sexual interest because she contains her unpleasant feelings too strenuously.

The causes for anger may be obvious or subtle: obviously if a man is unfaithful or financially dishonest, a woman's anger may cause serious separation in the bedroom and a loss, sometimes permanent, of sexual interest. Real rage leads to active sexual shutdown in a non-masochistic personality; hidden anger leads to repression. If a woman does not recognize that she resents her husband's smaller outrages, such as coming home late without calling, or not interceding to discipline the children, or allowing his mother to take over the household, she may find herself rather distant in bed. If a woman's husband spends too much time with "the boys," is too addicted to spectator sports, is too much or too little involved with his work, or procrastinates home repairs, she may find herself cold and unresponsive when she is supposed to be feeling wordless and ecstatic union. Dissatisfactions may mount to such a height that the best lovemaking techniques in the world cannot free sexuality.

Sex may also be devastated by a woman's failure to resolve her own identity problems. The overqualified housewife and her ideal, the supermom, are both usually compulsives. Intellectually unchallenged by her role, a woman can find her sexuality going down the drain along with her education. Conversely, the woman who tries to meet immense intellectual or business competition, while still responding to the full spectrum of her family's emotional demands, may see sex as another challenge. She is unwilling to admit that sex and everything else are burdens because she must see herself as perfectly capable in all areas. So she becomes covertly depressed and mysteriously unresponsive.

Secondary sexual inhibition is virtually always a consequence of some hidden anger. Of course, it is the major premise of this book that unjustified anger arises out of that mélange of repetitive experiences known to most of us as our "past." We develop our defenses in accordance with the emotional hardships we experience; we have a continual reserve of anger to release when we expect to have to deal with those insults to our integrity again. But sometimes the anger and the defensiveness arise without the insult. That is our personality trait, our disorder, perhaps. We defend ourselves before our perfection has been questioned, our emotion unrecognized, our privacy invaded. We become angry when no one but a parent—perhaps in the distant past—has made us uncomfortable. This is the anger that most mysteriously destroys excitement; it is the rage most difficult to resolve because first it must be dredged out of the mysteries of the past, then it must be identified, and then it must be accepted as having a real effect. The fear and hurt behind the rage need to be known, too. That is the most difficult task of psychiatry, if not of psychoanalysis.

There are, however, cases which imitate the disorder, against which the reader must be gently warned. There are women for whom sex gradually becomes peculiarly unsatisfying. Neither they nor their analysts can sort out the cause. A frequent solution to the mystery lies in the husband's secret and varied extramarital life, an activity which he feels is part of his cultural privilege. So long as he gives sexual "service" to his wife, he feels free to find erotic adventure elsewhere. The psychology of his difficulty with attachment has been previously discussed. Women should be warned against misdiagnosing their own abilities to love. It is difficult for most women to respond with passion to a man whose highest excitement is found with other bodies.

A less subtle source of repression may lie in a woman's own difficulty with monogamous attachment. Accustomed to five or ten years of premarital adventure—teasing, attracting, conquering, rejecting—she may find the play hard to give up. Certain compulsive women often convict themselves of unholy debauchery for continuing to be attracted to men other than their husbands. Some convert their feelings into jealousy toward any woman with whom their husband may have a conversation. Others simply lose libidinal interest, in guilt and confusion. They cannot meet their "ego ideal" of constancy, yet life no longer seems a chancy kind of music, filled with unexpected rhythms and surprise harmonies. Rather, it beats away with the frustrating dullness of practice scales. Their husbands may come to seem jailers of body and soul.

This unimaginative situation may worsen with the birth of each successive child. Caring for babies is at once a source of immense maternal satisfaction, a huge erotic stimulus, and a tedious drudgery that makes some mothers feel like sewage-disposal units. It becomes routine to shut off the sexual arousal afforded by intimate body contact all day long. Many mothers masturbate regularly at their children's naptime to relieve the sexual tension generated, although they are not aware of their children's role in nourishing it. This leaves them less interested at night. Others attempt a total shutoff, an even greater effort than excluding extramarital fantasies. Sexual guilt and the incest taboo add a new dimension to the sexual Bastille. Body contact with anyone can become a chore.

A new mother may also lose her erotic impulse through jealousy. Most women, being too dependent, achieve sexual excitement from playing child-mistress to their husbands. Now they are no longer the "only child." Indeed, at this critical time, their husbands distinctly crave more mothering themselves. As much as all the paraphernalia of infancy arouses old longings in men, it redoubles them in women. In this needy mêlée of baby's cries, bottles, Pampers, nurses, parents, and in-laws, sexuality retreats to a small cold place in the refrigerator, behind the Similac. The scales become weighted too heavily in favor of the antagonisms of rivalry. When these antagonisms do not get resolved, sexuality may be frozen out permanently.

Selective Inhibition   We may think of the sexual system as formed by many erogenous components: the mind, the sensual receptors (skin, nipples, clitoris, etc.), and the involuntary sexual reflex pathways. Selective inhibition is at work when one of the sensual receptors or pathways is nonfunctional. For some women, excitement may occur only under special circumstances: dreams, fantasies, solitude. Many of these women can become excited, but only when alone. Another person's presence extinguishes passion.

Inhibition among nonorgasmic women, however, need not take such an extreme form. Many do experience some kind of excitement from kissing or fondling or genital caressing. Yet they may not be able to become aroused in all of the ordinary ways. They may enjoy being kissed but resent having their breasts touched. They may like to have their genitals touched but be unable to accept body stroking, claiming exorbitant ticklishness. They may be able to achieve some pleasure with their eyes closed, but opening them, seeing what is happening, inhibits response.

Even women who have orgasms may suffer selective inhibition. There is an excitement disorder when only one place on a woman's body becomes the focus of her sexual receptivity. Only if stimulated in that one area can she get excited. Other so-called erogenous zones may never become receptive. Women may inhibit sexual response from any part of the sexual system: lips, breasts, anus, skin, clitoris, vagina, fantasy. Like a driver who always takes a familiar route rather than attempting newer shortcuts or highways, a woman becomes accustomed to, or allows, one path for pleasure. Change is unpleasant—perhaps she will not "get there."

Most women develop erotic focus in the clitoris, anatomically an available and sensitive place. Freud felt that it was necessary to switch the erotic focus to the vagina in order for a woman to become psychosexually mature. While there is no such thing as a "vaginal" orgasm, since all orgasms are triggered by the same mechanism, there is such a thing as an eroticized vagina. Indeed, the controversial G-spot may be a primary source of intravaginal eroticism. Many women really do inhibit the development of erotic receptivity in their vaginas, just as they may inhibit breast sensitivity, for a variety of psychological reasons. Though touch is largely absent inside the vagina, the sensations which are available—stretch and deep pressure—can be immensely gratifying. "Having something inside" can be quite fulfilling. But a woman must desire her vagina to be the source of pleasure, must want "to be full," must wish for vaginal pleasure before she can receive it. She must also be excited by the idea of giving pleasure to a man with her clitoris. This takes nothing away from what she receives from her clitoris directly. Clitoral eroticism is in no way reduced or replaced by vaginal eroticism, which adds a deeper dimension to the experience. Even if vaginal eroticism is no guarantee of psychosexual maturity, it is certainly an aid to pleasure on intercourse.

Why are some few women's mental pleasure centers stimulated most by vaginal stretch, pressure, or stroking of the anterior vaginal wall, while most others receive more from touch and direct clitoral manipulation? Why is sensation from one area inhibited or not eroticized, creating a selective inhibition, while that from another is allowed?

The simplest conjecture is that most woman are conditioned to clitoral sensitivity. Young girls are generally afraid to masturbate by putting "something inside." This is not paranoia, but plain fear of hurting themselves. An older generation was also concerned with the premium of virginity. Losing a valuable asset is a commonplace fear in the memory of many mature woman. Finally, although vibrators are now available in phallic shapes in most drugstores, only a few years ago dildos of any kind were not readily obtainable. A young girl had to have considerable courage and ingenuity to fashion their own.

The religious and societal taboos against all kinds of masturbation are additional factors. Women are brought up to believe, by some invisible cultural osmosis, that self-gratification is demeaning. Not having a man to do it for them reflects on their self-esteem and female attractiveness. There is overall feeling that clitoral masturbation is not so diminishing to sexual identity as vaginal masturbation.

There are, nevertheless, many women whose vaginal insensitivity is more than just a culturally induced habit. Just as in male problems, both sides of an emotional coin may cause the same disorder. Men who fear being too active or too passive wind up impotent. Women who fear being too independent or too submissive emerge with selectively inhibited excitement. For example, women who are clitorally sensitive only may fear being close. And women who insist on vaginal penetration, without enjoying other pleasures, may need to be too close, too dependent.

Many extremely childish women are able to become aroused only though penile stimulation. This can be a condition of severely constricted women, who have never explored themselves. They may not know they have clitorises. They may not have clitoral sensation. Some have it but have never directly experienced it. Others have clitoral inhibition, a relative numbness of the erectile organ but not of the vaginal entrance. Frequently these women prevent their partners from indulging them in variety. Acceptable sex, to them, is the missionary act. Anything else frequently seems an unpleasant perversion. Being afraid to know themselves, and more afraid to expose their bodies fully to a man's curiosity and creativity, they cloak their more obvious selves in untouchable distance, keep their needs and emotions altogether private by allowing only the most primitive, uninteresting, and monotonous union.

Vaginal sensitivity alone, without acceptance of other stimulation, therefore, may represent intense fear of exposure. It may be a consequence not only of cultural training but also of excess timidity, unassertiveness, and an absent sense of valid identity. It can be a sign of total passivity, dependence, and immaturity. It may compass countless fears of both self-knowledge and self-revelation.

Clitoral sensitivity, by contrast, may be equally anti-thetical to true bonding. Closing one's interior to pleasure, restricting contact to externals, can be the most effective guards against intimacy a woman possesses. While clitoral responsiveness does not always signify such closure—and on occasion may be the hallmark of a brave and independent girlhood—as a sole source of pleasure after years of attempting to enjoy intercourse, it may be symptomatic of strong inhibitions that need extensive psychosexual treatment.

For a woman to allow herself to be deeply penetrated, filled by and aware of a man's penis in a totally receptive sense, while at the same time grasping it, closing around it, moving it with all the intensity of her body and spirit, in a totally active sense, seems to me to be a reflection of her capacity to enjoy the most intimate sexual union.

Orgasm, as far as we know today, has only one final physiological path. It is very much the same orgasm no matter where the stimulus originates, although intensity, frequency, and uterine contractility may vary.

When selective inhibition causes sensitivity cutoff at some time after excitement has begun, a woman experiences a feeling of "going down," very similar to the distress of the impotent man. She may go through a beginning excitement phase, but abort before plateau. In this disorder, the linear progression toward orgasm is interrupted. The system works for a while, then stops. One part, the initial phase, works; later steps do not.

Excitement is relative. Time, speed, and place depend on so many variable forces that it would require a cosmic computer to tabulate all of them. The source of all this complexity is the mind, with its infinity of chemical and electrical circuits. The mind is the great doorway through which sexual stimuli may or may not be allowed to pass. Pleasurable arousal is largely a mental function with all joy stemming from that great source. While it is true that the physical signs of excitement and orgasm may occur as a simple reflex, without any help from the brain, the experience is incomplete and as totally without eroticism as a kneejerk. The mind is the only pleasure center, and the treatment of sexual disorder is purely an effort to alter a person's sexual psychology.

Vaginismus

Vaginismus is a rather formidable term meaning that a woman unconsciously tightens the muscles around the lower third of her vagina so as not to permit penetration. Although women with other dysfunctions can on occasion be more distraught than those with vaginismus, in clinical practice it seems to afflict a more disturbed patient population than the other disorders.

A woman may have long-term vaginismus, in which no one has ever been permitted penile entry. She may also acquire vaginismus after a painful experience, the memory of pain compelling the introitus to seal off.

Although at this time vaginismus is considered to be separate from other sexual problems by the American Psychiatric Association for the purpose of easy diagnosis, it fits logically into the category of excitement disorders. One part of the sexual system is impaired. The rest may be functioning quite well. Vaginismic women usually enjoy a sexual contact, or the idea of it. Only pleasure through entry is inhibited, although by muscle contraction rather than sensory anesthesia. This tension is as unconscious and involuntary as other psychic impediments to sexuality.

Many women who have never allowed a penis into their vaginas tend to be paranoid. Some are actively or latently schizophrenic. They clearly see the penis as a destructive force, a cudgel, a sword, a battering ram. Entry might rip them apart, pierce through their intestines. Direct harm to the self is just a beginning. One patient had

the fantasy that her womb contained a fetus which had
been placed there through paternal insemination. If she
allowed entry, her father's child would be destroyed. The
fetus would abort, a bloody and inverted mass of tissue.
Though she was sufficiently sane to recognize this as a
fantasy, it was a strong enough belief to cause vaginismus.
Another patient, whose childhood had been spent in Ger-
man concentration camps, where she had been witness to
the sexual humiliation and abuse of her mother and sisters,
viewed insertion, understandably, as a total violation of her
being. She could only repress and contain her memories of
despair if she did not allow intercourse.

At a less extreme level, vaginismus, like repugnance to
deep penetration, may be a way of preventing feeling
"open" to closeness and attachment. The woman vaguely
imagines her interior as a silent, enclosed space, a private
and peaceful world. Though no overt destruction, no tear-
ing of flesh and muscle, no cutting or piercing is envisioned, there is a sense that penetration is an intrusion.

Many vaginismic women are merely "uptight" about
sexuality. Habitually, they walk about with tightened buttocks and rigid pelvic musculature. Just as many people
grind their teeth, tighten their jaws, hunch their shoulders,
or curl their toes in an unconscious somatic response to
anxiety, these women clamp their vaginas. Because the
thought of intercourse arouses anxiety, they close up automatically without even realizing that they are doing so.
Their genitals present a solid barrier against entry.

Yet these women are often quite sexually excitable.
They are not afraid of orgasm. Rather more easily than
most, they have one or many climaxes. With muscles already tightened, all they have to do is relax to initiate
release. Their vaginal "clench" is a habitual response to
tension. Any problem or difficulty, related or unrelated to
sex, will do.

Acquired vaginismus is often caused by a lover who is
naïve, inexperienced, or—less frequently—simply brutal.

Entering before the woman is reasonably excited, expanded, and well-lubricated can create pain. Women who don't know that this pain is unnecessary begin to consider it an inevitable part of intercourse. They tense in anticipation of the ordeal to come, and vaginismus begins.

Some women have an arousal inhibition that may prevent excitement no matter how hard a lover tries or how skillful he is. They may finally allow entry out of embarrassment, or the lover may become impatient, trying even though the vagina is not ready. Again pain occurs preliminary to the pathological tension. If the experience is frequently repeated, vaginismus may result.

There may be, of course, vaginismic women who simply do not wish to be excited or to have sexual relations in any form. I have not encountered one yet in clinical experience, but in that case the vaginismus would be a disorder of desire, not of excitement. Most women with vaginismus who come to treatment at least wish to enjoy themselves.

Women have many generations to go before they are sexually liberated. Freedom is far more than a willingness to accept new ideas, or the abandonment of undergarments. It means something different to each of us. To those on an analytic couch, it may mean freedom to love and feel sexual simultaneously. To others it may mean freedom to have sex without love. To the vaginismic woman its primary significance is freedom to begin.

ORGASMIC DISORDERS

Never to have known love is, today, a regrettable but hardly embarrassing circumstance. Never to have had an orgasm, however, has become, for many women, the ultimate humiliation. Orgasm currently implies all manner of competence with which it really has very little to do, because it is essentially a reflex. Without it, women feel, love is not attainable nor is worldly success quite true. Without it, the physical self is perceived as a mutilated fragment rather than as a complete being. The woman who says that she enjoys sex but doesn't have orgasm and doesn't miss it is virtually an extinct species, with some few preserved in cloistered pastoral or ghetto settings.

The concept that orgasm will confer upon a woman magical powers to love, be loved, and enjoy her work, is an illusion. Nevertheless, overcoming orgasmic inhibition is frequently a key to working through serious personality difficulties.

Inhibited Orgasm

Inhibited orgasm is not an excitement disorder. A woman may be thoroughly aroused, but not able to release. Excitement begins, its warmth touching nipples and clitoris, reaching into the vagina and fluttering upward. Ascending, increasing momentum, finally nearing the peak, the sexual flight is suddenly stopped. No further arousal is tenable. And yet there is no relief. This is by far the most frustrating type of sexual disorder.

Orgasmic inhibition may be a primary or secondary dysfunction. Some women reach a highly excited state both on masturbation or intercourse, but cannot climax either way. In other instances a woman cannot climax on intercourse but can do so on masturbation. Difficulties with liberating orgasm, whether on masturbation or on intercourse, usually have characterological roots. In the vagina, in the home, in the broader world, the same psychic demons that mess matters up are always gleefully at work.

When an excessively dependent woman cannot bring herself to climax, the superficial reasons are transparently clear. She can't do anything for herself. Unless the world does for her, life ceases to have meaning. Her self-worth plummets. Giving herself satisfaction would be a road to abandonment. In adolescence, most curious females explore the wonders of their own genitalia and emerge in triumphant discovery of their singular gifts. The passive-dependent doesn't begin to try. She expects all bounties to be bestowed upon her. She may ultimately lead a life attached to such dependencies as will insure her survival, like her parents or welfare. If she is attractive enough, a man may assume the burden, not suspecting her deficits.

When a woman inhibits orgasm beacause she fears being too much in charge, too dominant, too much in competition with mother, masturbating to orgasm can seem a final and terrible act of self-control and independence.

Mother's presence may remain in the bedroom long after she should reasonably be excluded from the minds of most daughters. To create a maternally induced Oedipus complex, or what I prefer to call a Venus complex, she can play a part that has innumerable variations. At the bedside, mother's image may sit knitting and frowning. She warns her daughter against pride and hope. She, after all, got no pleasure from the dull and viscous act; she gave herself in duty, disgust, and despair, to a man who was worth very little in the ledger of character. "Don't be foolish," mother whispers. "You will not have it better than I did. Love is not true, and sex is the messenger of deception. I failed, and so must you."

Or so she communicates many similar themes. "I gave him my youth and he gave me an allowance." "He used me and threw me away like a dirty Kleenex. Don't be any man's Kleenex." "Protect yourself against men. No one else will. Pray to God."

On the other hand, mother's phantom may seductively remove a stocking or unhook a bra as it sits at her daughter's sexual bedside. Mother may have known one man or many, but hers was the definitive experience. Her daughter must not have more or better than she did. Whatever her child does will never be as a great as her own perfection. As Venus exiled her daughter Psyche to a lonely mountain because she was growing to be more beautiful and gaining the love of Cupid, so the aggressively sexual mother intimidates her offspring.

Fear of disturbing maternal dominance is only one side of the issue. Father has as often been the major protagonist on the scene of early life. Happiness lies in pleasing him, or at least in obeying him. Existence without the fullness of a man's praise, approval, or even tacit acceptance may seem void. There is no life without a man leading the way. Men are supposed to be in charge of everything. An orgasm without a man, or not produced by a man, seems a lonely obscenity, a devaluation.

Fear of assuming a "male" role can inhibit both self-induced orgasms and those experienced with others. Such fear begins early in a woman's life, with a great spurt in adolescence when girls begin to fail so that boys may protect and feel superior to them.

Success in sex, as in business and in art, makes women unwelcome competitors. One sexual theorist, Mary Jane Sherfey, posits that history is based on male control of female sexuality. Men, feeling like waterspouts by comparison to the majestic falls of women's capacity, imprison feminine lust in wedlock and throw away the key. All rules of fidelity and sexual morality are to keep women's appetites dulled while flattering their own poor endowments. A woman, after all, can have sex day and night, with time out only for sleep and food. No man is a woman's sexual equal.

Some women fear multiple orgasm as a goad to a man's fury and retaliation: he will become domestically tyrannical; he will be chronically unfaithful to prove the glory of his brief, one-time ejaculate. He will become selfish. Other women avoid orgasm altogether, the way they might resist good grades, promotions, the exercise of authority. Better not to wave a red flag, or even a pallid pink one.

The shadow of a domineering father may also inhibit orgasm by inculcating guilt with considerable force. Like mother, he too may be retained unduly long in the bedroom of his daughter's imagination. These fathers, under the guise of protectors, forbid sex to their daughters, warn them of its evils, chase enterprising young men from the doorstep at the slightest hint of erotic interest, insist upon modest clothing, prohibit ornament—jewelry, high-heeled shoes, makeup. In condemning "lewdness," like the pornography critics who must see every film they eradicate, they demonstrate an excessive interest in what they are trying to overcome. To pay such attention to daughter's body means to be obsessed by awareness of it. "Wipe that paint from your lips. Don't look like a whore. Be in by 10:30 P.M. Don't get germs from kissing. Don't let any man touch you. Don't be alone with a man. I don't want any daughter of mine to be seen in an outfit like that. . . ." Father paces the nuptial chamber, watching, disapproving. To have an orgasm under his surveillance would require as much daring and ingenuity as escaping Alcatraz in a Goodyear blimp. Few women can do it. Most relinquish the attempt.

Passive-aggressive women are those who hurt themselves or others more by what they do not do rather than by what they actively contrive. In masturbating, they become aroused, up to a point, and then stop. Such a woman "can't go on" even though she is "almost there." The purpose of stopping seems to be to defeat by inaction whatever the world expects of her. She may also defeat a man by allowing him to bring her to the same high excitement and then stopping him with equal determination.

Women whose parenting consisted largely of tyrannical demands often become passive-aggressive. Fathers who imposed their wills are the most effective, although brutal injury to self-will by either parent may serve as a cause. As if to defend perpetually against the idea that anyone, or any mechanism, even one's own body, can take charge, orgasmic release is prevented in a magnificent act of will,

an assertion of self that is founded, like all defenses, in the
need for human pride and dignity. We must be our own
masters, at all cost, even relinquishing the act that, properly
construed, most affirms our selfhood. Human beings have
a tendency to bungle their highest aspirations in a most
disagreeable fashion.

Aggressive women win at everything, even solitaire.
They learn to be proficient enough at orgasm to be entirely
intimidating, or they resolutely shift their competition to
other spheres: home, business, social skill. The important
goals are superiority and control; they magnify sexual occasions to the status of Olympic marathons or devalue them
entirely. That rivalrous women are timid in bed is a myth—
they really do perform better than others. If not appreciated, they manage to degrade a man so subtly, or with such
skill, that he does well to escape with his trousers and his
wallet.

Aggressive women shun masturbation as a waste of
time, unless they think of it as a method to relieve tension
en route to greater accomplishment. They may also make
an imaginary sport of it, counting orgasms and comparing
their achievement with national averages. Many, however,
avoid the solitary vice because it lacks a specific opponent.

In the toils of intercourse, such women may express
desire for 9 inches of perpetual solidity, or compare their
partners' abilities unfavorably with former lovers, imaginary lovers, or Harry the porno star. To be satisfied would
allow their men to feel as though they'd done a good job.
Many never permit even one orgasm to escape. If they do
succumb to one or two, they always imply that total satisfaction would entail so much more that it would be useless for
the poor man to try. Other gambits include making the
man feel that his way of stimulation is so inadequate that he
couldn't arouse a nymphomaniac, much less a woman with
certain problems, or that he is so clumsy and inarticulate
only the most patient woman would endure him. If she

impotizes her man, he won't be able to function with other women, or have the courage to try. He is, she says, clearly a mama's boy, a repressed effeminate, an insensitive male supremacist, an aging satyr, a body without a touch of soul.

Tough dames fear orgasm because being satisfied may deplete them of control over their partners. They will not have orgasm or pass out sexual commendation for the same reasons that tough bosses go light on building self-confidence in their employees. Of course, by the same token, they may send their lovers headlong into more receptive arms, but these women are uncanny in their choice of devoted men. According to marital studies, the dominant-submissive bonds are the strongest, whoever is doing the ruling. The flayed husbands in such alliances most often never venture, never speak out against their captors. In effect, they are often very much like the women's parents.

Parents of these viragos often appear to be the nicest people in the world. Mothers are sweet, amicable, gentle, caring. Fathers are regular, consistent, businesslike, even affectionate. Daughters get away with everything. They live out their parents' hostile fantasies, gain credit by doing everything mother and dad ever wanted to do but didn't. Such parents tacitly encourage their children to be absolutely vile by secretly admiring their "spunk." They don't want to destroy their offsprings' spirits, as they were destroyed. In the name of creating the strong-willed titans that they themselves never became, they bring up spoiled brats. Often, since few people have a real taste for bloody victories, these harpies succeed materially. Their neighbors are jealous. Their husbands are devastated, but faithful. And they have gained that most precious elixir, their parents' approval.

To the severely schizoid woman, for whom closeness is an acutely painful reminder of emotional impoverishment, orgasm often represents self-annihilation. Beyond loss of power and control, it may mean an entire loss of identity. Such a woman fears that the experience will change her to a shadow whose substance has been devoured, leaving only a gossamer shape. She fears being poured into the vessel of a man's desires, losing the shape of herself, evaporating. The man will take his pleasure. The woman will, without the bones of ego, the structure of personality, disappear.

At a less nearly psychotic level of the same feeling, many women stop their orgasms because they cannot identify with their partners. All good mutual relationships, even those that are largely sexual, require some ability to feel like, to understand, to identify with the other person.

The woman who cannot identify cannot project that the man is enjoying her. She hasn't enough self-esteem. Believing that a man experiences pleasure during sex play or intercourse requires a high, or at least an agreeable, opinion of oneself. Women, even very beautiful ones, often feel that they are ugly, unattractive, too thin, too fat, too smelly. They may be self-conscious about breathing, coughing, blowing their noses. Caught up in their own inferiorities (but not drowned by feeling that they are or can become nothing at all), they inhibit release of orgasm.

Many such women suffered critical mothers and rejecting fathers. A woman can often survive a naggingly perfectionist mother if her father appreciates her, but few escape the deprivation of a totally disinterested father. These women are confined to a lifelong search for an affection they have never felt. Sometimes they are capable of orgasm as a physical spasm, without the resonance of love, without the flowing and embracing that make life harmonious. More often they are captured by their empty childhoods. They cannot grow to nourish others with their bounty. They cannot come.

Severely disturbed women, then, feel that an orgasm will confirm the idea that they can become total nonentities. Less disturbed women, judging themselves deficient, but not potentially absent, cannot project that a man does, indeed, enjoy them.

* * *

As I have mentioned, the French phrase for orgasm means "little death." It is not, therefore, extraordinary to consider that some women fear it not only as a loss of command and an extinguisher of identity but, more, as the final moment for the grim collection of souls.

Fear of dying through orgasm is not quite the same as the fear of nonbeing just described. To be without an identity is still to be alive, in a continuum, while death is final. As one woman put it, "If I had an orgasm, I would be afraid that my soul would go out of me. I conceive of my soul as being not in my head or my heart, but in my womb. If I should touch it, or allow a man to release it, I would die."

Crazy? Perhaps. And yet the beginning, peak, and end, the cycle resembling life and death, is perpetually repeated in the orgasmic experience. When pleasure ends, after each act of intercourse, one is inevitably reminded that life's termination has come a little closer. Nevertheless, most of us go on making love in the knowledge that coffins, at least right now, are for others.

How can the *peur de mort* become so real? There is no single psychiatric answer. In the case of the woman quoted, the fear was a disguise for avoiding the pain of being alive. Her parents had left her early in the care of convents and boarding schools while they pursued dazzling international careers. She could become attached to no one, preferring brief liaisons with rich and powerful men to the complexities of longer-term human caring. She pictured herself as living inside a circular stone wall and peering at life through a slit in the stones. An orgasm would certainly kill her, she felt, until she realized that, if she invested too much in an attachment and it failed her, she might want to destroy herself. The fear of dying was real, but it was death by her own hand that she feared. The womblike stone wall behind which she viewed the lives of others meant to her that she herself was the living soul inside her organs. If touched, and deserted again, she would commit suicide.

For similar reasons, fear of death by orgasm may be a defense against homicidal thoughts. To want to kill the love that may fail can, by inversion, feel like being killed by union with that person.

Often the dullest of people, compulsives who fail to have orgasm can also be the most interesting. They may be obsessed with sex, trying everything, never succeeding, finally boring all their friends and lovers. Or they may direct their obsessiveness away from sex, becoming world authorities on supermarket prices or fifteenth-century harmonics.

The strongest motivation of the true compulsive is to be in control, not so much of others as of themselves. Control of body organs is certainly a compulsive device. Dancers who must practice unnatural contortions, anorexics who compulsively reduce their bodies to bone and integument, muscle men who develop the most unlikely anatomies—all share the desire to defeat nature and, perhaps, mother and dad.

Compulsive women are frequently quite adept at masturbating to orgasm alone. A private behavior, under no one's surveillance, it gives a sense of mastery. It satisfies the need for body command. Most important, the woman who can satisfy herself need not go searching through an anomalous world, on any random day, in any strange place, for sexual respite. She can pick and choose her time and person. She feels free.

However, not all women direct their personality traits to such logical ends. Orgasm is a release, an involuntary spasm. Some feel that any body action not absolutely subject to will should be avoided, if possible. If orgasm is a mystery, best for it to stay that way. To court orgasm would be like jumping on the back of a runaway horse. The journey might be a headlong passage back into the faraway darkness of a confused and depressed childhood, in which perhaps her parents paid attention only to the book facts of measured achievement. To control, with tight obsessional reins, all possible aspects of life has been the only path toward gaining the self-mastery her family respected.

The woman afraid of dire consequences from such a harmless delight as self-stimulation will be petrified of taking an erotic pilgrimage with a man. Under no circumstances can she expose herself to the possibility of his domination or to trusting that he will care. She has learned her tough lesson in the crucible of her past. She is bright. There is no need to repeat the instructions. Whatever she accomplishes has to be willed by herself alone. No one else may do anything for her. She may not lose control at any time. Thus it is that lives go haywire.

Female histrionics usually lack sexual confidence, even when they have some sexual responsiveness. They may behave as though no self-doubt ever entered their minds. They dress provocatively, smell of musk and myrrh, and seem to exude an almost tangible emotional warmth. Sexually, however, they can develop a sudden chill on close contact. On feeling the freeze, men may question their own sanity. Is this rigid, terrified, rejecting woman the same smiling, teasing, encouraging creature of an hour ago? How could she change so quickly? What happened? Most of the time the female histrionic doesn't give a man a chance to view her colors. She avoids overt sexual encounters. The hours people think she spends at sex are actually consumed by the creation of tomorrow's seductive costume. Women who really have an active sex life often look rather less refreshed. Occasionally they look and act downright tired. Good sex is, after all, an energetic business.

Orgasm, or even forthright arousal, represents to many histrionics a potential loss of emotional weaponry. If such a woman became sexually loyal or committed, she might have to withdraw from her accustomed rounds of tempting the population at large. The source might have to be limited to only one person, someone as unreliable and unrewarding as the parents with whom she developed her way of life.

Locked into a shell of absorption, such parents might have forced a child to perform with great artistry in order to gain the smallest hint of real attention. These parents are encrusted by their own defenses, preoccupied or distant. Only if the child is entertaining enough do they look and listen. When the show is over, they retreat quickly to their world. As a young woman their daughter can have no faith in the permanence of feeling. Sharing life with another, which often goes on in loving silence, and even over long times and distances, cannot be trusted. Silence is separation. The person who is not an audience, or making an active effort to demonstrate interest, is considered emotionally detached. Safety lies in immediacy. For such a woman all is lost if sex begins with its normally quiet and inexorable progress toward fulfillment, toward loss of ardent interest.

The histrionic needs the world for an oyster. To become monogamously, or even temporarily, attached, with the consequent risk of loss, is the primary danger. She only feels valid at the moment she has won a new devotee, a new friendship, a new lover. She lives to hear others say how attractive, engaging, delightful she is. Without conscious malice she goes about collecting admiration like the fisherman who returns his catch to the water. A few may die, but most escape with only hook scars, after a short bout of hemorrhage. No deep wound was intended, and frequently none is received. Occasionally, a susceptible sailor must listen (for his own neurotic reasons), and the melody is deadly.

Impaired Orgasm

A woman's orgasm itself may be impaired. This condition was described formally for the first time in the first edition of this book. It includes premature and incomplete orgasm, orgasmic anesthesia, and delayed orgasm. Women, as well as specialists in the field of sex therapy, too often aim at climax as the goal of female sexual pleasure. To limit joy to the attainment of orgasm—no matter what its quality—reflects a lack of insight. A woman's orgasm may consist of a few barely detectable spasms. It may also take her entire body into a convulsive release that rivals epilepsy in physical magnitude and may suggest, to some, a larger spiritual meaning. While not all women would opt for the grand experience every time, they should certainly know that the possibility exists. Some argue that what a person doesn't know won't hurt them, but when ignorance is deprivation, it rarely leads to bliss.

We all know that men who ejaculate too quickly may please neither themselves nor their partners. Women may experience a similarly aborted pleasure. In premature orgasm, the woman is able to have a small spasmodic release after only the briefest stimulation. It provides little, if any, pleasure, and certainly no corybantic joy. Such an orgasm takes its victim by surprise. A moment or two after intercourse begins, a few pulsing contractions ripple through the lower third of the vagina, and that is all.

After the rapid termination, it is a rare woman who goes on to the further enjoyment of multiple orgasms. Women tend to imitate the male model of the single orgasm followed by deceleration and rest.

Premature orgasm is caused by a disturbance in the arousal system which triggers orgasm. The sexual stages are: excitement, plateau, orgasm, and resolution. A woman may pass through excitement and plateau too quickly. This means that she only briefly savors her eroticism, the lusty delay that combines anticipation with enjoyment of the present. When what happens now is good, and what is about to happen seems better, life and sex are brightest. Orgasm, like all climactic moments in life, is brief. To climax without luxuriating in the events preceding totality is a form of sexual starvation.

We may attribute the cause of a female's premature orgasm to anxiety, most commonly related to a lack of sexual self-esteem and self-confidence. Fear of asking for longer foreplay, reluctance to request varieties of stimulation, determination to please a man by not requiring him to work too hard, aspirations to praise for rapid achievement—all desensualize a woman in the act of love. Why complaints of premature orgasm should be relatively uncommon in women, although so frequent in men, is an enigma. Perhaps women have been conditioned to be pleased with any sort of orgasm at all, and simply do not identify their problem.

Women's difficulties with orgasms go beyond having them too soon. An orgasm may begin, then stop or fade before total release. The woman seems to allow herself a tantalizing sample of ecstasy, but forbids the authentic experience. I call this "incomplete orgasm."

Female orgasm can be restricted at any point by conscious or unconscious forces. There need be no abandonment to an overwhelming impulse. If a woman decides, in the midst of orgasm, not to continue, the sensation will subside more quickly than if she wished the orgasm to go on. If unconscious fears interfere with the fullness of an orgasm, the experience will be abbreviated. Indeed, many women mistake minor orgasms for the entire involvement of mind and muscle that an unhampered climax produces. Perhaps the majority of orgasms that women have are incomplete, restricted to the pelvic area, brief, swiftly terminated after several spasms.

A true and complete orgasm takes the entire body into broad arcs of response for several minutes. It is a glory very different from the intense suggestion of joy that most women accept.

The argument that it must be normal to have limited orgasms because so many women have them is like reasoning that it is normal for over half the world to live in poverty. The sad truth of our condition is that what is statistically most frequent is usually far from satisfactory. It may be comforting to know that it is normal to have problems, but it would be an abdication of our ideals not to work for improvement.

In orgasmic anesthesia climax occurs and contractions are experienced, but they provide no pleasure. The orgasm, like the involuntary quivering of an overstrained muscle, creates no erotic sensation.

It is a deceptive experience, but the women who have it are often aware that something is wrong. Identification of this dull spasm is difficult. Some women suggest they have no orgasm at all; others persuade themselves they have reached the full measure of their capacity. For those who are of a mind that life's joys are beyond them, it seems an appropriate reward for sexual adventure. Still another group of women who suffer orgasmic anesthesia—perhaps the most wounded lot of all—have no pleasure for they would dare no bliss. Should they allow themselves the fullness of orgasm, they would be dependent upon another person for one of life's greatest sensations. Such women consciously inhibit delight in all their activities. The risks of joy—dependency, rejection, failure—are beyond their courage to attempt.

Like the numbing effects of a potent drug, the distortions of such women's psyches deny them true feeling.

It is important to remember, however, that disorders involving anesthesia are very likely related to organic causes, particularly spinal lesions. A physician must pay particular attention to ruling these out before making a psychological diagnosis.

* * *

Many women need long stimulation in order to reach orgasm, often more than half an hour. When the orgasm does arrive, it is psychologically unsatisfactory. There has been so much anxiety in its preparation that the unpleasant feeling persists even after the release.

Civilized people aspire to confront life's frustrations with dignity. We do not expect to succeed immediately at learning new skills. We try to accept our intellectual and physical limitations with equanimity. Most of us are slow in one or another area of life's contest, but we take comfort in the fable of the hare and the tortoise. We get there.

Sexually, however, we tend to such self-consciousness and insecurity that the smallest stumbling block suggests a landmine. We suspect that sexual efficiency is an absolute measure of our psychological maturity. Women who don't have orgasms in whatever they consider normal, standard stimulation time, often think they are emotionally below par, if not downright freakish.

In the disorder I identify as delayed orgasm, a woman cannot come as rapidly as she would like. She becomes anxious about her delay and sets back the onset of orgasm even further. Many of the cases contributing to this dilemma are similar to those in other inhibitions and repressions: fear of failure or success or competition; anxiety related to cooperation, dominance, submission. What is specific to cases of delayed orgasm is the patient's desire to conform to a male standard. If the woman were not measuring her performance by the brevity of normal male stimulation, she would not feel inadequate.

Delayed orgasm most often occurs in the woman who suffers severe doubts about meriting her partner's sexual attention. She fears that his finger, his tongue, or his penis will wilt of exhaustion. And it is not beyond her to fantasy that he will punish her later for making him work so strenuously. She tries harder. The more she toils, the longer the orgasm is delayed. She is a victim of the grim but familiar paradox: overwork leads to underachievement.

Inhibition of Multiple Orgasm

Those who would simplify sexual description told us, seventeen years ago, that an orgasm consisted of a series of contractions, usually about eight, occurring every eight tenths of a second, and accompanied by a uniquely intense pleasure. That was rather like limiting the definition of a house to a structure with four walls, two doors, eighteen windows, and a chimney, simply because such cottages are most frequently seen on the American landscape. Just as there are also huts and skyscrapers, so many varieties of orgasm may be experienced in richly patterned sequences.

It is cause for mourning that the female orgasm, one of the most frequently and universally acknowledged human pleasures, has been so rarely defined by poets or scientists. Music tells us most directly about its lovely complexities, but writers have largely failed to communicate the intimate message. Perhaps words cannot capture the changing meter and pitch of a woman's feeling as she moves through delicacy, turbulence, joy, and grief. The literature of the orgasm reads more like a road map than an elegy. If men may be forgiven for their ignorance, women must be accused of too much self-consciousness about revealing their delight.

Since 1977, the varieties of orgasm have been recognized by other experts. But in the years preceding 1977, orgasm was considered a standardized experience; I thought it pathfinding to suggest that female orgasms varied greatly in timing, texture, and degree of excitement. Perhaps the best that could be said for the "eight-contraction" theory was that it described the kind of orgasm that often occurs under conditions of scientific observation. These conditions cannot duplicate the harmonies, crescendos, and counterpoints of love and lust that transpire in the world between lovers without monitoring devices attached to private parts.

There are orgasms in which a single intense contraction may last for minutes on end. Or a peak with only one or two contractions may constitute a minor orgasm. A woman may have chains of minor orgasms that go on as long as she and her lover have the strength to elicit them. Minor orgasms may also occur discretely in the course of long stimulation. Major orgasms may precede and follow minor ones like pearls on a linked chain, or may occur at intervals by themselves after varying periods without orgasm.

The sensation of orgasm may also be quite diverse in intensity. Some are sharp, piercing, almost intolerable; others are warm and gently undulating. Still others engage the entire body in a convulsion. Some women attain supreme release on clitoral manipulation; others respond more abundantly to the stretch and pressure of a large penile head thrust deeply to the furthest boundary of the vagina.

Orgasms may become progressively more intense after the first. They may repeat with gradually decreasing force. They may startle at odd moments with unexpected profundity. Many women feel that after the first cataclysm is over anything more is so anticlimactic as to be disappointing. Others routinely find the second better than the first. Still others find themselves moving upward in chains of climaxes, with each orgasm closer and closer to the last so that finally every thrust of the man's penis may cause a new ecstasy.

Women have varying degrees of control over encouraging onset of orgasm. Some find that tightening the vaginal sphincter assists the development of climax. Others find that "bearing down" (which is really the sort of "opening up" one practices for childbirth) sends them into a more controllable ecstasy. Still others like to "hold in" their abdominal musculature as tightly as they can while tensing their thighs and breathing rapidly. Some women can delay the onset of orgasm, teasing themselves so that when they do allow climax it has greater force, while others can extend the length of a single orgasmic experience for as long as they have the strength and the partner to help them do so. Yet a large sector of women feel as if their orgasms must "occur" with no attempt at encouraging or eliciting them.

Whether one has a single orgasm or many, and whether there is any conscious, voluntary effort or not, depends more on character than on physiology. Having multiple orgasms is no guarantee of sexual health or freedom, though that ability can certainly encourage sexual sanity. Inhibition of multiple orgasms, however, is likely to be evidence of disturbance.

The most common cause is fear of assertiveness, of wanting too much. Just as a majority of sexually troubled women hesitate to ask for as much clitoral stimulation as they need, so the woman who has her one orgasm feels she ought to be content, even though when she is done she has a longing for more. After all, a husband usually has only one climax. For her to have several might set up an unpleasant rivalry. Women are not supposed to be better or have any advantage over men.

Another reason for inhibition is to exert a paradoxical control. A passive but rebellious woman may only be able to allow her husband to give her one orgasm. To stay longer under his sexual domination becomes severely uncomfortable, and so she must actively end the lovemaking.

Fear of becoming a nymphomaniacal sexual addict also keeps some women checked. The books now say that a woman is usually satisifed with one or two orgasms, and that if she wants more than four or five she is passing the borderline of normalcy. By too timidly adhering to these societal norms, such women remain ignorant of their full potential.

Indeed, excessive timidity may prevent other women who can experience more from doing so. Even when women have husbands whose erections do not endure long enough to put them in high climactic gear, they are often afraid to mention it, to seek help for the problem.

The experience of most of the women I have encountered is that although multiple orgasms may be clitorally induced, they are brought about equally often in response to a penis broad and deep enough to put pressure on the walls of the vagina as well as its deepest reaches. Women who cannot tolerate being thoroughly filled, or being thoroughly possessed by a desire to take a man "in" without setting boundaries, are less likely to seek them. Women married to men who are fearful of trusting the entire length and breadth of their penis to a voracious vagina also do not know their own abilities.

While an orgasm is an orgasm, the genus does not describe variations in the species. I believe that one day statistics will demonstrate that, for those women who are disposed both to trust men and to exercise appropriate self-control, the preference will be for that totality of union in which an unselfish man gives the full length and breadth of his organ to a woman who can receive it completely and encourage herself to have as many orgasms as love, strength, common sense, and desire permit.

Part IV

PSYCHOSEXUAL THERAPY

16

Techniques:
Pushbutton Panaceas

People have thought sexuality many things—power or whimsy, love or attraction, erotica only, the heart itself. It has been left for twentieth-century America to think it a science: a statistical science, a technical science. The past two decades have produced a best-seller textbook of sexuality and a spate of weak imitations. These teach us how to do it—or, better still, how to fix it. A new generation emerged thinking that if sex was not pornography it was higher hydraulics. A few odd persons even seemed to think it was something like cooking.

Many people who come to me for sex therapy bring their scientific problem and innocently hope it will be solved. They have been brought up to believe that sexual identity resides in the proper functioning of their genital organs. The brave new couples have read the textbooks. They know the language.

They often speak in tense polysyllables about manual and oral stimulation, making coital connections, and eliciting orgasmic return. Wounded and fearful, they sit on the office sofa. Fingers touching lightly in what seems to be a last gesture of defiant humanity, they can tell with scientific accuracy of how erectile function has decreased of late, or how clitoral manipulation may lead to orgasm, but vaginal penetration by the penis leads to failure. They feel hopeless. They are lemons. Factory rejects. Unable to be switched on, short-circuited, beautiful sometimes, but worthless.

People have begun to identify their sexuality with a mechanical model. Sexual feelings are to be tinkered with, adjusted, tuned up or down for volume, intensity, and speed. Chemicals are requested to turn sex on, reduce anxiety, increase pleasure. Concepts described by social satirists a few decades ago with mockery, fear, and loathing have become accepted ideals.

Technocracy has not only reduced man's image of what constitutes a sexual identity, it has also shrunk the stature of those who guide and help people toward sexual consciousness. Experts in sexuality have separated themselves or been separated from the philosophic thinkers and the compassionate sages. Sexual disabilities are now thought to be curable by simple mechanical means. All over the country, "sex clinics" are being set up and fostering a vastly oversimplified approach to the nature of sexual disorders and their proper treatment.

The "cures" for what is now internationally known as sexual dysfunction are so conceptually simple that any waif seeking a profession on the streets could soon understand and apply them. for this reason, in the seventies, practitioners handed out how-to-do-it sheets, telephone services gave information to any anonymous caller who could ask questions, and people from all branches of medicine, nursing, and social work rapidly set themselves up as authorities. In some cases that I was told of, patients, having been through treatment, felt that they knew enough to set up their own branch offices. Then there were the street people who become prostitutes and gigolos and rose to new heights as surrogate partners in splendid practice for themselves. Conversely, one might mention the members of the many legitimate professions who abandoned their formal training in helping the sick or the underpriviledged in conventional ways, and were to be located, of afternoons and evenings, eliciting "orgasmic return" from their patients and clients by various manual, oral, vaginal, and penile techniques, and getting paid for it. Some have had their credentials removed publicly; others may still remain in practice.

Not more than a dozen rules for sexual "cure" make up the basic repertoire of sex therapy. They can be summarized in a few brief pages. Anyone can learn them. In actual practice, however, extraordinarily few couples can respond to these elementary exercises without concurrent psychotherapy. Perhaps one couple in a hundred does not need help from the professionally skilled who alleviate psychic pain. A young premature ejaculator and his cooperative new wife may be sufficiently free of interpersonal conflict to obey the easy prescriptions. Or a man impotized and made anxious by a single unfortunate experience might respond quickly to the reassuring guidelines of behavioral method. For the rest—couples in mature and difficult marriages made even more complex by sexual trouble, women trapped in the mystery of their unresponsiveness, men whose entire character structure prevents them from giving their ejaculate to a woman—for them, the rules are the barest framework for the mosaic of treatment. As a discrete profession not requiring extensive training in psychiatry, medicine, religion, poetry, art, music, and all the humanities, sex therapy is often a dangerous and destructive concept.

A urologist, Dr. James Semans, presented a formal treatment for premature ejaculation in a brief unpretentious article in a 1956 issue of the *Southern Medical Journal*. Dr. Semans suggested that while a man stimulated his wife's clitoris she should simultaneously manipulate his penis with her hand until he approached orgasm. When the patient was close to ejaculation but not overwhelmed by the urge, he was to remove her hand from his penis. As soon as the patient felt ready to tolerate more stimulation without ejaculation, she was to resume stimulating him. Eventually, according to Dr. Semans's therapy, the patient should be capable of maintaining erection without ejaculation for an indefinite number of starts and stops. It was then that Dr. Semans recommended the use of a lubricating cream to simulate vaginal texture. Orgasmic delay maintained during prolonged periods of manual stimulation with lubricating cream proved to alleviate premature ejaculation in all but exceptional cases.

It was a commonsense approach to an age-old problem, a home remedy endorsed and verified by a scientist. Dr. Semans may not have suspected he was creating a new sexual era.

Masters and Johnson improved several aspects of this technique. They realized that it was too difficult for a man to stimulate his wife while at the same time being fully aware of his penis. Therefore they judged it best for the male patient to receive stimulation passively, without simultaneous concern for his partner's satisfaction.

They also prescribed a series of positions for intercourse to encourage the gradual development of ejaculatory control. First the woman mounts her partner. When the woman is on top, it is easiest for the man to delay his ejaculation. The vaginal walls tend to widen, causing less frictional pressure on the penis. After attaining control in the superior position, the couple has intercourse side by side. Finally, they have intercourse in the male superior position, the most difficult in which to delay orgasm.

Masters and Johnson complicated the original simplicity of Dr. Semans's method, however, by introducing the "squeeze" technique. In this version, when a man is excited during manual stimulation, but not necessarily near orgasm, his partner squeezes the base of the tip of his penis. This emphasizes a "stop." Later, on intercourse, he withdraws so that she can again take his penis in hand and squeeze. There is no limit to the number of times a couple may do this. Although this method effectively cures prematurity, there seems to be no clear rationale behind the application of digital pressure. If a man is too excited to delay, hand pressure does not prevent ejaculation. Improper squeezing may cause pain. And such brisk, often crude intrusion does not necessarily teach a man how to maintain high levels of excitement, a condition most helpful in encouraging a woman to coital orgasm. When a man sustains excitement with his penis at near-orgasmic level, the woman is intensely stimulated to orgasmic response.

The technique which I have accepted for treating premature ejaculation combines the best of Dr. Semans's method with the relevant contributions of Masters and Johnson. First the woman stimulates her partner with her hand. Each time she brings him near ejaculation, he tells her to stop. She does so without squeezing. They do this three times in the course of one coital experience. On the fourth time, he consciously allows himself to ejaculate freely. Once this is accomplished without lubrication, she moistens her palm and his penis with Vaseline, and repeats the exercise until he can confidently delay. The moist lubricant causes hand motion to feel very much like being inside a vagina. At least three manual experiences of delaying ejaculation are necessary. Each experience involves three stops, followed by ejaculation on the fourth round of stimulation. The woman then mounts, with her knees placed solidly on either side of her partner's chest, her hands braced on the bed. Thus she induces an increasing challenge to the man's delaying ability. The couple has intercourse this way several times, the man lying still while the woman moves back and forth on his penis, eventually the man is instructed to thrust slowly in rhythm with his partner's movements. If the man is still easily able to delay his ejaculation until the fourth round of stimulation, the couple experiments with a side-to-side position.

With the confidence achieved by these tactics the male partner is at last prepared to try the most difficult situation in which to delay orgasm—the posture curiously identified as the missionary, or male superior, position. Success in delaying orgasm while "on top" is tantamount to cure. The previously premature ejaculator now has a technique for controlling his decision to have orgasm. The time between stops tends to become greater. The controlled lover may stop as many times as he wishes, last as long as he likes, and ejaculate when he chooses.

The treatment of premature ejaculation can be summarized as follows: Learn to delay ejaculation by being stimulated to near the point of orgasm three times, stopping each time just long enough to be able to accept further stimulation without ejaculating. On the fourth, ejaculate freely. Do this while your partner manipulates you manually, and then again on intercourse in the female superior position, side to side, and in the male superior position. At least twenty-four hours should elapse between ejaculations.

The treatment of impotence requires less instruction and often less time than the cure for prematurity. The first injunction the therapist imposes denies the couple intercourse. Such as imposition on what is justly considered a personal right is often contrary to the patient's and his mate's impulses. Nonetheless this sanction from an "authority" relieves the patient from self-imposed pressures. It is not unusual for this simple precept to solve the problem. Because the doctor has insisted that there is to be no sexual union, the man is relieved of the necessity to perform, and with it his fear of failure often disappears. In this relaxed condition the man erects. The doctor's instructions are ignored and the couple makes love.

Most impotent males, however, require somewhat more attention to method. The procedure begins with the therapist's instructions for "sensate focus." This means that, without being allowed to have intercourse, the couple is guided through mutual gentle pleasuring. The woman lies on her stomach, while the man strokes her body, from her hair down to her toes. She then turns over, and he strokes the front of her body, but avoids her breasts and genitalia. When she has enjoyed sufficient pleasure, she reciprocates by caressing his back, then his front. The only prohibition is that she avoid his penis and testicles.

When the couple is comfortable with these sensual treats, and the man experiences erection, the woman proceeds to touch the genitalia, but they do not attempt intercourse. This seems the obvious method to reassure a man to potency, but it is one of the curiosities of unimaginative lovemaking that most couples never attempt it on their own. Instead of relaxing, the man is frequently determined to try harder. He worries about his ability to satisfy his woman. He belabors his fear that she will think him defective. The woman, convinced that something must be lacking in her feminine ability to excite her mate, toils to masturbate his penis to erection. Such attempts end in frustration, which may turn to anger and then breakup. Accepting that a man with an erection is not required to use it is the most curative concept in the therapy of impotence.

After several incidents of erections without intercourse, the man may lie on his back and allow the woman to mount. She gently inserts his penis into her vagina and moves slowly, making no effort to become excited or to stimulate him to any frenzied expression of his sexual vigor. Reassured by several "nondemand" sessions, the man is prepared to complete the intercourse. If the erections don't appear as predicted, or they do appear but soon fall limp, the man may be encouraged in the indulgences of fantasy to distract himself from anxiety about performance. Busy watching his own actions, "spectatoring" himself as from a distance, he tenses before this demand for proof of his manhood. He must accept the idea that his erection is involuntary, not an act of will. In the same way that we go to the movies or read a book to take our minds off disturbing events, the impotent male may need encouragement to fantasize about the postures or ladies who excite him. Such fantasies may be created as deliberately as we steer ourselves to the TV set for the relaxing balm of involvement in a synthetic melodrama. Lost in the erotic scenes of his own creation, relieved of concern for the specific responses of his partner, the impotent male's erection is most likely to remain sturdy. Once he has learned to use fantasy at will, and becomes confident of his abilities, the previously impotent male does not have to rely any longer on this device unless it pleases him to do so.

The treatment of retarded ejaculation follows a behavioral program that is essentially a simple deconditioning. The man is taught, by successive steps, to ejaculate closer and closer to his partner's vagina. First he learns to ejaculate within a woman's awareness. This means that he tells her that he is going to masturbate to ejaculation while she is in another room, occupied with other activities. But she must be aware that he is having orgasm. Although this may seem a remote therapy, the retarded ejaculator is so accustomed to masturbating to orgasm alone that this is significant to progress in sharing his private pleasure.

He continues the masturbating as his partner moves progressively closer to him. She sits near the bedroom door, then enters the room, and at last shares his bed with him. The most common technique for cure after a man can ejaculate in his partner's presence calls for him to learn to be stimulated by his partner's hand. She may then sit astride him and place his penis near her vagina as he ejaculates. If he is not inhibited by this intimacy, eventually she places his penis inside her vagina for the ejaculation.

Although this is the conventional cure for retarded ejaculation, many men are so inhibited they cannot give a woman this much control. They fear or resent having a woman bring them to ejaculation. It may work in some instances, but I rarely use this technique. More often I instruct the man to masturbate himself to a point near ejaculation and then place his penis near his partner's vagina so that some of his escaping semen may touch it. Eventually, he may choose to insert himself. The ejaculation is always in his control. He can begin to insert earlier and earlier. If he has difficulty ejaculating at times, he can withdraw and masturbate to near-ejaculation again.

Later, as a separate learning task, he can begin to allow the woman to touch and excite his penis.

Techniques for treating women have become increasingly well defined, although responses are markedly inconsistent. The woman who has never had orgasms at all must first learn to have them by herself (unless she is phobic of masturbation). One of the quickest and simplest ways to do this is with a vibrator, preferably a model with a disk attachment, used near but not directly on the clitoris. For most women, clitoral stimulation with a vibrator is sufficient to induce a first orgasm.

If this is not adequate, there are three paths: the route of helping a woman to become sensitive to her genital feelings, the route of encouraging her erotic fantasy to promote sexual excitement and relieve anxiety, and the major therapeutic route of assisting the woman whose main defense against anxiety is to deny herself pleasure by helping her to allow herself to experience joy.

With the first method, she learns to explore her body, observe her genitalia in a mirror, touch herself, and describe the qualitative differences in the sensations of her clitoris, major lips, minor lips, vagina, etc. She learns to pay careful attention to the increasing excitement as she stimulates her clitoris, to observe her lubrication, to concentrate on sensation and nothing else. This frequently results in orgasm because it frees many women of the guilt previously associated with all concerns for their sexual feelings. They are allowed—indeed instructed—to focus on their genitalia, areas forbidden to contemplation since childhood.

The second method, fantasy distraction, is, in my practice, more successful for alleviating impotence in men than orgasmic inhibition in women. Most anorgasmic women have difficulty imagining erotic scenes. However, when a woman is able to fantasize sexual adventures, she is encouraged to do so during vibrator and manual stimulation.

The ability to fantasize is often destroyed by guilt about a masochistic, unfaithful, or other fantasy whose meaning may be mysterious or frightening to the woman doing it. This guilt must frequently be alleviated by searching out the positive aspect of the unpleasant defense, i.e., in a fantasy about being, for instance, a queen bound and forced to have sex, a woman may be shown that her own imagination has created the force that lustily enjoys sex as well as the force that resists it. In the fantasy, she literally ties up her resistance (as well, incidentally, as giving herself a rather high social position).

If a woman cannot fantasize but has a willingness to try, she can also be taught the technique. When she learns, orgasms usually occur in concert with sufficient mechanical stimulation.

Soon after a woman has achieved orgasm with a vibrator, she should be weaned from it. One technique is to direct her to use her vibrator until near orgasm. Then she should try to culminate with her hand, to bring herself "over the hill." Once this method is satisfactorily mastered, she may use the vibrator for briefer periods and masturbate increasingly by hand. At last she achieves orgasm without a vibrator. Some women find that they then are able to approach and experience orgasm more readily by stroking their clitoris or that aspect of the front wall of their vagina known—accurately or not—as the G-spot. However she has attained her place, the woman has now joined that vast but no longer so silent community capable of self-induced gratification.

The next step is learning to have orgasm in a man's presence. A deconditioning technique similar to that used in the treatment of retarded ejaculation is most effective. The woman masturbates while her partner, who is aware of what she is about, retires from the room. On successive nights, he will progress from standing near the door to entering the room and at last join his mate in bed. Many women need not go through quite such an elaborate ritual. They can often start by masturbating in the dark, near their husbands. The darkness provides sufficient privacy to conceal hesitation and embarrassment. Later they masturbate while in some degree of body contact with their husbands—touching hips, touching legs. Ultimately, the husband mounts his wife while she keeps her hand on her clitoris and learns to stimulate herself while he is inside. Or she stimulates herself in any of a variety of positions which she finds comfortable. The goal is to experience orgasm— no matter how attained—with a penis inside.

Pelvic motion providing clitoral friction may be realized by instructing the woman to move her clitoris and vaginal lips against her man's pubic bones. If she is an adept student, she can learn to accentuate her sensations by contracting her pubococcygeal muscles (squeezing as though she is completing the act of urination). If she is well-coordinated, she can also learn to "bear down," the same muscular activity involved in assisting birth. Most women can gradually replace their hand stimulation with active thrusting in the same way that they weaned themselves from the vibrator. They can stop manual stimulation when near orgasm and either thrust to completion or tense themselves to reach orgasm in an isotonic way. They can then stop manual stimulation earlier and earlier on the path to orgasm. Coital orgasm without manual assistance does not often develop quickly, but women may be assured that it certainly will arrive in time, after practice, if they can have orgasms at all. In time, also, they may begin to enjoy the stretch and pressure of deep penile penetration as a source of intense sexual pleasure.

Premature orgasm is a relatively rare condition, unfamiliar to most therapists. It may be treated by teaching the woman to have multiple orgasms so that she does not emerge unsatisfied. Or the Semans technique may be adapted to women. They must simply stop before orgasm, wait until the urgency subsides, and start again. They do this three times and have their orgasm freely on the fourth. This both delays and intensifies the orgasmic experience.

Orgasmic anesthesia is treated by teaching the woman to associate pleasurable thoughts and feelings with her orgasm, if she is aware of the contractions. If she is not, she must learn to be aware of her sensations. She must slow the approach to orgasm and be alert to each increment of excitement along the way. She must also keep her body still if she is a woman who thrashes about so much in her excitement and anxiety that she misses the clear contractions which often signal orgasm. If orgasm is present, the slow, motionless approach will reveal it. Lack of sensation, however, is more often organic than psychological.

Delayed orgasm is not treated as such. The therapist simply helps the woman to the confidence that she is allowed to take as long as she likes. She needs reassurance that her husband's labor in satisfying her—moving his finger for half an hour or more—is hardly a strenuous exertion. Fantasy may also help the woman with delayed orgasm to distract herself from undue worry about keeping up with male pace or exhausting her lover's patience.

Vaginismus may be overcome simply by the introduction of an appropriate object into the vagina. Once a woman can tolerate something going in and out, she is usually prepared to accept a penis. Many methods have been evolved for helping a woman to allow entry. A gynecologist may insert graduated Hegar dilators over a period of several visits. A husband may insert dilators or vibrators of increasing length and width. The method I have accepted as most humane teaches the man to insert first a small finger and then gradually larger ones. Finally he may prepare his partner's vagina by inserting two or more fingers. When she lubricates and dilates she is receptive to his entry. Or a woman may first insert her own fingers and then allow her husband's fingers and penis. Hypnosis or relaxation therapy that teaches vaginal awareness is very useful here.

Creative therapists invent hundreds of variations upon these basic techniques. They prescribe footbaths, showers, shampoos, massages—any of the variety of human cleansing and grooming devices which may provide sensual contact. The goal is learning how to touch. Lotions, powders, and perfumes provide fragrance and texture to dry exercises. Assorted vibrators allow variety and different stimulation. Films and videotapes demonstrate techniques or promote arousal.

One must often teach or modify sexual language to suit both partners' sensitivities. Instruction in the art of fantasy can sound the depth of a teacher's familarity with erotic and pornographic literature, art, and film—indeed, the gamut of cultural and popular entertainment may be enlisted for therapy. But the riches of imagination are ornaments on the surface of understanding. A knowledge of personality, the dynamics of inner conflict, the obstacles to change, and some concept of a goal beyond mere mechanical cohabitation form the basis of sex therapy in its most complete sense.

17

Power and Intimacy

On the surface, it would appear that the overall goal of sex therapy is to improve the mechanical aptitude with which people function. Yet mechanical sex, as a goal, would titillate only a robot. And mechanical means to sexual aptitude do not really exist. Even a vibrator cannot stimulate sexual pleasure unless the person receiving sensation can connect the oscillations with some human joy.

How, then, does a therapist really do sex therapy? What are the major skills and the minor ones? What about the underlying philosophy?

Most sexual dysfunction can be seen as an aspect of ignorance, a cultural phenomenon, an accident of recent life, or a deeper symptom of disordered love. A therapist must, therefore, know how to educate the ignorant, to reassure the temporarily traumatized, and to help overcome cultural shibboleths. When the problem has more distant roots in adolescent or childhood experience, a therapist needs to be able to make systematic insight and to interpret on the basis of a helping ethic. The process of change may simultaneously be facilitated by behavioral prescriptions.

Simple behavioral method, resolutely ignoring the patient's past and focusing only on promoting the desired actions, is almost never enough. Analytic expertise is sometimes enough, given resourceful patients who can map their own changes. However, the best current model for sex therapy demands rapid and accurate analysis, a method for helping the patients resolve neurotic trends constructively, a set of values which defines constructivity, and behavioral prescriptions which are delivered in such a fashion that they do not provoke defensiveness, unexpected rebellion, or loss of self-esteem.

Many therapists are gifted with sexual expertise. A smaller number have analytic skill and training in behavior therapy. Few have any philosophy. Most are content with dedication to the quest for pleasure and leave questions about love up to the patients. Crude hedonism, however, died with the early Greeks. It motivates remarkably few people. In my experience, "cures" which postulate pleasure as a goal are never permanent. They break down. people are more complex, and far more miraculous, than simple organisms moving blindly toward the light.

Love is a curious old word to haul into a late-twentieth-century reflection on the state of sex, considering that it seems to be the mission of our era to replace it with more immediate considerations, or leave it to individual discretion, in much the same way that sex used to be a personal matter. The most important English derivation of the world "love" comes from the word "lief," meaning "belief." For English-speaking people, the root of love is belief, faith, and trust.

In other cultures, love has different connotations. In Latin, the essential meaning involves the act of pleasing (*libet*: "it pleases"), while in Sanskrit, the implication is one of desire (*lubhyati*: "he desires"). While most of us react to the word "love" as having kaleidoscopic significance, implying all manner of affection, for purposes of sex therapy the old English meaning is best, just as the Anglo-Saxon words carry most force in the practice of sex.

It follows, then, that "deeper" sexual difficulties reflect some failure of trust, of belief in another person. When love fails, when trust and belief are meaningless, we are unwilling to give power to another. We certainly cannot allow them to tell us what to do, nor can we even give them a mandate to protect us from calamity or evil. We are also, to the extent that we are damaged, reluctant to take power over others—they are not our responsibility. We build defenses and fashion personalities which exclude caring. And we engage in lifelong combat with the world. It will not touch us where we have been hurt. We will keep our shields up and our parapets high. We will do combat when challenged, and win the struggle for power over ourselves.

The sexual is the most intimate world between two people. Into this milieu, where injured feelings buzz at the rafters like angry wasps, the sex therapist must move with gloved hands to resolve the power conflict. Pleasure, arousal, mechanical functioning are only secondary side effects of some form of trust. There has to be a covenant if union is to be achieved, whether between new lovers in fear of their passion, old married people in search of it, or a lonely being hiring someone else's body to approach passion safely. In old analytic theory, the word "sex" embraced all affectionate and pleasure-seeking conduct. In sex therapy, I believe the word "love" in its broadest significance must be considered basic to all sexual conduct.

Superficially, of course, it would seem that getting laid, fucking, balling, screwing, banging, and all the other single-syllable activities that go on between frequently unrelated and disinterested people bear no thread of resemblance to love, an extremely responsible concept.

Yet in order to be sexually aroused at all, even on masturbation, a person must have experienced love at some time in his or her life, even if that trust was only enough to preserve the most fragile remnant of self-love. The person who goes out to "get laid," careless of a partner's needs or desires, must conceive of himself or herself as worthy of sexual gratification. Perhaps such people do not deem themselves worthy of a sexual companion possessing beauty or status, but they do feel they have at least enough merit to warrant acceptance by some human, if degraded, being. Even the most deteriorated back-ward schizophrenic, masturbating in the public hallway, presents some vestige of an ability for enough self-love to desire pleasure still. Only when self-worth and self-esteem die, when depression corrodes and destroys love, does libido expire. Only when there has been no love in early life, no warm handling received and expected, is an individual left without foundation for later affection. Sex therapy, no matter how rapidly accomplished, must build on remembered or forgotten memories of early nurture, whether patients are made aware of them or not. For an individual who has had no such experiences or who, for some bizarre genetic or constitutional reason, has been unable to receive them (as in the autistic or early schizophrenic child), sex therapy is useless.

We will illustrate, by discussion of the passive personality in distress, how treating people burdened by deeper conflict can be handled in psychosexual therapy. The contributions of Erikson, of systems and transactional theory, learning theory, and behavior therapy will be self-evident to those who recognize them. My own philosophic bias is that the capacity for sexual pleasure of any kind, even the most forbidden and obscene, springs from some knowledge of basic trust and represents a desire to recapitulate love. This is the formulation which works empirically best in treatment. Perhaps it is a truth.

When passivity impairs sexual performance, it is usually because action was met with rejection in a person's early life. In the first or second session of therapy, the patterns can be established. "In your family, who ran the house, who made the money, who decided where to go and what to do? How did they relate to you?" The passive patient will often describe one or another dominating parent who could give but not receive affection, orders, or any other currency of love.

Patterns of emotional trust or intimacy in early life can also be readily established. "In your house who could you tell when you were hurt, felt abused, felt happy, felt angry?" The passive patient will often describe a parent who "read my mind" too readily, answered needs before they were even consciously felt, sometimes created need by too rapid anticipation.

Once the fundamental parent-child transactions have been clarified, the system between the couple must be examined. "Who makes decisions in your marriage? Who handles the money, decides what movie to see, who to invite for dinner, how the children shall be disciplined?" How often these activites are governed by one member is impressive.

Passive people are most frequently married to dominant ones. By dominant, I do not necessarily mean aggressive or commanding. Dominance can also be related to mood, degree of verbosity, exhibitionism, paranoia, intellect, or indeed any other prevailing characteristic. Dominating a passive person is not difficult. Even the most wildly captious histrionic creature, totally dependent and longing for reins and limits, may overwhelm a quiescent partner. The therapist must determine just how the partner dominates.

The pattern of intimacy also requires direct evaluation. "Who confesses a need for help, for relief, for consolation? Who boasts, expresses distrust, relies, becomes angry with the other? Who seeks approval and metes out praise?" Again, one person in the partnership generally risks the lion's share of intimate involvement. The pattern virtually always correlates to that established in the patient's own family, unless psychotherapy has previously altered a way of life.

The sexual system may then be defined in like manner. "Who arranges the sexual ambience, if any? Who initiates sex? Who makes sexual demands, gives instructions, offers suggestions?" The overt power relationship (as contrasted to the covert methods of control by passivity) need definition. The person who has been a passively overwhelmed child will usually be the one who waits for the other to make the first move. The person who receives rather than gives, paradoxically, may be generous with giving pleasure to a partner, but only on request.

The basis for sexual intimacy can be reviewed next. "What is the emotional need that usually accompanies arousal? Do you want sex mostly when you feel lonely, isolated, unloved? When you feel triumphant after a great day? When someone has hurt you and you need reassurance? When something has gone badly and you need to make conquest? When you are angry and want distraction? Do you want to routinize the process of feeling good, as by having sex on Tuesday night and Saturday morning, the way you might schedule tennis, movies, gourmet dining?" These are often the most difficult questions for patients to answer. Most people defend against their need for intimacy. They do not know what they feel because they are often ashamed or afraid of their feelings, and if they do know, they are incapable of expression. People are not accustomed to analyzing their sexual behavior along the familiar lines which they might apply to any other transaction. Our culture creates sexual schizophrenia: sexuality is considered a "function," like eating, digestion, or breathing. However, sex is clearly not a vital life function, except in the broadest sense of preserving humanity. We can live without it. We cannot live without food or air. We don't have sex because we need it. We have it because we want it. Sexual schizophrenia is that condition in which people consider their sexuality to be an impersonal and automatic function.

Passive people generally want sex thrust upon them. They enjoy receiving. They like to get. Emotionally, they use sex more as palliative for injury than to express the joy of conquest or success. Receiving warm and tender feelings causes sexual excitement. They have been well trained to respond happily to what has been given.

The passive person often struggles inchoately to describe the need that promotes arousal. It is an emptiness that wants filling, a desire for the sensation of encircling arms, a sense of too much interior silence. It is a curiously exciting state resembling nonexistence.

Once a therapist understands the transactions, familial, marital, and sexual, relating to power and intimacy, therapy on the sexual problem itself, can be initiated. With experience, it need take no more than a session or two to establish this basic information.

In most sexual unions not requiring therapy, the balance of power and closeness is well adjusted. A passive man and his assertive wife may be perfectly content to go to bed when she is ready, on the nights and in the places that she chooses. Each may feel quintessentially loved through the message they are getting. She may give him exact information on how and where to stimulate her, and she may direct the pace and rhythm of their intercourse. He may be allowed to climax, but only after she has had hers, or however many she wants. When lovemaking is done, she may, like a familiar parent, note how he could have done better. Both may be fully satisfied with the sincerity of their love because their childhood power securities are reinforced with each act of coition. Security in patterns of intimacy may also be reinforced. The passive husband may come home feeling anxious about an incident at work. He may say nothing about it, but demonstrate his unease by tiny signals: an extra ounce in his cocktail, a quicker retreat to the evening paper. His wife knows his intimate needs immediately—she brings him out, they talk, she offers support. In bed that night, she is especially giving. He follows all her instructions and appreciates her ministrations. Life is good.

* * *

In the sexually dysfunctional couple, the balance scales either swing back and forth with such momentum that equilibrium is impossible, or they are so heavily weighted on one side that no balance can be attempted.

A passive person who is sexually dysfunctional has usually developed disturbance or conflict about his or her passivity. This conflict may have been born in childhood, when parents were so overly attentive that a sense of being smothered caused ambivalence: on the one hand, it was good to have so much care; on the other, it was paralyzing. Or parents may have been so neglectful and disinterested that the child became passive in sheer helplessness about reaching them. Eventually, they had to go to the child—to feed, to buy clothes, to insure attendance at school. This also created ambivalence, since human beings, by and large, do not enjoy obtaining fulfillment through helplessness.

When the disorder has begun in childhood, a mate who continues the old pattern is usually selected. Marriages combining love and loathing in equal proportions are commonplace. Sometimes, however, passive disorder erupts during marriage. A person may have been conflict-free about parental gifts. He or she may even find employment which suitably compensates passivity. In marriage, the system may break down. Not entirely comfortable with an assertive role which feels too demanding, too responsible, the more active marital partner may begin to demean and degrade his or her passive charge. The choice which seemed so right, so secure, buckles at the core. Conversely, the active partner may be too demanding, too aggressive to suit the needs of an only moderately passive individual, who then begins to feel repressed and controlled. The important point is that not only does such conflict influence sexuality from without, but it also takes place directly on the conjugal bed. For example, the man who married a dominant woman for security may have functioned well at first. But now, when she tells him what, and how, and when

to have sex, by direction and by indirection, without regard
for his will, his unease grows. He doesn't want to do as he is
told all the time. His erection goes down, or he comes too
quickly, or he cannot come at all.

The passive woman may suffer the same dilemma.
She has chosen an assertive man who gives her his organ on
the slightest hint of readiness, and most of the time when
she has made not even a breath of sexual suggestion. He
wants her everywhere, at all times—in the kitchen, in the
shower, in bed, and especially when she is all dressed and
groomed to go to a party. While difficult to give up, this
constant desire and adulation also imposes a pressure. His
sexual desires, like her parents' attentions, magnify her
self-esteem. They also reduce her to being an object.
Arousal comes, then inexplicably disappears. The inner
battle defeats it.

For passive but conflicted people, the behavioral prescriptions should usually be delivered with emphasis on
training the active, neglected aspect of their nature. The
premature ejaculator must feel himself totally in charge of
his partner, telling her strongly and succinctly when to
stop. His partner must be helped to give up the dominance
that elicits his ejaculation virtually at a thought. The passively impotent man must be helped to gain control over
that which he can voluntarily do: give his partner pleasure
through sensate focus, bring her to arousal with his touch,
his voice, his lips. The passive man who cannot allow his
partner to take his ejaculation must be taught to give it to
her, of his own free will, by his own hand. And women, torn
between reluctant passivity and forbidden action, need the
most sensitive encouragement to take charge of their own
sexual destiny by allowing themselves erotic thoughts and
sensual feelings. Few therapeutic skills require as much
tact, delicacy, and determination.

Sexual intimacy may also be destroyed by basic personality conflict. The passive person, experiencing grief or

loss, for example, might want to affirm life through long, loving sexual experiences combined with great quantities of tender care. An assertive partner may not be able to meet that need, too busy with commanding his or her own satisfaction. Intimate starvation may result. The more acquiescent person will continue to give and respond, but with less enthusiasm, less drive. Indeed, sexual interest may decline altogether—not so much from "depression" as from emotional unrelatedness in bed.

Similarly, under conditions of happiness, triumph, joy, or achievement, passive individuals may be inclined toward more sexual spontaneity and experiment, more fun, perhaps even more assertiveness. They may need to be "brought out." Some dominant partners are insensitive to changing nuances of temperament. They either continue to require the same sexual pattern as before, or insist on their own intimate needs, without regard for the mutabilities of their mates. This kind of blindness can destroy sex by insidious degrees, making people wonder what happened to their love.

For the therapist, techniques which help people to understand their emotional needs are very useful to nourish sexual intimacy. Prescriptions for helping people to feel "hot" by reading pornographic literature and seeing erotic films—such as are often routinely made at sex clinics when couples complain of low libido—are worse than irrelevant. They are a destructive travesty of human feeling when used in this fashion. People can, with effort, comprehend the unique structure of their own sexual motivation. They can learn to communicate it and to gratify both their circumstantial and characterological needs. With such compassionate self-knowledge, the sexual confusion that is presently ravaging our society may be vastly relieved.

It takes considerable self-love to have the courage to love someone else. Helping people to value the early bonds which gave them the ability to enjoy some form of sexual pleasure is the first and last essential part of the therapeutic process. They must learn that for all its limits and paradoxes, what they received in early life was fundamentally real and good. Were it false, they would be among the living dead, incapable of pleasure, without the comfort of a grave.

The therapist's most important work is to assure patients that their character developed in search of love and to insure emotional survival. If a man became passive, it was in order to feed on the only sustenance that was offered. Not to have done so would have denied his humanity. Choosing to change need not mean giving up fundamental traits or risking loss of all the old safeties. Parsimony rarely becomes extravagance, nor would Odysseus have been content to stay at home. Change means only some small alteration that makes life's plumage stand a bit taller. If it leads to more trust in self and others, it will inevitably increase joy.

The kinds of change required (in order to enjoy sex optimally) by people who tend toward the various personality types are simple to observe, difficult to accomplish. An obsessional male and histrionic female, for example, frequently unite in a marriage that becomes sexually dysfunctional. What may have started as a blissful union of opposites, one person stabilizing the emotional waywardness of the other, may eventuate in deep personal and philosophic antagonism.

The therapist, on the surface at least, may be faced with a "classic" syndrome: a premature ejaculator and his nonorgasmic wife, or an impotent man and his nonorgasmic partner. However, therapeutic instructions could be delivered until the doomsday book was closed, and no one would listen. The histrionic woman feels too injured and vindictive to consent to the self-denial involved in either the Semans-type exercises for prematurity or the sexual self-restraint necessary to cure impotence. She finds it unacceptable, if not impossible, to become aroused by a man to whom sex is either a feat to be admired or a routine elimination of wasted seed. He sees himself as a fumbling buffoon on the dual-mattress playing field. His wife either defeats every strategy or boos it from the stands. He will never be able to give her enough. Her dependent and narcissistic demands, combined with her critical views, keep him in constantly humiliating thralldom. To attempt change and to fail might be worse than present woes, which are at least defined within a marriage. Failure might lead to divorce. For many obsessional men, the idea of divorce— the shattering of routine, no matter how unpleasant—is intolerable. Perhaps it would be better not to try.

Restoration of trust is the first therapeutic task. The couple needs reminding that each once found in the other some missing aspect of parental love. He needs warmth, she needs controlling attention. His parents gave him self-discipline without self-love. Her parents gave her a way to love herself without self-discipline. They both have much to give and to learn from each other.

Often the histrionic woman has to be taught that she need not put on a Barnum and Bailey show of emotions, a display with colored lights and calliope, in order to gain her husband's attention. She could trust him to care for her even if she were a brown wren of a girl, wet-feathered in the rain. He needs to learn that she would care for him even if he expressed his frustrated rage and ordered her about in a fit of temper that belied all the "niceness" he has spent his life cultivating. In making therapeutic prescriptions, therefore, the personality problem which has usually come close to or reached the stage of classifiable disorder must be coped with. The cure of premature ejaculation involves sexual activity at defined times in a specified manner. The histrionic wife must give up, at least temporarily, her fantasy of wildly lustful and spontaneous sex. She has to be patient, friendly, giving. Sex must be seen, for learning purposes, as a moderately pleasant conjugal act. Until she can control her need to dominate by drama, no improvement can be made. She must learn the same lesson if her husband's impotence is to improve. She cannot demand, insist, or recriminate about his inadequacy. She must cooperate with composed and tranquil warmth. Either she learns to give up the destructive power she now wields and to become intimate in a new way, or sex therapy is useless. Sometimes she can do this, and it has a ripple effect on other life transactions. At other times, the characterological conflict is so great that sex is too fragile a field on which to practice, and pscyhotherapy must move into other domestic areas before it can come back to bed.

The obsessional male must give up not only his quest for gargantuan performance, but also his compliance, the need to please his wife no matter how unpleasant she may be. He need not give munificently. He can lie back and receive his partner's measured stroking to alleviate prematurity; if impotent, he can be the recipient of all the sensually ingenious ploys that a wife and therapist may together devise, without having to perform or win approval.

Couples in sexual trouble tend to act out their complementary neuroses in bed. Simply teaching one partner to behave differently, to oppose the neurotic pattern, is not enough. The other partner must also learn to satisfy the unmet need that created the neurotic pattern in the first place. It is insufficient to teach a passive man to be more assertive, or a histrionic woman to display and demand less. The partners must learn to give the kind of love whose absence created such a deviant style. The dominant wife must learn not only to allow but to applaud the emergent self-will of her husband. The obsessional husband needs careful and patient tutelage in expressing emotional responses so that his wife need not try so hard to elicit them. Sex therapy, at this level, is the therapy of personality disorder.

* * *

The number of personality combinations in marriage is prodigious. If one adds complicating neurotic features, like depression or anxiety, which may afflict one or another partner independent of basic personality trend, the types of amalgams multiply. If one considers, in addition, that personalities are often fusions of several types, the total is overwhelming indeed.

To try to describe how each and every variety of couple could be treated would require volumes. Suffice to summarize that a therapist should rapidly establish patterns of power and intimacy as related to familial, marital, and sexual functioning. These should be correlated with personality type. Instructions can then be given in such a way that the patient becomes aware of the unique functioning of his or her personality in bed. Correcting patterns which led to dysfunction may then proceed along predictable and rational lines, without the waste of time and emotional energy, both for the patient and therapist, that accompanies now popular methods. These "offer behavioral prescriptions" and proceed to "deal with resistances" by confrontation, bypass, joining, and other psychic sleights which, in the end, cheat patients of true improvement and deprive therapists of a job well done.

Sex therapy, properly practiced, is probably the most direct route to the resolution of personality disorder and in some cases even of neurosis. Unlike most of the other areas of life with which psychotherapy concerns itself, sex provides primitive, direct, and gratifying reward. One may learn to work and to survive while still suffering immense psychological pain. Having good sex is, at least at the moment of pleasure, incompatible with true suffering. Most people are very strongly motivated to want it.

The new dimension of sex therapy, then, brings us back to where psychoanalysis began: emphasizing the importance of sexuality in human affairs. Since then we have given much attention to developing efficient tools for probing and analyzing. Pragmatically, in the most philosophic sense of the word, we have discovered the modern implications of an old truth: love is a prerequisite for sexual feeling. It is not necessarily the love of one sexual partner for another. It is love received in some form, no matter how distorted, from another human being early enough in development to lay down a neurological pathway. Sex is not the basis for all pleasure-seeking conduct. Love, in some verbal, tactile, or even punitive form, is the basis for all sexual conduct. How we have received it in childhood and how we seek to get it in adult life form the environmental basis of personality and often the core of disorder. Psychosexual therapy, in its most complete sense, can enliven far more than a recalcitrant penis or a quiescent vagina.

18
Sexual Fantasy

Sexual fantasy, the amusement of the contemporary sophisticate, is also the traditional passage to the unconscious. It may be a way to promote sexual feeling or to avoid sexual action. It can tell us what we are, yet prevent us from becoming what we do not wish to be. We may indulge in it immoderately, or avoid it as a foul contagion. Whatever our use of the sexual imagination, its content can provide more graphic and immediate psychological self-knowledge than any other mental activity.

Fantasy may be a therapist's most powerful tool for defining personality traits, improving communication, releasing inhibition, and alleviating sexual anxiety. However, therapeutic intervention into sexual fantasy has so commonly proceeded along a path both destructive to erotic life and demeaning to human dignity that it seems appropriate to describe the pitfalls of good intention before suggesting constructive alternatives.

Misuse of classical interpretation is the most frequent culprit. Some incompletely trained analysts believe they have achieved their therapeutic objective when a patient slowly and laboriously reveals a previously unspeakable fantasy. The excesses of sexual fantasy are as diverse as the eccentricity of personality. A patient may speak of stretching a potential partner on a torture rack or urinating or excreting into a mate's mouth. These may be among the more conservative of premortuary unkindnesses imagined upon an erotic victim.

When these fantasies are not aroused by a mate's distasteful behavior, they may be clarified as signifying repressed or suppressed anger toward a parent. It is not uncommon for a therapist to proceed by searching out and at last affixing these hostilities to their source. Properly associated with the original parental object and the appropriate oral or anal stage, the fantasy is expected to vanish. Once the patient realizes that the victim stretched out spread-eagle and bound securely with harness and bracelets is dad or mom, both the fantasy and the guilt about it are supposed to disappear. Unfortunately it is often only the sexual excitement which evaporates, dissolved not only by the heat of still unresolved Oedipal attractions, but also by continued self-reproach for the offense.

Helping a patient to realize that he or she fantasizes blood lust during coitus for hate of mom or dad is like telling a crying child that the pain is caused by an open safety pin. It is as sadistic as it is ineffective.

At the opposite end of the spectrum are those still extant "new" sexual therapists who take their cues from pimps, prostitutes, and other commercial sexologists. In the name of "behavior therapy" they declare that any mental aberration which promotes sexual excitement is not only acceptable but should be universally encouraged. Whether the object of the fantasy is a rhinoceros, a mutilated geriatric specimen, or a cloven-hoofed hermaphrodite, the injunction is to enjoy freely. No interpretation is necessary. The measure of psychological truth is an erect penis or a lubricated vagina. Pleasure is where you find it. Consequently, masses of innocents accept the doom of spending their sensual lives in grisly contemplation of morbid erotica. The degradation that people will tolerate appears boundless. The new sex therapy offers us a highway to the new psychopathy. Anything goes.

An assessment of sexual fantasy begins with consideration of its relationship to the character of its creator. What is the content of the fantasy? More important, what value judgment does its author pass on imaginings which may vary from grandiose sadistic exercises to humble anatomical fetishes?

Fantasy can reveal character both directly and indirectly. Sometimes it is merely an extension of a person's lifestyle: a man accustomed to having many women may simply dream of having more; a woman desiring one true love may create impassioned scenes of ideal union. When real life and fantasy are synonymous, or at least proceed in the same direction, one may identify a well-integrated personality. One may also identify a true personality difficulty by the clarity and persistence of certain erotic creations.

The person who dreams of a singular love and works hard to achieve one good relationship in actuality would seem to be both unified and psychologically sound. The person who fantasizes hurting others emotionally, and also does so in real life for the sexual fun of it, may have a unified character, but hardly a healthy one. In either case, when fantasy and reality are closely related, the diagnosis is simple, even if the neurosis is stubbornly resistant to treatment.

For example, one may often identify a histrionic by a profusion of exhibitionistic images. Though not all histrionics are capable of sexual imagination, the ones who are may have extraordinarily vivid internal lives. In women, "showing" themselves is characteristic. A patient described to me her vision of lying naked on a grand piano in front of a male audience; another patient fancied herself dressed in a transparent white wedding gown, arousing the onlookers as she sauntered down the aisle. She also invented an image of herself in elastic stockings and black garter belt, entertaining the burlesque house audience with views of her vulva. Histrionics are often the most creative dreamers, building stories about themselves in every role from madam to vestal virgin desecrating the sacred trust. Their most frequent role in fantasy, sketch or scene, is exhibitionistic.

Male histrionics seem most often to spectate erotic scenes in which they may or may not take a part. Perhaps to defend against the desire to win approval for the sight of their charismatic genital, they fantasy the opposite of demonstrating, which is witnessing. They are stimulated by every variety of scene that pornographers suggest. In roles ranging from pimp to seduced adolescent, they mentally play out their erotic visions of sin. Male histrionics, more often than females, act out their fantasies. However, when free to do so, female histrionics as eagerly transpose their imaginings to reality.

Obsessional fantasy is characterized by repetition and a lack of diversity. The same fantasy, be it of violence or tenderness, is retained as a favorite security object, like a blanket or a teddy bear. For some, the aggression they avoid in life enters their sexual fantasy in dreams of fastidious torture chambers where they, as victims or tormentors, methodically complete their unions. For others, the tenderness that they are unable to express in their ordinary lives emerges in an ideal bonding of complementary bodies and souls. Whatever the content of obsessional fantasy (sacred, secular, or profane) a single genre, a single scene, or a single person is likely to be a stimulus over the course of months, even years.

For sociopaths, narcissists, and aggressives, fantasy more often resembles a plan than a release or wish fulfillment. Their fantasy is more a working daydream than a random assortment of images or feelings. If such a man imagines having a beautiful woman brought to a hotel room for a fifteen-minute tryst, it is not long before he has a lackey escorting her to him (providing his public name or private resources afford adequate magnetism). Men more often than women regard sexual conquest as sufficient motive for active pursuit of their fantasy. When an aggressive woman hunts her imaginary quarry, the aim is frequently more than emotional and sensory satisfaction. Whether it is nobler for a woman to pursue a man for property or for a man to command a woman's sexual receptivity, when both are consenting adults, is probably not an ethical concern. There are those who moralize on the subject, but in the meantime the dreamers who long for an assortment of spoils have long since gone on to the next adventure. Fantasy and reality, for these active personality types, have a complementary relationship.

Problems multiply when fantasy, as it so often does, contradicts or belies reality. Though it may be one function of fantasy to remove us from reality, the distance of the mental trip can be bewildering and disturbing. The dichotomy between people's lives and their imaginations can be a significant key to personality as well as therapy.

We are all familiar with the extravagances of Walter Mitty's wanderings: the timid and conventional soul who lives a majestic inner life. We are less likely to recognize our own inconsistencies.

The schizoid, locked into a lonely life of sexual abstinence or emotionless promiscuity, may dream of the tenderest adoration. The passive-aggressive, bound in psychic or economic servitude, may rebel in perpetual mental flights to other partners and other lands. Tied to a ritual of monogamy, self-sacrifice, and order, the compulsive may create a universe of obedient sexual servants, graded for performance, and available on demand. Busy attracting and, often, seducing everyone in sight, the histrionic can suffer the fantasy of one perfectly fulfilling love to satisfy every need for care and attention.

Most of us are disturbed by the divergence of fantasy and reality, but do not trouble very strongly to make them coincide. Our sexual fantasies are often concerned with something we would forbid ourselves to act upon, or they may fulfill that which we regretfully acknowledge as too difficult to obtain. In any event, both the content of the

fantasy and our reactions to it tell the struggle we have
been through to reach our present personality, defenses,
ego structure. What we are may not be what we would
choose to have been, but it is the best we can do.

Therapy is not usually sought for pruning a fantasy
life to order, but rather for improving reality. In the process of psychosexual therapy, however, one must frequently
both relieve guilt about fantasy and dispel confusion. Often
the difference between fantasy and reality is so great, or
the fantasy is so guilt-provoking, that sexual disorder results from the malaise.

The truth of the therapeutic experience is that, for all
the satisfaction associated with the mystique of sexual fantasy, most people are disquieted if not pained by guilt and
confusion when they make love to one person and consistently stimulate themselves by imagining relationships with
others. The man or woman roused, for example, by
thoughts of homosexual fantasy while engaged in heterosexual love frequently questions his or her sexual integrity
or identity. "When I am held by my husband I close my
eyes and get excited by the dream of being licked and
touched and manipulated by another woman," a female
patient confided. "What's wrong with me? Am I really a
lesbian?" Although the script may have the resonance of
melodrama, the pain is real. The answer is rarely achieved
by categorically accepting extravagances of the individual's
fantasy. For most people there must be authentic correlation between what they feel and do and what they imagine.
When the patient who envisioned herself in another
woman's bed accepted her sexual fantasy as a projection of
a need for the tender loving of another woman which was
denied to her in childhood, she was able to accept her
fantasy as a search for love rather than a perverse
eroticism.

Most of us require the comfort of physical reassurance
from both sexes. Although the degree varies, once we

perceive that this longing is frequently expressed as fantasy, we may be free of confusing and impotizing guilt. In recent years increasing numbers of people have accepted the overlapping quality of male/female identities. For all the traditional stereotypes, it makes sense both intellectually and genetically that male/female qualities and needs vary among individuals. As we become less arbitrary about the styles and characteristics associated with gender, it becomes less difficult for a therapist to help women accept the "male side" of their nature or men to enjoy their "female" proclivities.

When a therapist encounters a patient who discloses fantasies of a violent, if not bestial, nature, the therapy is more complex. "I want to beat a woman, to tie her to a bedpost and smash my fists into soft mounds of female flesh. I know I must be a sadist because that is just the beginning. I tell you, doctor, when I consider some of the things I imagine doing to a woman, I scare myself." Little wonder that the male patient who elaborated on this fantasy suffered impotence when he was engaged in "lovemaking." What relationship is there between what the storybooks tell us are the sensitive and tender exchanges of sexual union and the butcher's block this hapless fellow imagined as his mating bed? For some robust fellows sex is aggression. It is one of the tragedies of mating that the bedroom is often a battlefield, but I have found that it is a rare individual who is satisfied with exchanges of injury in the name of love.

Again the subtle wiring of the human psyche may be untangled by a search into the past. The man who was impotized by his imagined sexual mayhem did not find relief when the anonymous female of his fantasied abuse was identified as his domineering mother, although that was true. His guilt was exorcised only by the realization that this primitive mental violence was a means of freeing himself from her restrictions but not from her love. Once he had mentally eliminated her shackles, he was free to experience his need for union. In the shorthand of psychic integration, however, the need to love had become synonymous with the need to hurt.

Many people, therefore, frequently have fantasies which are incompatible with the dictates of their individual consciences. They suffer, without fully knowing their handicap, through sexual experiences which feel erotic but somehow not "true." The woman who allows a homosexual fantasy into her lovemaking with a man may think she is being aroused by the stimulus of the forbidden and perverse. She can respond neither to the totality of the fantasy nor to the intimacy of her partner. Yet she would be loath to give up the fantasy because it seems to be aphrodisiac.

Women with such fantasies usually do not seek therapy unless they have some practical dysfunction, like inhibited orgasm. Only then do they generally discover the relationship of their fantasy to early sexual and affectional memories. Only then can they become free to integrate the joy and excitement of early childhood with the strength of adult love. The experience they then become able to have is far more deeply satisfying than the queasy titillation once identified as "erotic."

Similarly, men with aggressive fantasies think they are enjoying guilty pleasure when actually the guilt interferes with the pleasure. Whether the source of the fantasy is fear of passivity, the need for freedom from restraint, or the contact involved in fighting with a parent, understanding and being able to feel its affectional and sexual origins without guilt can create a new sexual fulfillment.

Most theorists on human relations, and particularly authorities on marriage, agree with the universal mandate that, whatever else is lacking, there must be "good communication." People must, in other words, be able to tell each other what they feel and think.

They must be aware of their emotions. They must make them known in an acceptable way. They must test their responses against a value system in the painful process called thought and present conclusions to one another in speech and writing. A decision can then be arrived at, a compromise achieved. Thus people live together.

In psychosexual therapy, fantasy can be a powerful tool for mutual understanding. Knowledge of a partner's most intimate preoccupations can raise the curtain behind which is staged the real self. Yet clearly, if so few therapists can handle the content of sexual fantasy constructively, one can only imagine the paranoid bonfire that unguided exposure may create in the susceptible. Unless there are safeguards against inappropriate negative interpretations, "telling," either at home or in the therapist's office, is more likely to cause disruption than unity.

The taxonomy of fantasy may be a help to those who wish to try to communicate. Fantasy may be impersonal, deviant, or deeply meaningful. It may involve an action with some story to it, a picture, or a feeling. It may be related to reality or entirely detached from any real circumstance or person. For most of us, the difficult fantasies to reveal, of course, are those deeply personal imaginings about real people which may truly threaten a relationship.

The most common fantasies are detached: impersonal thoughts about other people or other types. Imaginative fantasies—stories about fictional or movie characters, and visual erotica—also fall into this category.

Women's most frequent impersonal fantasies are "romantic." The gist of romance, of course, is to be away from all anxiety and conflict: either too rich or too poor to care about material things, and certainly uninvolved with housekeeping and child raising. A man usually spirits a woman away to a romantic setting. If it were not for romantic fantasy, perhaps half the world's women, dependent, harassed, overworked, underpaid, tied to life's tragedies and boredoms, would not become sexually aroused.

The most common male fantasy is of an exciting, shapely, and nameless female body (or two), with whom he dallies. The setting is less important than the degree of female assertiveness. Depending on character, the fantasy ranges from completely docile and receptive flesh to actively seductive sirens.

At this most elementary level, fantasy serves as a playful separation from nagging anxieties. There is no active desire to change the conditions of life or have other partners. All a person may want is to be in a tension-free situation. The imagination is an appropriate path for getting there. Without such occasional fantasies of variety to alleviate normal life stress, perhaps half the men in the world would be sexually indifferent. Such stress is usually the result of a disturbance that cannot be immediately resolved, like troubles with inlaws, children, or a spouse's personality. Sometimes it arises from problems that are not even recognized, like unconsciously feeling dominated or abused. The result is an impersonal fantasy which, when not an obsessive preoccupation, makes most humdrum burdens tolerable.

The next large class of fantasizers, both male and female, may be identified as deviant. They find arousal in power or submission, violence or suffering, exhibiting or spectating. Not merely a method of relieving ordinary discomforts, these fantasies are attempts to repair lifelong problems with sexual guilt and parental love. They are usually quite intense and are ordinarily kept private. Telling them rarely improves sexuality unless a partner has a similar or complementary disposition. Two people who are stimulated by thoughts of sexual spectating, for example, may share imaginary friends or acquaintances in bed; a person with sadistic inclinations may find a mirror mate in a masochist. However, circumstance does not always decree such fortuitous combinations and the vagaries of one sexual dreamer may stir severe paranoia and distrust in a partner who has no intuitive clue to understanding. Communication would be enhanced, of course, if we could freely share the intimacies of our daydreams; but we must judge to whom we disclose our secrets. Rarely is the catharsis of confession accepted by a nonjudgmental partner in harmonious benediction. Unless a helpful professional or a supportive group is present, many people will be deeply shocked and intimidated by their partner's erotica.

Whether or not one shares the third level of fantasy, the deeply personal, depends on the solidarity and terms of a relationship. My experience indicates that most people become infatuated or fall in love with others an average of six times in the course of a long marriage. More often than not, they do not share these loves with each other because they are too threatened. Fantasies that are very nearly realities, unshared, allowed to become either obsessions or sources of pervasive discontent, are usually symptoms of the need for change in a relationship. They presage either battle or extramarital involvement. When a wife persistently dreams of salvation through the charms of a single other person (often her husband's best friend), investing him with all the love she cannot feel on the marital bed, something is seriously amiss. When a husband regularly eliminates his wife from awareness, pretending that she is another person, there is, if nothing else, a problem. To share the dream is to face reality, a harder task than dreaming. Yet rarely can a union continue unruffled or undiluted when one partner is not really there.

Historically, sexual theorists have taught us that fantasy is a way to control behavior and to reveal unconscious conflicts. Contemporary sexual pundits suggest that sexual fantasy is a guide to action. They propose that, no matter how destructive or self-indulgent the dream, it should be expressed to some degree: if dangerous, game playing can suffice; if merely promiscuous, the fantasy should be played out whenever possible, like dreams of wealth or glory. What are fantasies for, they reason, except to act upon?

Encouraging a man or woman to play out a sexual fantasy without a realistic appraisal of the emotional consequences is either naïve or pernicious. In today's culture, where elaborations of sexual possibility provide entertainment as well as sexual stimulation, the unsophisticated imagination sometimes adopts the erotic film or lascivious novel as a life-style.

"It seemed like innocent fun to share my husband with my best friend," a beleaguered wife explained. "We read about it and saw it in the movies. Our sex life was getting a little routine. So we agreed."

Fantasies of numerous lovers and diversified sexual situations are not uncommon, but once the dynamic of recoupling is introduced the relationship always changes. Regardless of their initial confidence in each other, in my practice it is unusual that one or both partners do not experience genuine pain or rejection on first seeing their mates have sex with someone else.

Certainly there are people who can feel their strongest human affections in the context of group sex or a swinging milieu. For most of us, however, a momentary mental excursion into sexual detachment, homosexuality, or sadomasochism is sufficient. Those who encourage "the real thing," regardless of the person to whom they suggest it, do a disservice to both reason and morality.

Narcissistic, aggressive, and histrionic personalities, especially those with a touch of psychopathy, often pursue their fantasies, without any organized permission or encouragement, especially when they are away from their spouses. Reveling in the grandiosities of politics or other theatrical professions, they have given new meaning to the term "sexual congress."

The trouble with pursuing fantasies is that they are often trysts with the forbidden. What is forbidden is usually harmful to someone. If taxpayers are not harmed, there are other victims: wives, husbands, employees, friends, even the performer himself or herself. There is no new morality, although there may be new kinds of open agreements. Casual violations of trust, public or private, generally exact a price. Or, at the very least, they should.

If there are some who act too impulsively on their dreams of paradise, there are others who not only do not act but dare not dream.

While inability to fantasize may sometimes result from absence of cortical equipment, this degree of impairment is rare. Even severely retarded individuals have the capacity, though their creations may be emphatically ungilded. Not IQ but largely fear restricts the pleasure of dreaming for both the simple and the wise: fear of retribution, of loss, of discovery, of punishment—vague, nameless, unsystematized—but nevertheless a terror not unlike the persecutory forests of insanity.

Women more frequently than men suffer complete paralysis of fantasy. They report having never visualized an erotic scene, never imagined themselves even mildly attracted to another person. On further questioning, a few will recall having been stimulated by a romantic movie kiss or a passage in a novel, but that's the extent of it. Active fantasy—creating a lusty scene, or even a mildly arousing circumstance—can be almost as taboo as incest.

Very few men draw complete blanks. Almost all have imagined some sexual act and found it arousing. The act may be only suggestive—a faint outline of a sensual woman, in softest focus, barely discernible, sliding in and out of the dreamer's contemplation—or it may be a quick surreal contact with a single body part, a breast, a mouth. The point is that even the most inhibited men can recall these brief illuminations and remember that they were exciting.

Neurosis may impede as well as encourage fantasy; dependent personalities, perhaps, allow themselves the fewest excursions and sometimes suppress their faculties

entirely. Just as it is one of the functions of a therapist to
tame unmanageable fantasy, so it is also a goal to release
severely constricted fantasy in the service of sexual pleasure. Such limitations are most common in women. Again,
the key to fantasy release, as well as to relieving the guilt of
deviant fantasy, is not simple permissiveness. It is the therapist's ability to connect the mental production, however
confined and tentative, to the best of early experience.

The most common use of fantasy in sex therapy is as
an adjunct to the treatment of impotence. Men are encouraged to fantasy in order to distract them from fear of
performance. If they can imagine an erotic scene instead of
worrying about their erections, they may be able to complete an act of coitus. Another frequent use of fantasy is to
help inhibited women realize the effects of mental stimulation upon physical response. As I have suggested, this
therapeutic use of fantasy seems currently in danger of
becoming a universal prescription for unlimited erotic de-
viation. Popularizers of what has become virtually a cult
promote sexual fantasy to "turn on" the hypersexed and
the undersexed indiscriminately. Conversely, strict religious sects still preach mental abstinence, regardless of
the individual. Perhaps the answer lies in the old Aristo-
telian plea for moderation. Too much or too little of anything can be a disease or a deprivation.

We need to be free to fantasy to fulfill the best and
exorcise the worst in ourselves. Advising the repressed to
allow themselves freedom of imagination should not be
construed as a mandate for those without controls to ca-
reen madly at the borderline of reality. One must still hold
a small faith that the best sexual relationships are those in
which flesh-and-blood partners are desired. For all the
commerce or art achieved in its name, sexual fantasy remains a pale substitute for the complexities of joy and pain
which are requisites for loving a real person.

19

Women's Web

The web that creates sexual suffering has many strands. Men are usually caught on only two: their parentally fostered personality disorder, or a crisis precipitated by some traumatic transaction with another person later in life. The struggles of early intimacy or the perils of later relationships are the major threads on which male pleasure depends. A therapist can rather easily determine whether a man had contact with a specific woman who brought his erection or ejaculation to grief, or whether the performance demands of his parents, particularly his mother, were so impossible as to create a permanent sexual wound.

Women, however, suffer not only the effects of early and later blows to self-esteem, but must also cope with societally and parentally induced sexual guilt and shame, cultural misconceptions about sex, and a high level of ignorance. They are caught in such a complex net of repression, inhibition, and fear that each element must be dealt with separately.

We are all familiar with the societal taboos. The older generation of women, married, divorced, single, has to be helped, regardless of individual personality, to overcome the simple notion that sexual pleasure is wicked and forbidden. The middle and the new generation must be helped to undo parental disapproval or the memory of it. The therapist holds a powerful transferential position for accomplishing this: giving permission, support, and encouragement, in the role of physician and healer. These are the only tools for combating ancient pressures. That they so often work is astonishing, considering the brevity of therapeutic contact compared to the lifetimes of guilt and shame, caused by old and new cultural misconceptions about sex.

When a woman is culturally conditioned to believe that sex should be one type of experience, but becomes aroused by another, she often inhibits herself in sheer confusion, if not total despair.

Many woman believe that the only circumstance worthy of excitement is a "romantic" liaison. What exactly constitutes romance is usually a bit vague. Romance may be a picaresque activity in an exotic place, like going down a dangerous African river with Humphrey Bogart. It can compass the tragic aura of star-crossed lovers like Tristan and Isolde, Romeo and Juliet. It seems to require that the woman feel both more serious than death about her union, and at the same time gayer, less responsible, more elegantly carefree than she has ever felt before. Romance is more moribund than the grave, and more prescient than birth. It is total honesty, and total deception. It belongs to the young, the naive, the untouched, but is best with sophisticated and worldly men. Romance is a penniless journey on which kisses must suffice for food; it is a private jet to the sun of a personal island. It is acquiring all the silver and lace of bridehood and tossing them out for love of a wandering spirit. In short, romance is an unattainable paradox. Devotees of romantic action must, by definition, repeatedly destroy what they have in order to follow the new adventure.

Still, women persist in the idea that, when their lives become romantic, they will have enjoyable sex. A major complaint is that life with John Doe, thirty-five, plump, regular, and trustworthy is about as dull and frustrating as making a meal out of sunflower seeds.

* * *

Pleasure is often dammed up because some women feel that, beyond romance, love is the only permissible emotion accompanying such a vast gift. And loving is not enough. Being loved, by words and deeds, must also be a part of the contract, which, to be valid, must be unwritten. Only perfect human love will do, a state beyond games and infatuation, an attachment beyond courtship, a union in which each would die for the other and yet neither would ask the other to give up life. Love must be a selfless condition which at the same time authenticates the self. Like romance, it has many impossible paradoxes.

Love must be a dedication to someone else, yet gratify self-love. It must surround a couple with transcendental unity, yet spotlight the individually divine. Love must be a giving and a taking, an end and a beginning, a cosmos and a speck at the brink of infinity. Love must grow with every abuse to its strength. It must be infinitely gentle, yet implacably tough. It must attain splendor in adversity. Love, to be true, is warm, flaming, life-giving, radiant. It is also the cold, austere meeting of souls in the grayness of eternity.

While such love between physical and spiritual equals is much to be desired, and represents a healthier aspiration than most of the other inanities we dream of, it is hardly ever to be got. It is there in mythology and literature, but life afflicts us with pride, covetousness, lust, anger, gluttony, envy, and sloth. We can be sure it will also so afflict our soul mate. The expectation of true and perfect love, as a criterion for sexual pleasure, is rather like needing the Aegean Sea to mirror a classical Greek morning in order to learn how to swim. Most of us make do with the local swimming hole. While early love may be the basis for all sexual pleasure, as adults we must content ourselves with trust, laced with the understanding that human perfection does not yet exist.

The need for a unique form of "being in love," known to psychiatrists as "transference neurosis," may also blockade sexual fulfillment. Strictly speaking, this condition is tied to that which happens in the course of an analysis, but the symptoms are so ubiquitous that it is well to understand them wherever they occur. A somewhat lesser state than the love of equals, transferentially neurotic love requires believing that one's idealized partner has attained perfection, is magically all-powerful, can protect, heal, comfort, befriend. He can handle the world in the most masterful way. Transference neurosis implies that the lover is less than the beloved, but shines by reflected glory.

Most of the time, the object of transference neurosis is rather difficult for a woman to capture since he is usually too busy and successful to notice her. She is also generally so awed by him that her tongue will not form the appropriate words. Or her legs seem to carry her quickly out of the room. Occasionally, however, such sexual unions do take place. In them, the woman often feels herself so inferior, so minuscule, so unworthy, so worried about pleasing and retaining her ideal, that pleasure, not to mention orgasm, is stifled at the source. Of course, frequently the masochism of a transference neurosis arouses intense sexual pleasure and brings on orgasm after orgasm. The woman's need to feel degraded is satisfied. She enjoys herself. But, more often, such relationships don't even get started. If they do begin, they end in fiasco. The hero may plunge from his pedestal, or he may glide down gently by imperceptible degrees, but the obsessional infatuation is over before the orgasm begins.

Sometimes transference neurosis directed at an unattainable man may not only defeat orgasm but destroy a marriage. It is not uncommon for a woman to be so deeply "in love" with her psychiatrist that she rejects her husband. He is not splendid enough to be worth a response. Among the dilemmas of nonorgasmic women, this is probably the most enigmatic torture of all. Unethical or inexperienced therapists can keep a woman embedded in transference and out of her marital bed for years. In any event, the belief that a woman should be "in love" before she permits sexual pleasure still constricts many women. There is no doubt that such a state can be the most powerful natural aphrodisiac known to man, especially when shared by two people who regard themselves as humble in their beloved's shadow, and as gaining stature by association with each other. As a prerequisite for sexual pleasure, however, it would certainly limit joy. It has been approximated that many people fall "in love" an average of twelve times in their lives, and the sensation ordinarily lasts three to six months (although in some rare instances it may go on for a lifetime). Such short-time bliss could hardly do as a prerequisite for sexual arousal. Clearly, other sources of erotic feeling must be considered very seriously.

That the modern woman has a sexual advantage over her counterpart in the forties and fifties can be a myth held by women in midlife. The myth is that being allowed to have casual sex frees erotic passion. Unattached lust is revered as the highest achievement. To be rid of parental grasp, to be free of any affectional statement, is thought to be the highest nonneurotic good. Only sex, pure and simple, is the goal. Wanting sex to be "just sex," however, can be as inhibiting as wanting it to be true love, or idealized love, or romance. Sex is never "just sex." Even the loneliest masturbatory experience satisfies some psychological requirement, such as a need for isolation. Sex-at-first-glance more frequently reflects a need for reassurance or conquest than a bland touching of heated parts. Women who think they can respond to biology alone, like "simple" animals (and men, as well, for that matter) haven't updated their anthropology notes. In mating, mammals with a cortex are always concerned with some form of dominance, submission, or protection. Without Psyche, Cupid does not function. Some women must be taught that they cannot be aroused by dispassion.

* * *

As much sexual pleasure is thwarted by misconception about love for a parent as by fear or antagonism toward that presumptuous individual who decided, among other things, that we were to be born.

The incest taboo merely prohibits sexual intercourse with an offspring. This prevents inbreeding and the inheritance of undesirable traits. Incidentally, it also prevents mayhem in those nuclear units governed by possessive jealousy. To obey the legal statutes, however, simply means not to copulate with a blood relative. For thoughts, fantasies, or feelings, there is no secular punishment. If there were, most of us would have to serve our terms.

Nevertheless, many admirable people grow up without allowing a single incestuous impulse into consciousness. While I do not believe, with the early analysts, that sex is the basis for all human bonds, I affirm that sexuality exists from early to late life. It can strengthen all other ties. When a nursing mother has an orgasm while her infant sucks her breast, we cannot call the relationship between mother and child primarily sexual. Yet sexuality certainly coexists with protective maternal feelings. When an infant is comforted to sleep by being patted on the rear or rocked, we cannot say that the parent is deliberately providing a first sexual experience. Yet the baby's pleasure in the motion of his or her genitals is inescapably there. When a mother powders and diapers her boy-child, and he lies in quiet delight, his legs spread wide, his tiny penis erect, it might be blasphemy to call the act a sexual encounter, but there is no denying the responsivity of nerve endings. Sex and maternal or paternal attention are inextricably bound. The sexual response cannot develop without concurrent affectional care. Their perpetual union is also heavily, actively, imperiously, and often belligerently denied. One is "supposed to outgrow" the "Oedipus complex." Or so many frightened women believe.

Psychiatrists consider it healthy and normal for a woman to marry a man whose best qualities remind her of

her father. If she has repressed all erotic feeling for her
father, her chances of erotic joy with her husband may be
limited indeed. She cannot undo years of nonfeeling just
because the state has licensed her conjugal freedom. She
has the experience of "something missing" in the relationship. Desperately confused, such women often take lovers
who do not remind them of their good parent. Some have
their first orgasms that way. Others fantasy a man different
from their fatherlike husbands, often in guilt and secrecy,
and reach climax through complicated indirection. Still
others are so bound by their unconscious incestuous feelings and the sexual guilt imposed by cultural inheritance
that they feel nothing to husband or lover or phantom
antidote.

These, then, are the wages of love. If, in addition, a
father has been actively seductive although sexually absti-
nent with his daughter, the result may be creation of a
female Portnoy. All hope of relating sexually to a fatherlike
figure is destroyed, yet such strong sexual ties are formed
that no one else but father will do.

Nor does it help for a father to withdraw his physical
affection from an adolescent daughter. She responds by
feeling unclean and rejected. She may spend the rest of her
life in search of that unattainable intimacy.

As long as there are repressed incestuous feelings
toward a father, there are potential sexual problems in
later life. The key that often unlocks arousal is helping a
patient to identify her sexual feelings toward her father,
and to accept such feelings. Many times a first orgasm
arrives simultaneously with a freed fantasy of having sex
with father.

An equally bewildered group of women still believes
that familial commitment should enhance sexual response.
They regard themselves as emotionally disabled because
they cannot always combine domesticity with eroticism.
Why they should struggle to try to mix eros with negative

two-year-olds, chicken pox, mumps, critical in-laws, dirty dishes, and lots of garbage is rather mysterious. Bacchanals take place in atmospheres freed of anxiety and responsibility. When things are going well at home, a vacation—a day at a country inn or a city hotel, or a weekend at home without the children—might be expected to revive the old lust. During a normal week, however, most of us settle for brief and friendly intercourse largely to express affection. There is no particular reason to believe that babies, mortgages, taxes, and all the other equipment of a marriage should stir pelvic flames to any white heat. And if a woman has had difficulty becoming aroused before marrage, it is only reasonable to expect that becoming a conventional wife, cleaning, cooking, doing domestic labor, and producing babies, will not accelerate her passion.

Masters and Johnson recognized the aphrodisiac effect of departure from sobering responsibilities in their two-week program of sexual therapy. The couple would abandon their worldly concerns and go to a motel in St. Louis. Sex therapists working with couples who live at home instruct patients to put aside their anxieties and arrange for relief from domestic struggles in order to free their sensuality. This should be a cooperative venture, not a task left to female initiative and organization. Unless a woman is "in love"—experiencing an adrenalized euphoria of devotion and identification—a chore is a chore. She does not prepare her food and her bed in that haze of delight that makes work feel like loveplay. She sweats, gets backache, headache, and fatigue. Nothing is more alien to carefree copulation than housework for the woman who resents it.

The "Total Woman" concept that revived the corpse of the fireside siren in the seventies seemed to contradict what has been stated above. A "total woman" could, theoretically, greet her husband in boots and bikini after a day of dirt removal and tell him what a splendid antihero he was. This concept occasionally yielded startling results—initially.

Novelty has always been a sexual stimulant. The new martyrdom lost its fascinating impact very quickly, however. There weren't enough martyrs to swell the ranks of the homey harlot. If a woman was going to trouble to learn the lore of the geisha, perhaps she concluded that she deserved the courtesy of practicing her profession in a proper house, where she could rest, anoint herself, and perfect the art of pleasing men in luxury and dignity.

Beyond shaping concepts of emotionally appropriate circumstances for sex (romance, love, being in love), culture and tradition also govern a woman's mind. They prescribe what a woman is to think during the sex act. The actual rules come out of religious codes written centuries ago, but many women absorb them by some intangible mental osmosis. This phenomenon suggests, more than anything else, the Jungian notion of archetypes. It is as though medieval ancestors are able to speak through their present-day reincarnations. These women have no idea where they acquired their ideas of mental propriety. They only know that they have obeyed laws which they never read or heard.

The first law requires that they think of no one else but their partner while making love. No matter how repetitious this thought may be, no matter how many thousands of times intercourse has taken place between a pair, boredom is a sin. Women who would not dream of reading the same book, seeing the same movie, or even serving the same meal twice in a row attempt to confine their thoughts to the very same man, night after night. Men, influenced by a freer heritage, are generally more sensible about their erotic imagination, allowing it to roam over girls passed on the street, movie queens, old loves, new possibilities. Women tend not only to rein their passing fancy, but to keep it at dead halt.

If, in the more liberated, fantasy is permissible, it is often kept well within the strictest confines—a romantic kiss, courtship preliminaries, the first genital touch—mo-

ments of arousal, always, rather than times of consumma-
tion. These are the delicate pictures with which many
women attempt to achieve robust sexual fulfillment. It is
rather like trying to cross the Atlantic in a rowboat with one
oar.

Women, in general, need strong encouragement to
use their great human gift for creating imaginary scenes of
sensual luxury. That so little art and literature of any vigor
has been produced by women over the centuries is a probable result of this repression.

In all of literature, there is almost no celebration of
the male body by female writers. Painters and artists have
begun, but the poets and novelists lag far behind. Perhaps
the only detailed literary love of the male body from a
female viewpoint comes down to us in the Song of Songs,
and that was very likely composed by a man. Women,
writing of sex, cry about betrayal, despair, and punishment
after joy. They are not free worshipers. They are still
confined.

When a woman has both a personality problem and
also suffers the inevitable cultural inhibitions, the therapist's job is complex, indeed. Masochistic fantasy, for example, represents the most intricate scheme to untangle. The
provocations to it and the bans against it are so great that it
may well be the singularly most important aspect of female
sexuality for a therapist to understand.

Most rape and bondage fantasies originate from the
cultural taboo against a woman taking initiative to satisfy
her own sexuality. If she need take no responsibility for it,
if a strange man forces her to the act, then she is free to
enjoy it. The brutish stranger, the ripper, the obscene
juggernaut, will unrelentingly crush her to submission.
Having no choice, she cannot be guilty of choosing.

A passive personality will magnify society's impress.
She may spend her entire sexual creativity on the building
of monsters and giants to tie her and force her. Still, one
must be careful not to assign the passive label to anyone

with rape and bondage fantasy. Societal influence has been
so strong that it may, in a woman, create a sexual personality entirely at odds with anything else she may do in life.
The fiercest female initiator in business or politics may be,
in her bedroom thoughts, the prototype of the humblest
and most helpless femininity.

Punishment fantasies, as distinct from rape and bondage, still exist to expiate the societal crime of having sex.
Sex as sin continues to permeate the hearts, if not the
minds, of many women. Intellectually they understand biology. Emotionally they are concerned with wrongdoing.
The fantasy of being hurt is the way to forgiveness, and the
size of the crime is related to the punishment. If sex is a
minor felony, a few flicks of the strap will do. As a major
felony, it may require burning, gibbeting, or crucifixion.
Only while the scourge is going on can pleasure emerge.

Masochistic fantasy may also occur for other reasons,
most prominently as a way to experience love. It is not
unusual for a woman never to have known the touch of a
father's hand except through spanking or slapping. Some
only experience paternal closeness at an even greater distance, through a hairbrush or a belt applied to bare buttocks. Pain, then, is associated with an expression of male
caring, a negative statement to be sure, but caring nevertheless. If this is the only manner of masculine attention a
child has experienced, her erotic self may be firmly conditioned to it. Human love and sexuality are remarkably
sturdy and difficult to eradicate. We survive on the merest
threads of unity, the shortest rations of affection. Our
minds can transform the agony of bristles and belts into a
primitive succor that enables us to procreate and be with
others.

Sexually exhibitionistic fantasies of degradation by
public viewing of private acts often come from early notice
by a girl's parents of performance only. These parents do
not supply other sources of self-esteem. Fathers who are
proud of the way their daughters skate, dance, or otherwise

exhibit their bodies, but who do not give further encouragement or affection, sometimes create women whose sexuality is released by thoughts of having coitus on stage before an audience. Occasionally, not only coitus but sexual abuse in front of others must take place.

Parents who devote attention to their daughters only as potential bait for a rich husband, or who are concerned largely with financial success, to the exclusion of warmer attachments, may create daughters who marry the local banker—but they also run the risk of schooling their daughters in strong fantasies of prostitution and slavery sale. Sometimes their bodies go for a high price on the marriage market to satisfy their parents; in other instances they sell themselves at nightly mental auctions for exorbitant figures. Or they may choose to be sold for a pittance, as if to rebel against their inhuman parental promotion.

Whatever the masochistic fantasy, it can usually be traced to some bastardized form of parental love. Even that most subtle masochism of all, erotic fantasy about a physically unpleasant but highly intellectual man, can be related to overemphasis on academic achievement in childhood. "Get good grades and we'll be proud of you," can be translated as, "Achieve a bright man, and we will be pleased with you." This transformation occurs whether or not the woman herself was able to satisfy her parents' scholastic ambitions.

Masochistic fantasies arise, therefore, from two sources. Sexual guilt is the first and less pathetic source of self-wounding imagery. It is formed in the female psyche by subtle messages from the outside world and by not so subtle injunctions against pleasure: "Don't." "It's bad." "Your reputation will suffer." "Men will think of you as a whore-slut." "You'll go to Hell." "You'll jade your feelings." "You'll be worthless." "They'll only want you for your body."

The second origin is the need to recapitulate the care expressed in old punishments, or to satisfy parental expectations. The images arise in what must be a fantastically complex rerouting of neuronal circuitry. They are a way of saving a tattered shred of childhood love.

To complicate matters even further, feminism demands that women respect themselves and give up masochism, just as psychoanalysis once pointed out that self-diminution was not precisely a healthy activity. Today, masochistic fantasy is not only an analytic but also a political no-no. The surface appearance of hitting and hurting and moral abuse is genuinely appalling. At the first hint of masochistic fantasy, these days, women tend to roll in their beds as though they were caught fornicating in the family pew.

Although repugnant to the sensibilities of those who can enjoy sex directy for love and intimacy, masochistic fantasy is, for those who need it, a perfectly acceptable gateway to pleasure. Many women might be erotically freed by imagining that they are being flagellated, crucified, interred in a harem, exhibited, prostituted, sold on the block, and otherwise exploited. Although these fantasies seem entirely demeaning, they actually reflect an unusually stalwart need for love that is not at all degrading, and a need for sex that seems to be the human condition. According to one interpretation, if everything in a fantasy represents the self, then the aggression is the internal force that compels a woman to have sex "against her will," when her conscious will does not truly represent what she desires. She must rape her resisting self. If, to enjoy a man, a woman must imagine rape, bondage, punishment, or those first encounters with a physically harsh parent as a stimulant, then she should not only be free to do so, but helped to feel proud of the delicate and intricate nervous system which has preserved her ability to relate to others. When such fantasies are wholeheartedly embraced and accepted as a positive aspect of personality, they tend to diminish in time as the conditioning reverses itself. Rather than becoming reinforced by repetition, they fade toward extinction. Good real touching and caressing gradually replace pain as a stimulus. More natural ways of loving take precedence in the imagination. Only when the masochistic fantasy is rejected as an unhealthy perversion does it persist to torture and deprive. Even when allowed as a stimulus, but with reluctance and guilt, it may remain forever. There is no need to be political about suffering as a key to sexual liberty. After a time, body and mind come to accept the genuine and reject the disease. Denying oneself such fantasy can be the most masochistic act of all.

Compared to men, relatively few women fantasy sadistic and terrible acts. When they do, it often frightens them, and sexual pleasure dissipates. Women are not supposed to be aggressive. To be truly feminine is still considered, by many, incompatible with destructive urges. Analysts have long since amended their starched position on this issue, allowing that women may growl and claw and still be quintessentially female. But the popular psyche still clings to old ideals, whether or not intelligence rejects them. It still feels unfeminine—and, by implication, inhuman—to be fierce.

Destroying the man, or woman, who soured the grapes of joy may sometimes be obligatory. Orgasm may be liberated, not by poison, gun, or butcher knife, but by a simple act of imagination. With every bloody entertainment we pay for, we accept the manacled violence in our hearts, the self-righteous indignation and the need to kill our enemies. Though we no longer accept watching the sacrifice of Christians or the punishment of criminals as amusements, we do avidly consume movies and books with bodies strewn recklessly through frames and pages. We are savage. Our controls are limited. Yet we, and especially women, feel ashamed of the perfectly good mental mechanism which permits pleasure without hurting a single one of earth's creatures. When, in imagination during the sexual act, a woman lets herself break her parents' shackles, she may be on the way to freedom.

Women have sadistic fantasy more to take power away from others than to rule over them. They dream more to protect their mendicant inner selves than to catch others on the web of their supremacy and gloatingly watch them beat their wings to death. In subtle distinction to most male sadistic fantasy, which repairs a felt defect in the ability to subdue and conquer, female barbarity fights a defensive battle to afford survival.

Virtually no man is propagandized, by his parents or anyone else, to believe that his sexuality is a filthy, crawling sensation that must be decimated in the fires of renunciation. No man is encouraged to murder the roots of his being. No man is expected to develop the protective spines and emotional water supply of the cactus, surviving in the morbid sun of abstinence. Women, in spite of *Cosmopolitan* and Masters and Johnson, still are burdened with sexual selves which have wearily survived drought, plague, and pestilence. The new generation still has old-generation parents. Acts performed as a matter of principle are not always accompanied by congruent feelings of sexual freedom.

20

Psychosexual Change

Observers of human nature have always marveled at the tenacity with which our species clings to the familiar. We love our old shoes, habits, and friends. We collect memorabilia from the high moments of our lives: important remembrances, symbolic objects. With even greater passion, we seem to embrace our miseries, indignities, and deprivations. The miner stays below ground. The New Yorker breathes endless dirt. A daughter gives up life and love to care for a possessive mother. A married pair engaged in daily violence to each other's emotional integrity remains locked in perpetual battle.

Given this propensity to preserve the status quo, however stagnant and unhealthy it may be, the psychiatrist who focuses on sexual problems faces the dilemma of imposing change. If people could simply go home and do as they are told, there would be no need for any therapeutic skill beyond a memory for the instructions and a voice loud enough to give them.

In the arena of sexual disturbance, it is most often the woman who first fears salvation. While male pilgrims also handicap their progress toward heaven, they usually don't begin by doing so. Women start out by loading themselves with impediments as capaciously as cargo ships. They cling to the security of their burdens: sexually incompetent husbands, sexually unfulfilled selves. Male mythology promises reward after battles successfully fought. Female tradition relies on a payoff for endurance, for patiently transporting the freight of adversity.

By far the most overwhelming obstacle to the alleviation of a man's sexual disorder is the woman's fear that when he improves he will leave her. Armed with an old spirit of adventure and a new capacity for it, he will foray into the world of seduction, temptation, and romance. She will be left behind to smooth an empty marital bed and cry on its pillows, while he explores new destinies and delights.

Nor are her fears usually groundless. At some time in the course of therapy, though not ordinarily at first, the man with premature ejaculation, retarded ejaculation, or impotence will at least fantasize testing his new skill on some impressionable member of female society. Out there are the women he never previously dared to transfix, the free young things, the liberated older ones, the harem slaves and Amazons of his particular sexual imagination. The courage to imagine such boundless union is born quite slowly. Images do not start to form, flesh out, act their parts until the man begins to feel assured of his virility. Sometimes as a transiently soft vision of acceptance, more often as explosive drive to conquest, the impulse to exploration seems universally present. Fear of not containing such primitive and powerful lust, of destroying basic security, may reduce all further effort at therapy to inconsequence.

The therapist's first responsibility is to elicit these awful fears of abandonment and to encourage a new ambience of trust and mutual affection. Basic bonds other than the transience of erotic pleasure must be affirmed. Emotional attachment, respect, achievements together need reinforcement. The prognosis for success in sex therapy can frequently be given at this time: if a man and his wife, both threatened by the temptations that success may awaken, reach out and touch lightly, or look at each other in a warm and reassuring way, the outlook is good. The basic texture of the relationship shows in the nature of the

look or the touch that promises commitment. Any holding
back, hesitation, or failure of support must be explored
before further sexual instructions can be given. People may
not be able to swear fidelity, and this promise need never be
exacted. But they can deliver their hopes and profoundest
efforts to care faithfully for each other. They must know
that this is all which can be given.

New barricades spring up at each step forward. The
next potential loss is far subtler than the naked fear of
desertion. It is the loss of neurotic safety. Again, women
tend to be the first to protect the crystal house of their
illusion, the garrisoned asylum of their pain.

As much as it protects a woman against being alone,
male dysfunction gives a woman the power to dominate the
blood bond of her family. A deprived woman feels that she
has exorbitant rights and can exact every penalty. She is
sexually frustrated. Others must pay.

Passively, she may cry, complain, feel anxious at the
slightest provocation. Her helplessness can operate with
the effectiveness of Wehrmacht authority. She must be
served, given extravagant gifts, petted, made allowance for
on every demanding occasion. She is not getting what she
needs—can never get enough. Furs, breakfast in bed, jew-
els (whether or not affordable) are her rights and privilege
for the sacrifice she has made of her body. For her husband
to become sexually competent might, to her inverted way of
thinking, place her at a disadvantage. She will no longer
have the right to require compensatory tribute. He will
expect her to service him.

Maintaining sexual deprivation may also be an excuse
for avoiding receptivity. A woman may be so conditioned by
the distance, coldness, or rejection of her parents that she
cannot take the chance of accepting the fullness of a man's
offering. The danger of taking, of being exposed to the
empty echoes of earlier unfulfilled needs, can prevent all
but the beginnings of cooperation in sexual exercises, and
may preclude even starting.

Sexual impoverishment can feed the aggressive woman's need for mastery. Perhaps she chose a man incapable of piercing her with the shaft that might cauterize her destructive will; or perhaps she created a castrated eunuch groveling at her irritated commands. If her husband could really satisfy her, she might be expected to be sweet, giving, submissive, in return. That would be intolerable anathema.

The compulsive woman fears her husband's new gifts will disrupt the order of her defenses, the daily rounds of tasks that must be done, the pride in perfected accomplishment. If sexual pleasure was allowed to contaminate the predictable order of life, to interfere with clean dishes, shining pots, or a career pursued with the same impeccable vigor, who knows what specters of decay might foul the pristine compartments of her soul? She might have to face the terrified void that she enamels with work, routine, and enough inevitable interruptions to make her perfection a chaos. There can never be time enough to make a new world. When accomplishments are miracles squeezed from the miserly hours in each day, the luxury of sex can seem more wasteful than wondrous. So can the time-consuming comfort of love.

Thus resistance to therapy emerges in the now-familiar list of personality types. Histrionics fear losing not only their dependency but also their role at the center of the stage. What excuse will they have for not being able to respond to their lover's ardor, for decorating themselves in the bright plumage that coquettes contrive to arouse and frustrate male mating instinct? How will they rationalize their constant flirtation with what is for them the impossible? And how will paranoids retain their victimized state, their suspicion that men—being woman haters—take every opportunity to hurt them, especially through the unconscious route of sexual punishment.

Males, too, must protect their neurotic safety, though they tend to do it less and later on in the course of their therapy than women. The premature ejaculator, most often an obsessional fellow, has compartmentalized his life into work, domestic duty, and play (usually tennis). His work habits regulate and routinize the day. He rarely demonstrates excitement or anxiety. His voice pitches at a medium monotone, and his facial expression is bland.

Cure might destroy his compartments. Like repressed rage, which makes some people feel as though they would murder if they became only slightly angry, repressed, sexuality threatens to erupt as promiscuity and defiance. Regularity, loyalty, fidelity, and efficiency might be compromised, even shattered.

Impotent men must protect their position toward women who are, in their scheme of things, better than they. They conceptualize the feminine, or some aspect of the feminine, as a source of overwhelming power. The schizoid fears a woman's power to nourish, the obsessional fears her power to control, the passive-dependent her power to abandon, the aggressive her power to destroy. The defense reveals what is defended against. Potency is the hurricane at the ramparts, the danger from without that might disturb the safe equilibrium within.

Should a man become potent, he could concretely be able to be closer to a woman—indeed, to get inside her. He might be trapped by the generosity of her womb, by her need to give herself to him, a gift he finds too painful to receive. Or again, he might be led around, as it were, by his penis. A woman could enslave him through the old enchantment, control his actions, his mind, even his purse. And if he gives himself to her, in passively erect obeisance, she might leave him there, someday, waiting desperately for sustenance, like a solitary tree in the desert. Should he take her forcibly, press into her with the rage and fury of life, she might retaliate somehow. She might find a way to castrate him.

Ordinarily an aggressive man with a severe authority problem, the retarded ejaculator feels that shooting his semen into a woman both destroys her and fragments himself. The bed is a field of warfare on which a woman advances against reluctant artillery. Cure is delayed, again and again, by retreat to the trenches, submergence, camouflage. When a therapist begins work with this disorder, a long battle can be expected, requiring every nuance of skill to preserve the marriage. As often as not, in my practice, such couples are so poorly mated that divorce becomes a welcome relief whether or not therapy is successful. Paradoxically, these marriages can also become the most devoted unions conceivable, if trust can be established.

In the treatment of female disorders, the man rarely impedes therapy at the start. Again, women—shackled perhaps by their dependent concepts—create their own impasses. In rare cases, a man may feel himself diminished by and in competition with the vibrator that seems an inhuman and insurmountable competitor. Generally speaking, however, men have less resistance to women's sexual development than women have against male fulfillment. This may have more to do with what is still extant of the double standard than with individual sexual patterns. Men trust that their wives will remain committed or faithful more often than women trust men. Indeed, frequently the matter is not nearly so important to men as to women. It is my experience that more men are willing to allow, and even enjoy, the thought of other men having intercourse with their wives than women enjoy the idea of their men having sex with other women. More men actively fantasize their wives with other men than women imagine their husbands with other women. More men encourage their wives to have extramarital learning experiences. Whatever the cause—a greater unconscious acceptance among men of their latent homosexuality, a greater tendency to see women as tradable objects, greater female dependence, or less male guilt about sexuality—men seem also to demonstrate less resistance to sexual improvement in their wives.

Women bind their sexuality in a far more complex fashion than men do. It is the rare man, for example, who cannot have orgasm at all, while this condition exists in enormous numbers of women. Men who cannot have orgasm on intercourse—retarded ejaculators—are also relatively scarce. The cause may be as frequently biological as it is psychological. Experienced and uninhibited women have orgasms rapidly and frequently—with little fanfare and concern. It seems reasonable that, given such marvelous and capacious apparatus, women would be lusting, copulating, and having orgasms almost nonstop were it not for the unusual and extraordinary restraints on their feelings and behavior.

Personality difficulties probably make similar contributions to female and to male dysfunctions, but the effects are far more profound in the female. There are more female than male histrionics because society has only recently sanctioned female sexual pleasure. There are said to be more male than female obsessionals, but I feel that the numbers are becoming equalized. Nevertheless, they manifest different sexual symptoms. Male obsessionals seem more concerned with pleasing their wives than with losing control, and are more likely to develop prematurity or impotence. Female obsessionals often fear orgasm itself as a loss of control.

Both sexes may tend to withdraw and be afraid of each other in schizoid-avoidant fashion, but women, by far, lose more orgasms in the process. Whatever the contribution of a skewed personality, men can almost always climax in one way or another: the therapist need only help them adjust and moderate their arousal system. Treating male dysfunction is far simpler and, in my practice, yields a high percentage of rapid good results. Treating women—eliciting and working through the important blocks—is often like searching for a fugitive from justice. Just as the clues take one to what seems the exact place, the culprit escapes in a new disguise. Results are equally good, but the therapeutic process usually takes longer.

Part V

SEXUALITY TODAY

21

The "New" Impotence

If character is related to an individual's sexuality, are there generalizations one can make on such themes as "Impotence in America at the End of the Twentieth Century"? Or is sexuality such an individual matter that no single rule applies? If one man's aphrodisiac is another's saltpeter, how is it possible to generalize?

Without adequate statistics one can only hypothesize on the basis of experience. Such hypotheses suggest that, in spite of Masters and Johnson's heroic crusade, there will be at least as much impotence as ever at the end of the twentieth century. With all the "new sexuality," alas, there are also new sources of impotence.

Many women who formerly did not feel capable or worthy of sexual satisfaction now demand fulfillment. They aspire not only to intercourse, but also to orgasm on coitus. Some women request it gently, asking a partner's help *sotto voce*, in sweet dependence. Others demand the right to coital orgasm along with the equal jobs and equal pay. Still others reject the penis summarily as a threat to emotional and physical autonomy.

In response to the gentle approach, some men cannot tolerate "the new dependence." They develop impotence caused by anxiety and an excessive desire to please.

In response to the more severe pressure, many men become hostile. They develop "the new impotence," an entity which has been blamed on the female movement. Anger reduces their erections.

Although sexual therapists rarely hear from the sexually satisfied, we can be sure the articulations of the liberated woman's dependencies and demands have excited flaccid penises, too. Men traditionally respond to their partners' verbalization of sexual need and excitement. A woman's breathless demand—"Give it to me," "Make me come," "More, more . . . "—may inspire man's sexual strength. One can, therefore, reasonably anticipate an eventual improvement in sexual union as a result of an increasing number of women's newly discovered sexual voice.

However, the current trend, as reflected by the number of patients requiring psychosexual therapy, would seem to be toward increased feelings of inadequacy, particularly among sensitive men who are overanxious to please. Passive-dependent, schizoid, obsessional, and paranoid personalities are the most severely affected.

Though it may be true that "only the problems arrive at the office," it is equally significant that sexual therapists are exposed only to those brave enough to identify their problems and work toward solutions. There may very well be vast numbers of men, identifiable as the personality types listed above, who suffer sexual inadequacy while silently imposing pain and self-denial on their mates as on themselves.

Sex has lately become more and more of a public as well as private performance. While the effect of publicity and dramatization is often beneficial to individual sexuality, there is certainly a scatter of impotence in the flash of such stellar light shows. From the first brown-paper-covered manuals to the live color portraits now available in bookstores, from a dry celluloid kiss to a wide-screen wet coital closeup, from a stage embrace with "risqué" lines and wandering hands to nudity, prurient dialogue, and posi-

tions which do justice to a pretzel factory—the entertaining
and exhibitionist potential of sexual union has been produced, promoted, and exploited. No longer is it necessary
to peek through windows; sexual performance in books
and on stage, videotape, and wide screen opens doors to
the bedroom. Although pornography sometimes has the
tendency to become a spectator sport, it also affords an
opportunity for comparison as well as education.

Perhaps the most reassuring aspect of exposure to the
performing male on celluloid and wood pulp is destruction
of that ancient and often impotizing myth that only men
with enormous penises may satisfy a lusty female. Indeed,
if pornographic films have done nothing else, they have
verified the medical dictum that penises tend to equalize in
size when erected. But there are always those who demand
bad news. Some men, instead of admiring or being stirred
by the cinematic machinery of sex, compare their own
abilities with Harry the porno star, then retreat in despair.
They can never equal the demonstration, so why try. They
are unable to thrust continually without ejaculation. How
then will they ever find a respectful place in that spectacle
of male and female bodies, writhing and maneuvering?

The educational benefits of visual information are
considerable. A movie or book may reassure the sexual
adventurer that he is neither strange nor alone. For the less
imaginative, an author's or screen director's creations may
suggest new approaches to sexual satisfaction. But to the
unsure and self-demeaning, exposure to sexual performance is often impotizing. The more some men know, the more
there is to think about—and for them thinking is worry. How
they worry! They worry about muscle flexibility, wind, coordination, fitness—a virtual glossary of the skills and talents of
an Olympic athlete. And after they pale before those mea-
sures, they worry about the intricate demands for timing—
when to turn around, up, down, sideways.

When the format is less erotic—more scientific—ad-
ministered by a doctor rather than an author or theatrical

person, the vulnerable man has other debilitating worries. Certainly the information is organized and coherent, but it smacks of academia. He feels he is entering a schoolroom rather than a bedroom, confronting a bluebook rather than warm human flesh.

He fears his blood is turning to oil, and what has a programmed machine to do with responding to a woman's sigh? Alas, the new sex education runs the risk of rousing new anxieties. *Plus ça change, plus c'est la même chose.*

Freud noted that the more a man's wife came to resemble his mother (feeding, caring, running a household), the less sexual interest he maintained. That may have been an example of Freud generalizing from his particular attitude or even a disposition confirmed by some of his patients. Perhaps Freud was ultimately only able to feel excited by types who did not resemble his mother. But his observation nonetheless provides the clue for detecting the cause of impotence for some men in the jet age, even as it did in Freud's Vienna.

A man married to a woman who comes to resemble "mom" can still be afflicted by loss of sexual enchantment as soon as the similarity becomes pronounced. But most people think that to be like "mom" means to be a domestic type: dusting, scrubbing, peeling, frying, broiling, baking, ministering to running noses and aching egos. Mother Earth wears a flowered apron across a bolstered chest that is more pillow than breasts. Mom, of course, could just as well be a bony starveling who requires help in deciding whether to have aspirin or cigarette smoke for dinner.

Certainly, whether mother ruled from the car pool or the steno pool, from the chaise longue or the swivel chair, romance may die when a wife arouses the same resentments a man's mother provoked. This interpretation, unlike the classical notion that romance flees because incest taboos grimace in the matrimonial darkness, extends the range of complication emerging from a man's relationship to his mother.

Another lapse into sexual disinterest and impotence may evolve when a man's attraction to his wife is based upon her physical as well as personality resemblance to his mother. Physical and emotional likeness makes him comfortable with a woman who might be mistaken for mamma. His erections rise with consummate ease. She is not only as good and familiar to him as his mother, but she is also sexually available. He marries in celebration of his sexual feeling for his mother, not in spite of it or to escape from it. All goes well as long as the illusion lasts. Ultimately, however, such a lover may discover that his woman does not actually care for him with the madonna's devotion his mother felt. Often he has misinterpreted his wife's feelings for him because of her physical resemblance to the matrilinear prototype. As truth emerges, potency may retreat. He is not at ease with his wife. He has married a stranger in his mother's "clothing."

It is, therefore, not only a woman's increasing resemblance to a man's mother that may interfere with a couple's sexuality. She may also fail to resemble her predecessor enough. Not observing the strict rituals of son worship may even prove sexually terminal. There is nothing wrong with marrying a girl just like the girl who married dear old dad, but when that precarious balance is off, women through the ages have suffered with mamma's boys.

We have been hearing with great frequency lately of new life-styles. In the quest for increased self-fulfillment, the traditional demands of marital fidelity have been challenged by those advocating sexual adventure as the last frontier. Certainly infidelity is not new to human temptation or experience. Open acceptance of a mate's philandering is no more unique today than it was in biblical days when Sarah "allowed" Abraham a concubine. But after all its vaunted advantages of honesty and sensual joy, there is obviously a great potential for marital stress when the strictures of the vows are relaxed.

Those who condemn, as those who proselytize, such mobile arrangements are limited in their view of man's nature. I have no desire to argue the case for or against mates cleaving to each other. For some, a sense of ethical satisfaction in being limited to one person may lead to physical joy, and for others the sense of being right, of being good, substitutes for sensuality. If one feels moral, other sources of joy and self-esteem may be secondary. In still other instances the question of ethics never arises: fidelity is spontaneous and the commitment to one's mate so total that ventures from the marital bed offer temptation in neither fact nor fantasy. Such relationships are rare, but they do exist. Degrees of sensuality and sexual need vary greatly from couple to couple even as the range of individual sexual appetite.

Married sex may be inhibited by hostility, economic pressure, the presence of a family, limitations of space, and the infinite complexities of parental relationships which may converge on the defenseless phallus. Outside the marriage, the search for exciting variety or a new and deeper love may lead to unexpected involvement, unanticipated hurt. What begins as a simple feeling of lust turns, for the susceptible, to affection and finally to emotional need. Or what may begin as a feeling of emotional need may turn out to be lusty craving for diversity. Whatever the beginning and the consequence, new partners offer the imposing possibility of new problems.

A couple may agree, in today's fashion of "apartness," that while he must be away (acting on the road, attending professional school, traveling for his company), he may have sex with others. So may she in the interim. The delights in such agreements belong to the naïve, who believe the unknown is bursting with happy surprises. Obviously, the chances for pain and failure are significant when marriages are conducted at separate headquarters. Sexual experimentation and the introduction of new partners increase the possibilites of impotence.

Most marriages terminate with sexual distaste but not inability. Couples who disagree characterologically may be perfectly able to copulate with each other, although they are not particularly enticed by the prospect. Only in the aftermath of separation and divorce, when proof of manhood, virility, and vitality are crucial, does the question arise. Precisely in those moments of question and self-doubt does impotence occur. Too scarred to try another marital marathon, too tired from the fight to engage immediately in what has come to be known as divorcé sport-fucking, the newly liberated man may find himself unenthusiastically in bed with a plum from Maxwell's or from some other singles' magnet outside New York City. He does not know quite why he is there, except to prove that he can still do it. These are the circumstances under which a man whose autonomic system responds with fear will find himself embarrassed. "Situational" impotence sets in, and may last a lifetime, unless he gets help. The challenge accompanying the journey and the search may prove far too great. Not only do all the old sexual bogeymen come to taunt (performance, conquest, desire to please) but a few new ones arrive in the interim. Am I too old for this? Can I do it as well as a young man? What will she think of my gray hair, my bald spot? Do I make enough money after alimony and child support for any woman to take me seriously? How do I feel about scoring with a woman who is financially independent, who has or earns more than I do? All these concerns do not, in general, enhance sexual prowess.

The sexual experience itself may also cause anxiety. When a man has been able for long years to bring his former wife to orgasm with his penis, he may become unsettled by the woman who requires clitoral manipulation, diversified foreplay, and a willingness to experiment.

A man whose former wife never found his penis important to her orgasmic satisfaction may find himself with a woman who wants his organ to provide the evening's entertainment directly. Duration, size, frequency of ejaculation—all become concerns, while in marriage they may have been ignored. As the divorce rate skyrockets, so does sexual dysfunction.

Sexual behavior may be instinctive or learned, but there can be small question as to the influence adult sexual values have on the young. Since Freud suggested guilt was a major legacy of parenthood, Western society has moved progressively to more permissive attitudes toward sexuality. It is certainly a boon to mankind to explore openly and intelligently the variety of sexual pleasure possible for consenting adults. But the injunction to be "sexually free" may wreak as much havoc with a young libido as the dictum "do not touch."

The sexual situation of the last half of the twentieth century is perhaps analogous to the wave of progressive education that influenced institutions of learning during the early part of this century. Freedom of choice demands an enlightened understanding of the alternatives. We may learn by doing, but sometimes the scars of failure are traumatic, and our elders impose a burden upon us when they fail to offer guidance. We are only now learning that freedom of choice benefits the well-organized, moderately obsessional children who can limit their own freedoms. Those with poor integrative capacities need a more defined system.

Young men today may find the new sexual freedoms a path to a rose garden or a maze. In the past, restrictions on sexual expression made it possible for a boy to have many encounters with girls without confronting the self-imposed demand to perform. Today, many boys feel that they are sexually retarded if they do not respond to "Hello" with

"Let's." Current sexual discomfort is caused as much by the demand to act as by remnants of taboos.

Young men are expected to know so much these days about technique and anatomy, it's a wonder they manage past a hug. Unmarried young men come for help by the score, impotent after a first attempt during which an even more insecure girl charged them with clumsy stupidity.

In response to these expectations, boys sometimes do manage insertion of their penises into tight young vaginas rather earlier than before. And the social consequences are often quite endearing. The young persons may cling to each other with firm tenacity for several years. The girl becomes emotionally committed rather too easily; the boy is afraid to test himself with someone else. What passes for young love is more an adhesive uncertainty, but it bears some vague resemblance to honest passion. The boy has found a warm and furry home for his genital; other values may become important in time.

The prothalamia to these unions are popular songs, which speak clearly to the point. The rush to early sexuality has brought a peculiar romantic agony to the young, a very different pain from much that has gone before. What used to be excited anticipation of ecstasy ("Temptation," "Blue Skies") has turned into the grief of union and separation. Endings to these "first marriages," long attachments with or without a legal contract, bring more than their share of impotence on parting. One cannot judge but can only observe these rather different facts of life, and wonder at the fate of most enlightened intentions.

Ceremonies of the past, like antimacassars, eight-course dinners, and the marriage proposal on bended knee, have given way to the expedience of the present. The trappings of ritual which frequently built confidence, as well as creating a sense of continuity, are now considered decadent and even pretentious. In sexual relations, trust is no longer something one is supposed to develop: it is expected to be present at the outset. The sachems of instant self-discovery suggest we begin by reaching out, touching, following our impulse to go all the way. For a rare few, such exercises in indiscriminate sexuality may provide a new confidence, but for others sex without familiarity is more a threat than a treat. New styles in sexual encounter may delight the confident and experienced, but to the young person making this first tentative step into a relationship frequently clouded by romanticism as well as lust, traditional rituals of courtship often prove a more graceful rite of passage.

We may consider that old customs become outmoded but not necessarily because they are useless. Long courtship, with intercourse forbidden, was a tortuous but relatively safe route to the marital bed. Gradually a man became accustomed to his partner, as she did to him. With intercourse forbidden, he did not need to worry about having an erection. There was no pressure. He was erect all the time. Long hours of sexual and affectionate play trained men to become good lovers. A woman could encourage her man to become a fine practitioner of the ancillary arts. Both had time to become physically and psychologically receptive for coitus.

Certainly there were disadvantages to such delay: guilt for breaking the rules and anticipatory fear of the great moment. But, on the positive side, erections were provided with a long and comfortable time to stabilize, to poke gently and partially, to explore and retreat. Mine is not the argument of a committed antiquarian. Indeed, the processes of traditional courtship, abbreviated and translated into medical jargon, have become the universally accepted (if not always successful) prescription for treating impotence.

Young adults today face abrupt coital situations. Everyone is doing it, and so must they. They know very little about sex and less about each other, but now is the time to perform. They are not supposed to be repressed or inhibited. They are expected to be "healthy," which means receptive to sexual experience, informed about contraception, wise about physiology. After all, they're supposed to have had Sex Education since kindergarten.

As many are damned as are saved by the new rites of early sexual relations. If the impotence of frustration is decreasing, the impotence of inexperience is on the rise. Sexual pressure is akin to moving at extraordinary speeds: the faster one goes, the slower time passes. At high enough speed, one gets younger. The more we advance, the more we regress or, at best, like Alice, stay in the same place. Perhaps the popularity of the Buddhist movement with the very young relates to its sexual code. Abstinence may be prescribed for long periods of time when a neophyte is in psychological trouble. Few others today (except for sex therapists) seem to understand the value of sexual quietude. Certainly it is relieving to life's novices, who flock to masters to receive peace from their struggles through edicts for abstinence.

Being single but older does not guarantee an increased chance for lifetime potency, either. Even in the last decade, before epidemic venereal disease like herpes and fatal afflictions like AIDS were feared as much as they are today, experience could be a dangerous teacher. The rate of partner change today is probably higher than at any time in the last few hundred years. It is not unusual for an American male to have explored fifty new bodies before he is thirty. Somewhere along the "garden path" to the ultimate relationship, a man must meet his witch. She might be a delicate child who makes his penis quake for fear of hurting her, or an elderly magpie who talks it to the ground. The witch is different for all men. She causes impotence. The more women a man tries, the more likely he is to meet her. With today's high exchange rate, she is sure to voodoo him at some station of the night. Yet this is no feat of dark magic—it is simply the mathematics of probability. For one man's witch may be another's passion.

Though I see far fewer sexual adventures now as patients than I did a decade ago because of the increased fear of disease, some are still finding it exciting to try more than one partner of either sex. The aftermath of this experimental scene is a familiar one in the therapist's office. A man may confront his homosexuality for the first time, or his jealousy, or his lust, or his love. Such experiences often reveal people most unpleasantly to themselves. Extraordinary as it may seem, few humans really understand either their sexual selves or their potential. A man may not consciously be sexually competitive, yet his erection may disappear at the sight of someone else's larger organ. Alternatively, he may discover in himself homosexual desires toward the more imposing organ, and in his guilt find himself impotent.

On display, his performance anxiety may increase. Sexual discomfort, far from being lost in the crowd, may develop into an illness. We need not have militated against multiple swinging relationships, for what people feared might happen in such wide-angled exposures often did indeed occur. The casualties reported from the playing field: "I couldn't make it for the first time in my life, and I haven't been able to since." "I'm disgusted—I don't know if I can ever touch my wife again after what she did." "I don't know what kind of a person I am anymore. I wanted him, not her."

Sex education, even from kindergarten up, didn't prepare men for swinging and swapping, nor even for the less structured forms of togetherness that living in cramped city or dormitory quarters can create. Nor can pornography, the army, barracks language, or locker-room laughter. Each experience is a personal one.

The young and the middle-aged, struggling against the dragons of the new sexuality, have an easy task compared to those further on in years. At least the young have a few extra decades in which to experiment and work through the new attitudes. Senior sexuality, especially among readers of popular literature, is under stress. Having learned that older people can function until they die, they begin a campaign—even an all-out battle—to ward off terminating their stay on earth, to prevent death with sexual action, as alternative to philosophic or religious resolution. Failing prevention, it becomes an inadmissible hope to transform the last rigor into a last orgasm.

Which of the older people are so concerned? Largely the obsessionals. The men calculate that their orgasms are no longer so frequent or so forceful as they used to be. They study their weekly pattern—ejaculation once is all they can manage. They measure the force of its emergence: it drops, like water off a ledge, rather than shooting with the geyser-like intensity of yesteryear.

Can they be helped? Only to check for prostatic enlargement or other possible abnormality with a urologist, and then to accept their mortality, to be reassured that less is statistically normal. They may continue to have sex until the end, but with limitations.

Those who do not accept limitations overstretch their capacities and become impotent. They must keep up the old pace. They will not believe that it must take longer to become stimulated enough for an erection. Sex twice, not once a week, is mandatory to their self-esteem. The penis to these men points to the coffin; down, it points toward the grave. They worry, causing, of course, the same kind of impotence everyone else develops in tense situations. Much of the impotence of old age, the difficulty that occurs past the age of sixty-five or seventy, is due not to physical incapacity but to fear of failure. That is why men who continue to have a regular partner to the end also continue their sex life. It is not necessarily true, as studies seem to indicate, that men without women atrophy into disuse as they near the end of life. Certainly sexual hormones are reduced and the arteries to the penis, like those to the heart, tend to clog. There are medical reasons for poor erections or ejaculations. Even so, it is likely that at this age, fear of death, fear of failure, fear of rejection by a younger woman, serve more than physiology to desexualize the last days of what might have been a fulfilling and vital finale.

Age, marital status, changing sexual ideals will all have an effect on the incidence of impotence during the last quarter of the twentieth century. As long as men have fear, the problem will be with us. Sex—in civilized humans—is an expression of feeling, and not a simple activity like walking, yawning, or stretching. Even economic conditions affect human sexuality. Penises tend to rise and fall with the stock market. Severe impotence after a large loss, accompanied by mental depression, is one of the awful results of intertwining sex with every other human function the way our brain does. In uncertain but not devastating economic times, however, before depression descends, sexuality tends to be stimulated. Mild anxiety provokes and excites. In our own economically precarious times, sexuality became a major preoccupation for many to defend against the possibilities of disaster that oil shortage and inflation might bring; then it preoccupied people in the throes of oil glut and recession. In eras like this, men play at the edge of impotence. They may run themselves out sexually to compensate the possibility of other losses. Will the men make it? Will their erections hold up through what may be the first grim days of a new and difficult civilization? Or will they be impotent to prevent what may also be the last days of our time?

22

Female Sexual "Liberation"

Matters were, of course, simpler when men divided women into wives, slaves, and sex objects. Respected wives, reaching a zenith as imperial Roman matrons, provided immortality by bearing children. Slaves helped to maintain the house in which children grew. Mistresses, prostitutes, and educated courtesans were welcomed reluctantly by the wife because they relieved her of bearing more children than her body could tolerate. They obviated the horrors of a sex act that might culminate in unwanted pregnancy in a time of high maternal mortality rate. Given a choice between an increased chance of death and the transience of intercourse, most wives preferred to shift that risk to concubines.

Men were stronger than women in those days. They used their strength to fight wars or do heavy labor to sustain their families. Structured, mammalian, incredibly cruel, this hierarchical system lasted many thousands of years. It is over now.

For better or worse, men created their own new destiny by discovering machines, effective birth control, and antibiotics. Their motives may have been purely self-serving: less work, fewer children to support, better health, and greater longevity. The side effects of these discoveries on women's lives have catapulted the world into a social disorder that baffles even the most obsessive systematizers.

Women would have to be blind, indeed, not to notice that now they can have sex as freely, be as strong (with a handgun), work as hard (with a tractor or a computer), think as rationally, and live as long or longer than men. But the traditional realities of female sexual bondage, subjugated intellect, restricted power, and abbreviated life span have prevailed so long that women who recognize their new estate often do so with resentment or uncertainty.

What work women will do, how they will improve their minds, which paths they will take to political power are predictable. Women will learn from the diligent and the lazy, the heroes and villains of the past. They will fight their way up a traditional ladder with much the same technique, if not the specific style, of men. How to cope with sexual freedom, however, has no precedent. Women cannot adopt the system of dividing men into three classes any more than men can continue that division of labor and pleasure. New life-styles emerge and vanish as quickly as they appear. The choices are innumerable, confusing, guilt-provoking. How to think, how to act, how to feel sexually are individual frontiers. Each woman must discover the way for herself, according to her personality and her beliefs.

Over the past hundred years, female sexual conflict has gradually altered in character. Feeling at all erotic created the Victorian sickness, a mutilating shame and guilt. Victorian ladies were not unlike Roman matrons, except that "rubber sheaths" were available to liberate erotic urges. Sex no longer implied pregnancy, although random sex offered the unattractive possibility of incurable disease. Men kept control. They even invented psychoanalysis to preserve monogamy, keep themselves clean, and maintain the social order. Prostitution, though vigorously banned, continued to flourish, but venereal illness made it unwelcome. "Good" women tried, with increasing desperation, to quell their sexual unease. Eros was still "bad," at least for medical reasons.

The first decades of the twentieth century popularized the diaphragm, flappers, and the ideal of "living and learning" before "settling down." One had to have experience prior to making a choice. What, precisely, one was supposed to learn was undefined. Nevertheless, the problem was not the quality of the sex act, but the right to have it. Those who were unsure of their rights responded to what remained of the cultural ban on sexuality. Schizoid women, fearing sex anyway, withdrew from it. Obsessives ruminated upon it—agonizing interminably over soul versus body, reason versus passion, good versus evil. As a tribute or a sacrifice, passive-dependents gave their bodies, almost as inanimate objects, to their protectors. Passive-aggressives struggled to obey and conform to the old societal code. However, they violated so-called decent standards at every opportunity and unconsciously arranged to have themselves caught and punished. Women with a tendency to paranoid thoughts, of course, did not indulge because they really expected punishment, and those with depressive spirits never felt worthwhile enough to act on their sexual needs. Sociopaths ignored the bans and used sex to their own advantage, while aggressive women managed to find ways to destroy men through sexual channels. Histrionic personalities teased, invited, displayed, but rarely acted. Given a rule, most people obey it, some ignore it, others destroy it, but the small minority who create history try to make a better rule.

The societal code loosened and improved. Premarital intercourse became virtually an establishment. Extramarital relations might have become more acceptable had it not been for World War II and Korea. The aftermath of war prompted women to try to be monogamous wives, mothers, slaves, and geishas, all rolled into one. One body, fitted with a diaphragm, could conceivably have sex while cooking, doing laundry, and mopping the floor. Even without the consciousness raising that scoffs at such a servile commitment, women failed. So did the ladies' magazines which

washed romance with the new detergents and sprayed it
with aerosol. All that remained were products for cleaning
and shining named "Joy," "Zest," and "Pledge." Watching
women at domestic labor may be aphrodisiac to certain
sadistic men, but women were growing wiser.

In the late fifties and sixties, with the popularity of the
Pill, chaos began in earnest. Middle-aged mothers wore
mini-skirts. Men less often felt obliged to pay for sex.
Everyone wanted to try everything, whatever that was,
whether they actually did it or not. Sexual anarchy reigned,
especially in urban centers. Marriages terminated because
"the sex was no more fun." Families got smaller. By the late
sixties, because availability was no longer an issue, and guilt
(intellectually, at least) was an anachronism, people began
to notice the quality of their sexuality. Heterosexual, gay,
bisexual, swinging, autoerotic, married, single—the rights
of consenting adults were acknowledged though not always
accepted. If a couple mutually agreed on extramarital freedom, no one challenged their privilege. But the sex act
itself often proved a disappointment, now that other rules
were no longer restrictive.

Today, toward the end of the twentieth century,
women suffer a peculiarly painful disturbance. The right
to have sex has been won, but a new transitional syndrome
has developed. What else may we call it but Political Sexual
Dysfunction? It is that disorder in which women misin-
terpret the goals of feminism and mold them to their own
neurotic impulses. It is also that disorder in which women
cannot respond to whatever psychological stimulus excites
them, for political reasons. The active woman, for example,
finds her passive longings reprehensible. The passive
woman, who has accepted a traditional role in sex, feels she
is a total disaster, a barnacle on the ship of progress. And
the majority of troubled women, assertive or compliant,
dynamos or drudges, tough or tender, are conditioned to
be sexually passive. Some may be stimulated by this role,

others numbed by it. All sentient women, provoked by politics, are trying to change it. The hardships of this change create the rigorous obstacles to finding a sexual peace compatible with our era.

Difficulty with becoming active may begin with a symptom as slight as a woman's reluctance to touch a man first. It certainly ranges through the paroxysms of pain and frustration as a woman—haunted by and sometimes secretly pleased by the ancient male code that a woman in bed may respond but not command—denies herself sexual pleasure. For all the manifestos of the contemporary women's movement, bold and commendable as they may be, the dungeons of yesterday still shroud the sexual expression of most women, impairing their feelings and perverting their pleasure. We are stuck with Political Sexual Dysfunction. It may be America's most malignant psychological disorder, a powerful relic of female bondage.

The feminist-activist ideal prescribes that a woman must never be sexually used. She must discard passivity, never be an object, eliminate guilt. A woman should be sexually active as often as she likes. She should initiate and speak her mind. She should never demean herself in any way. Masochism is unacceptable. A woman must go through a period of healthy paranoia about male intentions. She should consider the alternative of living without a man, even if she chooses to discard it. If she does have sex with men, she is entitled to orgasm.

This is an ideology, simple and splendid, but the passage to pleasure is not so direct. Not only must a woman choose a life-style consistent with her creed, but sexual excitement must accompany her choice. The undercurrent of delight must flow unhampered to make dedication a living reality. For some, joy in liberation has turned rapidly to sorrow at imprisonment. Poets have killed themselves for continuing to be chained by the dark demands of a frightened womb. Other writers and novelists take us on journeys through their fears, flagellate themselves for weakness, inscribe the misery of their archaic longings. And if we examine women's lives, the identifying marks in their personalities, the knots of winter in their souls, we can come slowly to a frail understanding of the complexities of freedom.

In the vanguard of revolution, the radically aggressive woman wrote her passionate statement in "The B.I.T.C.H. Manifesto." A bitch was strong-minded, nasty when she wanted to be, and always "herself." She sat with her legs apart, talked back, fought her points. She was Superwoman in baggy blue jeans and Earth shoes. She allowed no trace of the old, delicate image to remain, not even on her underwear. She was terrific. She was dynamic. She enjoyed sex. And she liked the way she smelled after a day's combat. The only question was, did she exist?

I never met a real bitch, probably because the real ones didn't come for therapy, go to New York parties, loll at the ocean, or seek genteel entertainment. I suspect they were all at caucuses and conventions, yelling mightily to change the world, God bless them.

In my office, I have only seen partial bitches. These are women who grew up wrestling with boys and pleased when they beat them, until one day the male fraternity no longer accepted them. They tried losing games, baking cakes, impressing others with their wit, but to no avail. Their firm opinions and loud voices scared the boys away. They intimidated the girls. Developing a permanently arthritic chip on the shoulder, they spent adolescence in limbo. No arms found their way around their waists. No kisses and caresses were deposited on their shining heads, held too high for easy stroking. Even their parents withdrew affection early, embarrassed by cuddling such a resolute being. Partial bitches talk loudly. They're tough. They walk straight. They return any insult, ounce for ounce, and more. They don't spill tears. But inside, if one listens carefully, they are crying perpetually the anguish of their deprivation. They dream of tenderness, soft beaches, and the gentlest winds of love. They also dream of rape and getting sex without having to ask for it. They are the most poignant victims of Political Sexual Dysfunction. When the time comes that a brave man's hand finds its way to their nipples or their genitals, they shut out the horrid, masochistic, dependent fantasies of joy. They lock up the undercurrent in concrete canals. They feel nothing.

Which way do such women go? What life-style do they choose? With therapy, they may learn that fulfilling their personal needs will not impair social or political growth. If, instead, they wall off these needs, they often overcompensate, giving what they never got by becoming teachers and caretakers of little children, or the trusted, maternal confidantes of countless friends. Or they may go the other way, picking up the rifle of a cause, developing their aggression to a peak. Both of these counterphobic behaviors generally do not result in sexual freedom. The impulse to arousal, the need to be a deserving recipient of warmth, nonpolitical and human, has been extinguished. The political has invaded the personal. These women must learn, as many successful men have learned, that intimacy has no rule except honest appraisal of need.

The woman who has chosen a life-style to harmonize with her passive conditioning finds herself at a most alarming juncture. The critical question of active sexuality threatens her entire dependent foundation. She has a suburban home and small children. She depends on her husband's income. He "takes her" on vacation trips and "gives her" presents on appropriate occasions. In return, she may draw his bath, serve him dinner, care for his wardrobe and his linen, and do all the chores that, when not shared, feminists abhor. In bed, she responds to his advances as a not unpleasant pastime, without any great lust. But she is content. Sex is in its place, like everything else. And she puts a big DO NOT DISTURB sign on her mental door. If her husband travels, or comes home too late occasionally, she believes his stories of hard work, long hours, late conferences. It is all for her.

The new sexuality, however, demands that she be more, do more, enjoy more. The books say so, the movies emphasize sexual ecstasy, even her husband tells her he'd like her to be more enthused, more giving. Maybe if she would initiate sex once in a while, instead of leaving it all to him, he'd be more motivated to fix the house, to cooperate in domesticity.

Exactly what does he mean? Does he want her to perform fellatio? She doesn't see why she should be required to do something which gives her the same feeling as mopping up spilled egg white—slight revulsion, sexually deflating. Does he want her to have orgasm on intercourse every single time? She can't. Especially since his foreplay has gradually become, in recent years, so perfunctory. Would he like creative new positions? She doesn't know. He always seems to prefer being on top. Anyway, she has lower-back strain from lifting the last baby. It was his child, too. Why should she feel self-conscious about her back? And does he want her to look more seductive, more glamorous, to lose the extra fifteen pounds around the middle, wear perfume, slink into bed? Spas and beauty parlors cost money and call for babysitters. Even serving spaghetti instead of steak wouldn't fit them into the budget. And if a man wants his wife to wear good perfume, he should buy it for her. Lingerie, too.

In fact, she could stand on her head, have orgasms with her toes, and catch his flying ejaculate in her mouth as he rushes off to the 7:40, and he would never fix the storm windows or put in a new kitchen floor. He'd promise, but after a week he'd take her for granted. Pretty soon she'd have to dye her hair, develop a foreign accent, and give the children out to adoption to make things more "interesting" for him.

She never asks any of her questions outright, of course, nor lets her husband hear the defeated answers. For his part, he only knows that the woman he met on the last trip to Chicago, and the little blond typist in his partner's office were satisfying enough, and different enough, to ease his boredom. He has no right to want more from his wife. She strained her back with the last baby. He feels badly about even asking.

The prognosis for liberation is very poor, indeed. And yet even "typical" housewives dream. In the past, as today, that elusive handsome millionaire can be summoned to take them away from all this. Now, perhaps, encouraged by the liberal women's magazines, the housewife closes her eyes and dares for a moment to become a svelte professional, doctor or lawyer. At five, she stops work, goes home to change, and then meets her latest lover for cocktails. They have dinner and dance awhile. After dinner they go back to his thick-carpeted bachelor's apartment. There, she kicks off her shoes, drinks a brandy, and starts to undress him. She licks and bites him, turns him on with bawdy words, eats him, teases him, tells him exactly what she wants. They fuck, and she has orgasms until exhaustion.

The housewife turns to her husband in the dark. She starts to stroke his thigh. He has an erection in his sleep, but turns away from her and hugs his pillow more tightly. He mumbles incoherently, something about bad breath, and suddenly the effort seems too great to be worth pursuing. It was only a promiscuous fantasy, anyway. Better to wait until her husband comes after her than to be rejected. She hugs her pillow and goes to sleep, embarrassed.

Becoming an active sexual partner, for such a woman, implies an entire alteration of life-style. She can barely fantasize without guilt, much less act. For her to be able to take charge of her sexual situation, make it exciting, she must think of herself as independent—economically, emo-

tionally, intellectually. Since that is terrifyingly out of the
question, assertive sex is also impossible. Liberation is for
the new generation, for her daughter, perhaps. Sex is really
secondary, anyway. The most important thing is for the
children to grow up healthy and bright.

Some single women today, of course, do not devote
themselves to caring for other people's children or fighting
causes. They work, and like the heroine of our dependent
housewife's fantasy, they do indeed meet their latest lover
in the evenings for cocktails and sex.

When a new man rings the bell of a single woman's
apartment, there is a moment of the old anticipation: something good will happen tonight, something she can rely on.
After the first cocktail, the visiting creature launches into a
discussion of his two former wives and his most recent bout
of affectional disasters. His wives were immature and faith-
less, the last being an incompetent mother to boot. The
woman he really fell in love with, two years ago, was beautiful, capable, on the ball, a great human being. She moved
in with him for six months, while her husband was on a
prolonged reportorial assignment in the Far East. They
were to be married as soon as she divorced the peripatetic
reporter, but she never divorced him. Instead, they started
life over on a farm in Vermont. Since then it has been one
disillusionment after another, hysterical women afraid of
sex, sadomasochists leading him on and turning him off,
women too young, women too old . . . he is really ready for
the *right* person.

What will be wrong with me? our single friend wonders. She sees herself already posted on his casualty list, if
she ever becomes important enough to him to merit a
plaque. At the consciousness-raising group last night, coin-
cidentally enough, the women were discussing just such
men, innocent, victimized, the best seducers in the world.
They set up the play for the woman to think she has a real
chance to win whatever the prize is. Though the third

cocktail has by now made her want to have sex even before they go out to dinner, she knows already that the game is over.

As single life goes on, suspicion increases. Axioms begin to emerge. Married men with children never divorce unless their wives kick them out, no matter how much they complain about their wives. Bachelors over thirty-five are either homosexual or mamma's boys. Millionaires and doctors want sex fast, between appointments. Artists and writers give love for money, or meals. Men being divorced will cling, and then become abusive, in retaliation against their wives. Separated men can't make their minds up about anything. Recent widowers are sincere, needy, and impotent. So are men without jobs, unless they want sex all day and night to reassure their virility. Bisexuals want a strong woman to seduce and take care of them, especially a woman with attractive young sons. Men who show off the Gucci shoes are in financial trouble. Bachelors with regular jobs, easy hours, and lots of time and money are lazy and dull. Show biz celebrities can't remember women's first names, much less their last. Falling in love with a psychiatrist is a symptom of transference neurosis.

In the single woman's world, paranoia flourishes like milkweed. There's some basis for it, too. And yet, how else is she to feel about the octopi on her couch? Had she been trusting, and signed up early for her course in marital mythology, she would not be in this position. Neither would her suitors. The only answer seems to be more paranoia, which leads to more consciousness-raising groups, until even women begin to seem dishonest. Eventually all sex starts to feel like a violation of the last integrity. Only by being completely alone, standing on the platform of solitary female dignity, can liberation be realized. The paranoia is a fixed political dysfunction.

For some years now, women have been "searching for themselves" through sex. Encouraging them in this fruitless pursuit have been the works of several generations of male writers. Creatively gifted men, with exquisite self-knowledge, have fooled the world and its women into believing that identity may be discovered by traveling through many lands and many beds. Unhappily, this is only true if one can write well about the trip. Twenty years ago, men made Spanish politics, French cafés, and the bedrooms between seem a sure solution to the problem of who they were. They were faking. They were writers, first and foremost, and they weren't looking for anything but experiences to write about.

Women recently went abroad to "find themselves," too. Again, the gifted brought back books. They were written before they left, and better ones when they returned. Inspecting oneself for literary purposes presumes having a self to begin with. The "search" is a masquerade, a play, an entertainment. When good writers start looking for their identities, they stop writing. They are depressed.

In the old bohemia of Greenwich Village prior to mid-century, having identity meant being an artist of some sort. The prerequisite for being an artist was to have strong emotional experiences. One of the ways to generate sufficient passion to be an artist was to have a lot of sex. In the process, someone was sure to be hurt, get pregnant, fall in love, be crucified. Then there was material to write, paint, and feel about.

Today the whole philosophy has become inverted, and is even more disastrous to mental health than "sex for art." Women, especially gullible ones, seem to think that a lot of sex (with all its potential pain in the area of human relationships) will transform them into artists, writers, actresses, or transcendental philosophers. They don't even begin with a conviction of identity. They are trying to find out what and who they are. Sexual adventure, as a path to self-realization, is about as reasonable as planting a field of potatoes and expecting to harvest orchids. The only truth these women can wind up discovering is that they have been screwed.

Intrepid sexual explorers can only discover, like the curious old bear, another mountain. Allowing no time for memory, for reflection, for sorting, sifting, and learning, they can't possibly find out who they are. One man elicits tears, another makes them laugh, a third makes them see the world as a hard, dry field of scattered bones. They are audience and actress in a shifting, pointless drama.

There was a time when psychiatrists would have called them nymphomaniacs.

Immaturity, dependency, inadequacy have many disguises. Sexual liberty, the banner of political freedom, is the most dangerous and deceptive. In today's chaotic world, it's best to know one's self before playing musical beds. The sex act, performed in a hotel room, on a yacht, in a Puerto Rican condominium, or at a married man's apartment, won't help with such decisions as what career to select or whether or not to marry and have children. If a woman waits too long to educate herself professionally, she may be doomed to a life of underpaid obedience behind a typewriter or a steno pad. And it is still true for those who select wifedom and, perhaps, motherhood that the pool of provident men diminishes with age. The only truth to be learned from a life with no goal is a bitter lesson. Getting vast quantities of sexual reassurance is not very fulfilling, after a while, by comparison to carving a more substantial destiny than a date book. Freedom can be an excuse for the immature woman to waste a lot of time being a sex object.

As the dim-witted accurately observe, bright people have no common sense—especially bright women who think they are going to beat the system. They will be feminists and traditional wives at the same time, pleasing everyone. They will have careers, rise through competitions, raise a family, and still give their men the dignity of

an ancient paternal role. Obsessional women are particularly prone to wanting to satisfy all demands. They have
rigid consciences and take everything to heart. If on the
one hand they want to be in control, on the other they want
to make everyone happy.

As any fool could see, the duality is impossible. Structural breakdown occurs, however, not at the job or in
providing order at home. Bright women get their work
done and keep their professional lives briskly chugging
along. Domesticity and business are usually negotiable
through good scheduling, high administrative skill, and
plenty of luck. The women can even find time to listen to
their husband's travails, to praise and encourage them.
The vulnerable area, sad to relate, is sexual.

When a woman efficiently relieves her husband of
domestic and financial pressure, he not only has an abun-
dance of libido but also a surfeit of leisure. While she
juggles schedules and deadlines, often putting in an eigh-
teen-hour day at the pace of a busy counterman at lunch
hour, he has a swim, comes home, has dinner, chats with
her and the children, and wonders what's next. He studies
his wife for a clue. She is clearly tired, drinking too much
coffee, smoking too many cigarettes. Her skin seems to be
wrinkling prematurely; her posture is going bad. During
the week she is virtually asexual, falling into bed late at
night and either sleeping instantly or churning with tomorrow's worries. Usually she remembers to brush her teeth,
but she may forget to insert her diaphragm. Her smell is a
sexless condensation of anxiety. He doesn't want to have
intercourse with her, although he would if she asked. She
ought to stop all this nonsense and try to live on his salary.
A smaller apartment, public instead of private school for
the children ... they could do it. ... Nevertheless, it is
pleasant to live in relative luxury and afford all the extras.
At the thought of all the extras, the second car, the summer
house, he puts an arm around her and pats her bottom
with some affection. It feels secure having a wife with an

earning capacity. Still, he wouldn't ask her to sacrifice for him. And he does anything, everything she asks.

For her part, she often experiences moments of enormous but transient loneliness and depression. The worse these become, the harder she works. If he would only step in, somehow, force her to let up the grind. He would make her slow down if she really meant anything to him. He would lock up her work in a big box, hide the key, and spirit her off to a week in Switzerland, or even a weekend at a local inn. He would take care of her, the way traditional men take care of their wives. Seeing her overworked, unable to cope with the momentum, he should assert himself, damn it. Why does she have to do *everything*? Well, this Saturday night, if she has a little too much to drink, maybe they can have a private orgy at home. But then, there's that party at the Bensons'. No matter. Even with all the work, there are occasional horny moments, quick and without pretense of romance, but they are there. And there might be more, if he really wanted her. He could massage her back occasionally, caress her slowly and gently, relax her, turn her on. But he is only interested when she is unequivocally receptive, on weekends. That seems to be enough for him. Maybe, after a score of years, the simple security of lying together in the same bed is warm and adequate.

Of course, it is not. And of course he sees another woman, or two, or a hundred (on weekdays) in a dozen years. How else could he survive? Sex is a personal thing for the traditional man. As long as his wife never knows, it won't hurt her. Besides, he would probably have other women whether she was always sexy or not. A man only lives once, and there are too many beautiful girls to resist in a big city. After a while, they get to be a habit—that's the way of the world. He wonders if she plays with other men. It would be a good thing for her, though for appearance's sake he says he'd destroy any man who came near her. But he would understand; after all, maybe women need some excitement, too. He is open-minded. He accepts her work. How she could fit a lover into her schedule is the only question.

The new passivity—wordlessly expecting a man to step in and ease the burden, help with life to make it more satisfying—is a modern version of the old female sickness. So is working hard and giving a man service and mastery. Any idiot could have told the beleaguered woman that. But she was too smart—she thought she could beat the system. Maybe she did. More likely, when she discovers her husband's curious philosophy, she will have to make up her mind between staying in the old world and joining the new. Let us hope there is time for her to make the right choice. Sisterhood needs all the support it can get.

Dressed in a shirt and trousers resembling army fatigues, her red hair cropped short, her firm character revealed in a face without makeup, she attends efficiently and without strain to the tasks of the day. It's clear that she was liberated early. It's also a thought that she might be a lesbian. She's not. She has been attracted to men, but her principles now keep her from swinging her hips, wearing spine-deforming heels, or placing shiny metal trinkets on her body to attract attention. Nor will she shave off the hair nature placed on her legs, between her thighs, under her arms. And the hair of her brows was intended, not for plucking, but to protect her eyes from soot.

After work, it is good to live by her own clock. She can sleep, read, take herself to a movie, eat when and what she wants, see friends, write in her diary, attend meetings. She can swim, play tennis, go hiking on weekends. Life is simple without marriage, children, or even going out very often with men. In any event, the men who seem drawn to her now are largely younger, effeminate types. The last one wanted to crawl into her lap while she read children's stories to him. It made her slightly ill.

She became a radical feminist ten years ago after a siege with men that would have made Dunkirk seem like the Riviera. First there was her father, a doctor in the small town where she grew up. In his rusty Ford, he was the last of the horse-and-buggy types, charming, charismatic. So irresistible, indeed, that it was rumored he sired more than half the town's population. There was an abnormally high percentage of redheads at school. They all did look like brothers and sisters.

Mother, cold and perfectionistic, hated him. She convinced her children to scorn him also, especially since he never seemed to collect his fees, which were too low to begin with. One day he disappeared, never to be heard from again; last year, at Christmas, there was a postcard from Hong Kong. Maybe Chinese women had dominant genes and couldn't bear children with red hair.

On coming to the city, she took a secretarial job. In keeping with her position, she displayed her knees and the fullness of her chest. Her long, flaming hair was a beacon for male attention. Although she didn't trust or even like them, she was attracted to men who reminded her of her father. Her first abortion was performed in a Pennsylvania trailer, the second in a Puerto Rican clinic. The men neither helped to pay nor stayed at her side. She realized her weakness and decided to date men who did not resemble father.

She married a man who was as reliable and kind as the good parents she never had. She felt a security with him that she had never known. But he did not excite her. He did not even arouse her. At first she pretended orgasm in order to preserve the secure feeling. Eventually, she told him the truth. His kind reliability turned to unexpected rage. He beat her savagely, then wept in remorse. They divorced amicably, although after the beating she had felt a sexual stirring.

The men who aroused her were the ones who abused her. She began to allow herself to be cheated, used, and occasionally whipped. She could become attached to a man only if she knew he would leave her in pain.

One day, she tried to kill herself. Since she had not taken enough pills, she awoke a day later. When her head cleared, she determined once again not to let men hurt her. Something in the experience of being near death had made her see that she was not inflicting the harm entirely on herself. Although she had to be psychologically receptive to pain to have a neurotic need for it, they had to be bastards enough to give it to her.

Staying away from men, as best she could, was the only answer. Joining the women's protest was part of it. At this time, she created her militant appearance, to ward off men who might think she was vulnerable. Sexually, it was difficult at first. The lure of being degraded to orgasm was immensely strong, and she would masturbate to her masochistic fantasies. Eventually, the fantasies tapered off and her sex drive atrophied. She went back to college, achieved a graduate degree in business administration, and then found an excellent job with regular promotions built in. People now feel that she is a very strong person. Perhaps they are right. She feels that men, with even the slightest encouragement, will reduce women as low as they will go. Perhaps she is right.

The woman in the middle generally walks about with a self-satisfied and modestly superior smile. She will not suffer the deprivation of male amenities that comes with being a staunch feminist. Nor will she go without an identifying career, a place in the world. She will fulfill her marital, maternal, and secular self, all in good time and good order.

First she trains herself thoroughly as a professional: an architect, a teacher, a composer, a mathematician. Then she marries and takes a small, noncompetitive position in her field, for which she is grateful. No use fighting for status now—when children come she will have to reduce her commitment. Working on a limited scale, she has plenty of time to devote to helping her husband's career. She learns all about his work, his maneuvers, his triumphs and disasters. She encourages, acts as a sounding board, even advises. She also has the leisure to dress well, keep her figure trim, and be rested enough to enjoy sex. Life is good.

The children arrive, a boy and a girl (in the appropriate order). She stops her small job for a period after the birth of each one, but is able to resume. Work is more tiring now, but she still looks bright, feels vital. Her husband's income is going steadily up. Life is fair to those who take just enough.

Now in his mid-thirties, her husband really pressures himself to advance. More responsibility entails more work. It begins to seem that he will become a superstar at the company and she is very proud. He needs her now more than ever, to entertain, go on business trips, be entertained, elicit helpful information from other wives. She's so tactful, so insightful, so much sharper than all the other women. She's invaluable.

With the children and the new work of being a corporate wife, there is hardly time for her to pursue her old interests, which, in any case, have gradually diminished over the years. Not applying herself competitively, she has not advanced. Her job is uninteresting. It's almost embarrassing now to do the work she was once thankful for. The added income is meaningless. She decides impulsively to give up the pseudocareer. Perhaps she will write, or paint, or take up a craft.

Her husband becomes busier, preoccupied, anxious at times, but always optimistic. His emotions seem to have acquired a veneer through which nothing can penetrate very deeply. The rounds of parties, theaters, dinners become work nights on her calendar. Entertainment has turned to labor. Relaxation is what she does at home, alone, on rare mornings when both children, well at the same time, are at school. Relaxing also means having declined to go with her husband on the latest trip.

On one such morning, the telephone rings. The caller is the South American diplomat who sat at her right at a dinner party a few nights ago. He had said he would call, but she hadn't known quite how to understand him. Would she like to meet for lunch at the Carlyle?

The question makes her tremble with an anxiety that suddenly turns to pleasure, almost a "high." She hasn't felt like this since she was at college. Though the diplomat is, in many ways, less attractive than her husband (a little older, a bit fatter), the surge of excitement is too much to resist. Yes, she'd be delighted to meet him.

There are so many things to do in such a short time. Her hair needs restyling: she feels elderly in the matronly cut she has been affecting to help her husband present a stable image. Nothing in her wardrobe seems to suit anything but tea with the ladies' auxiliary. Maybe that's why men approach her so infrequently. It's time, too, to stop concealing her breasts under jackets and to wear a silk shirt. By tomorrow lunch, it will be impossible to firm up her belly and her backside, but she will start a regular program of exercise on Monday. This could turn out to be quite a renewing experience, exactly what she needs.

At lunch the next day, exhausted but happy, she looks ten years younger. She feels as beautiful as the South American tells her she is. While they drink and banter about how different a respectable American woman is from the protected, chaperoned female prisoner in Latin America, she has to cross her legs tightly to ease the sexual pressure.

After lunch, his car and chauffeur are waiting to take her to his hotel. He doesn't touch her as they drive. Disturbingly, he keeps glancing out the rear window. "A man in my position never knows when he is being followed," he says. Her excitement lessens.

Their time together is short and interrupted by several calls. He also looks out the hotel window often to study the cars in the street below. Although he is a good lover, technically her husband is better. From the moment of nakedness, she feels depersonalized and inhuman. Intercourse is hardly arousing. She doesn't have an orgasm and doesn't want one.

Although she never sees the diplomat again, having affairs has begun. A pattern develops and becomes fixed. Parties are for seeing how many men she can reach. The sex is sometimes better than others, but the peak of excitement is always at the first call, the first lunch or dinner. Although she feels no attachment to any of them, one hugely attentive man encourages her to talk about herself. Suddenly, with a force she hardly knew existed, she is sobbing at her failed career, the lack of intimacy in her life, her inability to feel as close as she thinks she should to her children. She sees this man more than once and soon begins to long for him, to dream of a new life with him, a life where she will be understood. On their sixth meeting, without warning, he doesn't show up. He never calls again. A few weeks later, she tries his office, but his secretary says he's too busy to speak to her. She pleads, and he consents to talk briefly. "You are a very confused and unhappy woman," he tells her. "You want romance, something much more than I can give you. I don't know how to relate to you, and I prefer not to."

A few months go by before she is ready for a new affair. It takes time for the hurt to settle into a protected place. Soon it's mandatory again to provoke pursuit. This time, however, she sets it up so that she disappoints a man by not appearing at their meeting place. Oddly enough, instead of angering him to withdrawal, his calls and his desire become more intense. She has found a new game which is really satisfying, even more than simply inviting and receiving sexual attention, which has begun to pall.

The game may escalate and turn into a taste for sadomasochism. She may really start to enjoy seducing men into feeling strongly toward her, then becoming disinterested. This is a rather easy task for the uninvolved. (When a woman really wants a man, achieving him may be considerably more difficult.) She may also begin gradually to refuse her husband's overtures by showing less and less enthusiasm. His sexual and emotional discomfort at her reserve can become a gratifying source of revenge.

Ultimately, however, our passive-aggressive wife will probably become depressed and seek insight into her behavior. What she did with her life was to "act out" her furious resentment of her broken aspirations and her husband's distance. Not confronting him with her rage, her loss of dignity and identity was the passive aspect. Her aggression against him converted, in a complex and imperceptible human way, to the joy of deceiving him, the stimulation of conquest. Later, it turned to something more universal: a dislike of all men. Sexual pleasure emerged from watching their humiliated persistence as they tried, like rats attempting an inconstant barrier, to reach her.

For the woman who puts herself aside, to be "completed later," for the wife who passively allows her husband to slip into another world, life will provide another time of reckoning. What we neglect in ourselves will return, like some Shakespearean ghost, to tell how it was murdered. The qualities we fail to encourage in others will also return to haunt us with the treasure we have lost. A life lived by halves and sacrifices will itself become split and offered on the altar. Perhaps only the gods can help to cure the woman who starts out in the middle of the road, and winds up nowhere.

What is the prognosis for women at the end of the twentieth century? So far, it seems as though if it's not one apple for Eve, it's another. We may free her from the curse of spending her days in bloody travail for the quickening sin. We can teach her body to beat to the orgasmic rhythm that multiplied mankind. But the cure for the old ills of guilt, shame, and fear of sex rarely works, or lasts very long unless the rest of the dilemma gets solved.

If it was up to Adam to beware Eve's temptation, it behooved Eve not to listen to the serpent. It is now up to women to take more realistic charge of their destinies. Some are beginning to do so, though that is the hardest task of all.

The young are free to make choices without trauma to themselves or to others. In selecting a business or professional life, they may decide not to cultivate domestic relationships but rather to respond to more detached—or at least less formalized—encounters. They may opt to make homes and to bear children first, being sure to negotiate the terms of sexual and family life with their partners. They may choose any role they like, according to their abilities and their needs.

Like men, they are also free to become victims and to make mistakes. They may find themselves laboring inhuman hours to earn a pittance for the support of too many people. Like men, they may travel to do their work, satisfying themselves with the lonely obscenities of roadside solace, and calling it fun. Like men, they may become figurehead parents, giving the care of the family ship to others, and losing the love of husbands, sons, and daughters in the search after glory, success, or even simple competence. Young women can do anything—or almost anything—that men can do, when they don't really know what they want.

It is too late for the women caught in the political mêlée, the discontented middle and older generations, to make an initial choice, for better or for worse. They are only able either to radically alter their life-styles, or to make precarious "adjustments." The high divorce rate among older married couples may attest to new, if belated, identities. The high incidence of marital therapy for the middle years certainly reflects a need to work out solutions to changing problems.

The present unrest, as disconcerting and difficult as it may be, can be a source of hope as well as discomfort. No personal or philosophic growth has ever been achieved without distress. Perhaps the best of a more equal world will be demonstrable in a lessening of passive-aggressive female behavior. Maybe fewer women will encourage men to work themselves to an early grave, to eat their way to diabetes, arteriosclerosis, and myocardial infarction, to feel unfulfilled because Mr. Jones has more, and to slaughter each other for home and country on every battlefront. There are better stimuli for having orgasms.

At the end of the twentieth century true fulfillment for any individual—man or woman—remains, as always, a personal responsibility. Literature, science, art, and political discourse may offer us clues and options as to who we are or what we may become, but the most constructive integration of ideas and life-styles is achieved only when we are able to identify ourselves and select, from our resources for maturation, what we choose to cultivate. Our identity resides not only in what we seem to be, but also in what we wish to be. That is an ancient wisdom, but it is recent that women as well as men may consider an understanding of individual sexuality essential to this quest. It is a possibility for joy as well as dignity.

23

The Old "New Sexuality"

Less than a decade ago, sex was still a frontier to be explored freely and fearlessly. This research, involving personal experience, was considered necessary to form one's philosophy of love.

In perhaps the subtlest counterrevolution in the history of ideas, a reversal in our attitude toward the flesh is occurring. It is not a radical cause led by militant theorists, flooding our consciousness with headlines. Rather, it is a gradual transformation, like the change that occurs in the concepts of young reformers who, as their perspective matures, come to understand that traditional codes embody wisdom and that rules are mankind's collected aphorisms for survival.

The "new sexuality" of the sixties and seventies, far from being mindlessly immoral, was a profoundly idealistic movement proclaiming a utopia to which everyone could aspire. It wasn't necessary to join an organization, carry a card, or live in a commune, although communes for sexual freedom did—and still do—exist. All you had to do was buy a book and get the idea. Some people even appreciated the idea without books, but books were the first real proselytizers of the new sexuality. Glossy magazines and pornographic films had been circulating for decades as promotion for underground excitement rather than open sexuality. Books, with crafted covers, bold type, and unabashed illustrations conveyed the inspirational message.

They depicted lovely beings cavorting in timeless pleasure, on slick pages with abundant white space. This was our dream of Eden. The participants were unanxious, unafraid, sensual. They did not possess each other—they welcomed others to share their joy in ones and twos and tens. In games of bondage and aggression, but only games, they communicated the now-harmless vestiges of their barbarity. Relaxing, having fun, as cleanly and sweetly as though electrodes were implanted in their brains to deliver them from our ancient evils, they bathed together, and emerged shining like gods from the sea. Instead of clouds beneath their bodies, there were downy pillows or soft white fur. The banner over them was trust and friendship, and the voice of the turtle was the norm of middle-class morality.

It was a good dream the joy books sold to us, worth their price. As an aphrodisiac, an illusion to turn on by, it even stimulated some people, though most found it paradoxically unexciting. For we knew, even then and in spite of the convincing pictures, that it was a utopia, an ideal, and as such no different from older promised paradises of perfect love, romance, and marriage. Ideal sexual happiness is no more attainable than ideal justice or ideal truth. We unconsciously suspected that someday the copulating figures in those books would look as foolish to us as posed photos of pompous Victorian gentlemen and their well-corseted wives, presiding in moral splendor over orderly and obedient domains.

The sexual revolution, as distinguished from the new sexuality, merely called for freedom to pursue sexual pleasure, whether one was married or not, and whether or not sexual relations actually provided any joy. It allowed the young to explore their sexual life without fear of societal disapproval; it encouraged older generations to discard inappropriate inhibitions. Indeed, it was less a revolution than a legitimate sexual evolution that took place quietly and intrinsically, without hype or fad, in the normal flow of quotidian life.

But the new sexuality, in which penises blossomed in benign erections and vaginas gaped in open-mouthed trust, suggested a path as vacuous as any charlatan's panacea and as sure to disappoint. Its advocates proposed that sexual relations, in themselves, created happiness, especially when performed with skill and without particular attention to a partner's identity or character.

Something essentially human was missing. There was no pain.

If the new moralists neglected the deeper insecurities of being alive, however, the old sexual idealists had also ignored the prospect of pain. Our ancestors embarked upon monogamy behind a screen of flowers and white lace. The resonance of organs and the voices of prayer blessed their voyage. Love and marvelous sex would occur or continue with state consent and religious approbation. Childbirth would be a global experience suggesting the great moment of the world's emergence from chaos. Work would fulfill high creative aspirations. A great partnership would be a tale of exuberance and a chronicle of good will. Life on earth would be its own reward. But neither approach, new or old, was destined for much success. As Genesis made clear, marriage is no Eden.

Being human, and still in search of that blissful state, we have spent the past score of years considering whether the new sexuality would enable us to skip blithely through the circles of Hell, dance through Purgatory, and fly up the mountain toward Paradise. Many practical advances made such a leap seem possible: ecologically, we did not need to feel obliged to multiply our kind; mechanistically we could prevent the sorrow, labor, and expense of unwanted children being born. Women no longer were required to bind themselves to the marital bed in economic servitude. Crowded urban conditions made multiple sexual affiliations a social communication that was difficult to deny or resist. Such unions often promoted good business relations or relieved the strain of self-support. And we believed that sexually transmitted diseases were easily curable.

What with all these new freedoms, it was not surprising that an easy-ranging, nonspecific sexuality came into being, liaisons that were more pleasurable but not necessarily more meaningful than lunch with a friend. Sex was the ultimate recreation, the game of games. Of course, it used to be the song of songs, but that was in another country, a long time ago.

Not that the new sexuality denied the possibility of love occurring between two or more people. Love was a "positive" force, much to be welcomed in the ideal community, so long as it brought with it none of the old evils: jealousy, possessiveness, pride, rage, and all that. Most "positive" feelings and actions were also welcome: drive, pleasure, affection, fun, trust, and skill were the mainstays. Strictly forbidden to players at the great noncompetitive game were all the psychological ills known to be morbidly exciting to some people: using sex as a commodity, an aggression, a hunting sport, a sin; as rebellion, punishment, self-destruction, duty, death wish, manipulation, or escape. The ideology of modern joy was every bit as rigid as the tenets of religion or psychoanalysis. The only difference was that no deep bond was required, though such bonds were admissible if tamed.

At first, lack of sexual restraint seemed capable of immense benefit to many people. Perhaps in time it might break the shackles of sexual guilt that handicapped so many in their pursuit of happiness. It might increase not only the quantity but also the lifespan of human pleasure. If children were permitted to fondle one another freely, it was suggested, instead of having to play furtive and often sadistic games of "doctor," we would start to have sexual fun at a much earlier age. Indeed, if mothers were free to allow themselves to have orgasm during nursing, and parents were free to masturbate their children to sleep, a lot of "colic" might disappear. The habit of giving opium to babies in the form of paregoric might become an outdated form of child abuse. Teen-agers, it was argued, might not need to become so sullen and rebellious when hormones flooded them with oceanic sexuality, and the use of drugs by the young—the narcotics that they used more, in fact, to defeat their sexuality than to enhance it—might not be a national problem. Marriage might return to its former estate as a cooperative economic effort, since single life, though feasible, was becoming increasingly difficult to sustain under adverse economic conditions. Pledges of financial fealty and emotional loyalty rather than sexual fidelity might become accepted as a more attainable commitment by both sexes. Men had tacitly assumed this to be the issue for centuries. Now women might adopt the same position and make a single standard out of the old duality.

Early on, then, in broad cultural overview, the liberation of the sexual instinct seemed a good thing. Why did it turn out not to be so good? Why was sex not purified once and for all?

Many people did not understand the ideological complexities of the new sexuality, which were as respectable and difficult to live up to as any code now buried in the vast library of failed experiments. They thought that sex without bonding was a license for promiscuity, just as our elders used to think that marriage was a permit to hold someone in bondage. To be promiscuous means to be indiscriminate; in sex it means to exert no choice in one's selection of partners. Most of the people who practiced sexual freedom seemed not to have the faintest notion that there was any ideology involved at all. Serious-minded scientific folk stated categorically that "the sexual impulse should not be restrained." Lighter-headed gentlemen quoted Herrick's famous travesty on rosebuds. The general public, overwhelmed by a media full of anonymous breasts, penises, buttocks, and pubic hair, became, to say the least, disturbed. What was once a voyeuristic accompaniment to secret masturbation now seemed as though it might become the way of the world. A vocal minority began to call itself a moral majority.

The practitioners of psychiatry and psychoanalysis sat back behind their desks and couches and mulled over the new questions. In view of the characterological oddities that afflict us all, how would we react to group sex, multiple partners, mate exchange? It used to be that one could condemn—or at least subtly disapprove of—these activities under other names: orgies, promiscuity, wife swapping. If people were deprived of the old moral code, what would become of guilt, aversion, seclusion, rumination, hostility, and the notion of sin? Would they disappear from man's character the way polio disappeared in America after the Salk vaccine? Would freedom of copulation free us from despair?

Hardly. More people than ever began to fill the sessions in therapists' offices with sexually related anxieties and depressions. New villains as well as new victims arrived on the sexual stage. People who had formerly limited their aggression to other spheres now practiced it in sex; others who had confined their sensitivities to nonerotic relations now suffered for erotic reasons as well.

Sex without pair-bonding offered a broad range of activity to people with character traits that had made them deviates or offenders in the past. They could now express their eccentricities as lavishly as they wished. Histrionic folk, especially, could collect and discard new sexual audiences as rapidly as they got tired or bored. They could show off directly to real people or indirectly on tape and celluloid. They could call themselves by all manner of polite names—gregarious lovers of human contact, warmhearted appreciators, prophets of unlimited good will—but their pleasures came from being unconstrained exhibitors, always needy of praise, always searching for the thrill of new sexual admiration. By far, they were the most comfortable in the new sexuality. They could even pay lip service to the ideology, if they understood it, and their hypocrisy was hardly detectable.

In the old monogamous regime, histrionic personalities were the ones who were, as men, successful enough to acquire wives who tolerated their open sexual perambulations for economic reasons. As women, they were charming enough to acquire busy—and often impotent—husbands who allowed them lovers out of a sense of their own inadequacy. Histrionic personalities almost always marry—even though they need not—because of a strong dependent streak. Men like to have a "base of operations." Women want someone to "take care" of them. Without this security, they tend not to enjoy their promiscuity.

I say promiscuity in the full and harsh sense of the venerable word. For the person concerned with being always loved inevitably makes a precise and elegant choice, however random. He or she fastens on someone who truly responds with love. Often more than one fall under the spell. They know they will never, can never be enough. And they must watch, with mixed admiration and disgust, as their pretty, handsome, charming, buoyant, exuberant, seductive mate or lover goes on to other bodies and other praises, mindless of their pain. Not Don Juans or their female equivalents in the full premeditated and antisocial sense of the word, they are, nevertheless, the innocent ravishers of souls. Immensely sensitive and perceptive when they want to attract a new devotee or maintain a secure base, they are also abnormally devoid of feeling when they want to move on. Whether their sexuality belongs to the old naïveté or the new ignorance, they act the same way and perform the same devastations. They would be less troublesome to those of us who seek a sensible balance between admiration and self-respect if they chose only their own kind to mate with. But these actors and actresses require audiences full time. And when the show is over, they go home.

The men and women who are left behind mend painfully. Often the healing is rough and unstructured, without a guiding splint to prevent deformity. They become embittered. Sometimes they come for professional help because they can barely survive depression. If they are lucky they learn that life provides a "next time." Next time they can be wiser. They can select more carefully. They need not contribute their bodies and their souls so quickly to the new sexuality.

Narcissists fare even better with sexual freedom than histrionics. They lack the dependency that keeps the showperson juggling relationships. They also lack the sensitive empathy that wins transiently deeper unions for their more lovable competitors in the field of self-display. Wonderful, knowing everything, most right and most beautiful, blameless, untouched, they never notice the Stygian mud that clings to them in passage through their love affair with themselves.

In the old monogamous world, the narcissists ruled at home, either as male despots expecting homage, or as empresses practicing enslavement. Whether or not they married depended more on whether someone else took the trouble to court them lavishly than on their own decision. In the progress of marital years, if others wanted them enough, or provided a new jewel for the crown of their self-love, they simply moved into new arms, without the usual pain of separation from the old. They were attached to no one but themselves.

In the new, sexually free world, narcissists move through bodies with much the same carelessness and ingratitude. Ego-deficient women attach themselves to male narcissists and serve them as sex objects with the same masochistic enthusiasm that they used to spend in becoming martyred wives. Men continue to be challenged by the unattainable goal of "reaching" the narcissistic woman, and they ply her with whatever baubles of attention she demands. The chemistry of neurotic attraction continues to catalyze relationships, whether these are begun in naked incognito among human animals who don't know each other's names, or after careful introduction at a dinner party.

But the newly wounded seek poultices and remedies. They must learn to recognize their own reflection in the water, to distinguish it from that of the person who seduced them in the name of freedom. Next time, for them too, the new sexual frontier will not be so avidly pursued.

On the surface, it would seem that withdrawn and isolated people, who live in fear of the perils of intimacy, might profit from an ideal of sex without malice or meaning. They would be free to use their bodies in much the same way that they are often free to do technical work, without any interfering emotions. Schizoid or avoidant persons used to pay for sex to eliminate attachment. Now they might simply seek other agreeable transients, have sex, and part without friendship or enmity.

In the past, sexual union inevitably meant some brush with attraction, assertiveness, decision making, and all the other discomforts that schizoid personalities so assiduously avoid. Now there might be new possibilities—and, best of all for the men, the bodies were free.

Open sexuality does, in fact, attract a large number of emotionally disconnected people. Their hopes of finding a passion-free sexual outlet are, of course, destined for disappointment. The danger lies not so much in what these sorry beings do to others as in what happens to them. They do not break hearts in their faithlessness. Nor do others, usually, deliberately snare them in order to leave them writhing in the bite of a love trap. Just as they stay away from the world, so the world generally gets the message and stays away from them. The problem quickens when a solitary man or woman, who has been burying the pain of being alone for a lifetime, suddenly feels the pulse and momentum of wanting to possess someone else. More powerful than first love and less capable of fulfillment, the feeling may cause such acute pain that psychosis can be precipitated. Many of these crises have occurred through the organized sex groups that became more and more popular for a while to bring people together. Indeed, they became a familiar occurrence for most psychiatrists. Narcissists rarely require psychiatrists: they do not feel enough pain. Histrionics find their way to therapy only when their dependency is seriously threatened. Otherwise they emote their way through complex lives, rarely wounding or being wounded too deeply. But the shy and the pained, having no one to turn to, come to the professional. They cannot seek help in the free network of supportive friendships, but they can pay for help without feeling personal about it.

For the emotional isolate the peril of unhampered sex is emotional breakdown. This may not, in the end, be a bad thing; with help, he or she may reconstruct a more satisfying existence.

The victims of the more flamboyant offenders, as well as the timid recluses themselves—and anyone else who is intimidated by the new sexuality—may develop a crippling malady characteristic of our times. It might be called "sexual hypochondria." Instead of considering what is the matter with their relationships or themselves, the disturbed try endlessly to find remedies for sexual disorders, real or imagined. Just as an anorexic may blame all unhappiness on an improper distribution of fat, so the sexual hypochondriac thinks that his or her sexual disorder must be cured before happiness can begin.

Sexual relations would be tolerable, possible, or acceptable, if only an orgasm could occur, any way at all. Or it would be fine if an orgasm could happen on intercourse, or two orgasms, or one that happened a little faster. Or ejaculation comes too soon or too late to merit female respect; or sex would be pleasurable if only one felt less inept in the oral department. A penis that swells and empties at the wrong times is a curse; such an organ has to be governed better before its owner feels safe to take on the sexual competition. So the complaints persist, even after reassurance, even after their lack of substance has been demonstrated, even after it is quite certain that a partner feels that affection is more important than expertise. Among the personality types, sexual perfectionism has become a new preoccupation.

Compulsive personalities, of course, will be that way no matter what they do. As monogamists they are either uniquely successful or, more commonly, painfully loyal. Repressing all deviant impulses, they clutch their marriages with the same fearsome intensity with which they stroked their security blankets to a frazzle. Should they embark upon an affair after a long and arduous internal conflict and struggle with the forces of good and evil, they suffer as though they were about to be dispatched immediately to Hell. Sometimes they punish themselves by committing assorted parapraxes—for, when Freud spoke of the slips of everyday life, he was usually referring to the strange behavior of obsessional people. They walk into walls, break arms and legs, and all but do themselves in to avoid facing both their imperfectability and the wonders of their capacity to love. Their inability to accept themselves and their needs was the bulk of the materia psychologica that traditional psychoanalysts used to deal with for years at a time—and still do.

Once committed, obsessives will pursue sexual competence and experience as intensely as they may devote themselves to monogamy or even celibacy. They will have every kind of lover, every sort of sexual relation. Real obsessionals become supreme notchmakers, high technical experts, vast collectors of sexual lore. The new popularizations of what might be called "supersex" are probably products of the obsessional mind working overtime. Whether or not their findings have validity, scientists (or people who claim that estate) are writing books for the public with neat alphabetical abbreviations as titles. There is the "G-spot," to designate that precise place in a woman's genital system where orgasm may be further encouraged; there is also "ESO" to stand for "Extended Sexual Orgasm," an ability for marathon climaxing that you can learn to achieve by going into sex training the way runners work up to 25-mile jaunts. This is not to disparage the findings: Masters and Johnson noted that fifty orgasms in a night were quite attainable, and the first edition of this book, written in 1974 and published in 1977, described prolonged orgasm. However, until recently, there were no clinics for the purpose of achieving olympic sexual abilities, no seminars offered.

As yet, average people are not caught up in these prodigies. Rather than extend sex to wild extremes of performances, they are likelier to compartmentalize sex, to make it into an "activity" like swimming or golf. Just as the monogamous compulsive can routinize performance with a single partner (Tuesday and Saturday nights, between dinner and TV, or after the ten o'clock news), so the unattached can set themselves times for "purely sexual" recreation. Indeed, only the obsessive character could conceptualize the notion of "adult sexuality," undiluted by other motives, as one of the goals of maturation. Promiscuous sex as recreation would seem to be a largely compulsive (and often highly effective) defense against misery. It serves as well to defend against the admission of troublesome meaning to life.

As for how the obsessive compulsive has contributed to the sexual retreat, one need only read the magazines that have recently announced the end of sex. The articles tell us that the public has succumbed to workaholism, striving to keep business moving, to keep domestic environments clean, and most of all to keep sex (that dirty distraction) invisible. According to these popular essayists, the work junkies spend all their money on entertainment machinery. At home, they place themselves in the cockpits of their amusement stations, adjust headphones, flip dials, and take off into the eerie world of yesterday's movies and today's tragedies. It would seem that removing oneself from the electronic recliner for a go in the saddle has become too much not only for mother and dad but also for the youngsters. The magazines are very serious about this. For some, apparently, the demands of the sexual revolution are excessive. The best way of dealing with them is to deny them, in good obsessional fashion.

Marriage, monogamy, and staying at home offer the perfect havens, too, for dependent personalities. Clearly, if the essence of meaning in life is to rely on another's identity and support, especially as this is reinforced and proved out by sexual fidelity, random sexual encounter will seem the ultimate insecurity and degradation to the needy person. Many people exhibit extreme dependency on their mates, becoming helpless and hopeless for years after bereavement, for example. For such people, the notion of loose sexual liaisons threatens their justification for being alive: that they are worth someone else's care and devotion.

Dependents can adapt to open sexuality by having a variety of sexual friends to turn to in time of need or disappointment. This is not really an adherence to the true principles of the old "new sex," however. It is only a makeshift substitute for a preferred single attachment that doesn't work. And in the free sexual market, dependents learn rapidly that the sex act does not entitle them to reliance. Some are immensely hurt and surprised by that revelation and need to rely on a psychiatrist for a while to understand it. Most, however, guard themselves from the start and do not enter the larger game. It is enough to move very carefully from one person to the next in the search for a proper mate. As long as dependency, both male and female, is an important facet of the human condition, marriage and all the oaths, contracts, bonds, rings, and pledges that it entails, will remain an institution for the majority of people.

Paranoids, as one might suspect, have always had a dreadful time with open sex. They contributed very little to the sexual revolution because they were too suspicious of being had. They still feel that way. To them, almost everyone represents some form of danger. Thay are far too alert to the possibilities for disaster to appreciate the opportunities for pleasure. They do much better in monogamous sexual relationships than in multiple ones if they can see their partners as outside the persecutory system. Of course, not all paranoid personalities have fixed systems, but there is a tendency to regard any unknown person with considerable suspicion and hostility. Therefore, when such people find someone at all trustworthy, they tend to marry for safety.

In today's milieu, not only are paranoids afraid of being harmed by people, but they are also extremely affected by the possibility of being struck down by disease. Although this fear may be exaggerated in suspicious people, it is actually not at all paranoid at the present time to be concerned about the possibility of contracting an incurable or deadly disease through indiscriminate sexuality.

The threat of herpes is ubiquitous: everyone who has ever had a cold sore lives with one of the two types of herpes virus in his or her system and may be able to transmit that virus to someone else's genitals via oral sex. While it is most likely to be transmitted from an open sore, we do not yet understand viral "shedding" or the carrier condition when there is no obvious lesion. People like "Typhoid Mary" may be able to give disease to others without actively having it themselves. Oral and genital herpes have become epidemic, according to some observers, and as yet there is no cure. For most, the disease is mild and may not repeat its symptoms. For others, long sieges and dreadful complications are possible.

Far more intimidating is AIDS—acquired immune deficiency syndrome. The people who contract it will almost certainly die as a result of it. Their systems are lacking defenses, particularly against certain forms of pneumonia and cancer. At first AIDS was thought to be associated largely with male homosexual encounters; now it is known that women and children may contract AIDS. Drug abuse appears intimately related to transmission. Concern seems to be spreading faster than the disease. Because of AIDS, the promiscuous aspects of the new sexuality may soon reach a terminal phase, and many of the old restrictions may once again seem to make sense.

Scientists and philosophers have spent a good deal of effort trying to establish whether human beings are essentially a pair-bonding species or whether we are indiscriminately erotic. The answer, perhaps, lies not in studies of the copulatory habits of West Coast swingers as compared to those of East Coast academicians, but rather in a contemplative approach to history and literature. Human beings, far more than lower animals, develop individual character traits. No two people are precisely alike in their makeup, but one can generalize about predominant characteristics. I believe that it is character in human beings that determines the nature and durability of sexual unions. To what extent character itself is predetermined remains the most fascinating question of all.

Sex that reflects only the simple hedonism of biological pairing is not a human function. As far as I have been able to ascertain, even those of us possessing the most minimal cerebral equipment incorporate into the sexual act the sum of essential pain and pleasure. We may have a primitive memory of being spinal creatures who mate by instinct, but our glory and our tragedy is that we cannot return to those precortical days. Nor can we yet sift our pleasures from our sorrows, and act solely in pursuit of delight. We will not be able to do so until we have effectively conquered death, disease, disaster, and aging. Until then, our anguish always touches, deepens, enriches our gladness. We are, for all that science lies to us about our unimportance, a higher order of animals forever on the verge of immortality. Our uniqueness lies in our ability to conceptualize eternal joy; our community with trees and fishes rests in our inability to create it.

Epilogue

The sexual experience is different for everyone. Enjoying it means knowing how to make the best of one's particular—or peculiar—style. This may be difficult without misbehaving by hurting others, or suffering self-inflicted pain. We may be eccentric, slanted this way or that by our convictions about what is important in life, but these oddities need not become or remain neuroses. Indeed, developed and cultivated properly, sexual personality traits may express our greatest capacities for sharing ourselves.

An orderly and fastidious attitude toward life need not result in sexual extinction through overcontrol. Knowing one's best hours, seasons, and places for love, selecting the music, and readying the soul are occupations that suit any compulsive's finest dream. To take pleasure in detail, in promptness, in the mystical comfort of ritual, is a birthright, not a disease.

Theater, too, is a time-honored element of life. With or without a Greek chorus, we are very much entitled to play our parts as momentously as we dare. Talented thespians may capture and reveal our most vital spirit. Expressing emotions strongly, conveying sensuality with a performer's gift and a poet's heart, they may move us to ecstasies that fortify us for immortality. They must be the most deserving of our love—they work so hard for it.

Perhaps paranoia is the intemperance of the questioning mind. Such minds are responsible for all those delicate ruminations that we classify as introspection: the elegant dissection of motives, the uncanny insight into character, the self-protective suspicion that makes it possible to choose, finally, a secure resting place for trust. To be appropriately paranoid is to be at once exquisitely selective and totally pragmatic, relying only on the demonstrable. Highly refined mistrust yields a fascinatingly perceptive lover, alert to nuances, unwilling to take hurt silently, careful to trace all the subtleties of discontent that must be traced if sentiment is to stay vigorous. We call such people sensitive and deeply thoughtful. As lovers, it may take them some time to make up their minds about us, but once accepted, we may achieve that small company who glimpse the reality of their sexual selves.

Enough. This is a list of personality types, of erotic ideals as engaging and impossible as the Ten Commandments. People are rarely so categorical. Our personalities defy such convenient definition. You know—and I know—that we may only begin when each of us has a unique vision of love, that most enigmatic and least romantic of human passions.

Index

Acquired immune deficiency
syndrome (AIDS), 128, 306–7
Adolescent sex, 13–14, 22, 262–
63, 297
Affectional systems, 16
Affective factors, 103–9
Aggression, 93–102, 122–23,
129, 294; and competitive
spirit, 95; fantasy in, 220–21,
228; female, 98–99, 271, 274–
75; and female sexual disorders, 171–73; male, 95–97,
148; and male sexual disorders, 134–35, 137–38, 147–
48; parental influence on,
134–35; passive, *see* Passive aggression; sex used as weapon,
94, 97; women as objects of,
95–97, 134–35
Ambivalence, sexual, 115, 122,
126–28
American Psychiatric Association
(APA), 17, 113, 115, 132
Anorexia nervosa, 117–18, 302
Anorgasmia: in obsessional
women, 72–73; therapy for,
197–99
Antisocial personality, 93–94, 95
Archetypes, 238
Arousal, sexual, *see* Sexual
arousal
Art and sex, 280
Atom-smasher theory of
character, 17

Attachment, 14–16, 27–29, 33–
34; detachment mixed with,
29–31
Aversion, sexual, 115; female
disorders of, 116–18; male
disorders of, 117–18; primary,
114
Avoidance, sexual, 115, 122–26
Avoidant personality, 87n, 127,
128, 301

Behavior therapy, misuse of, 218
Birth control devices, 270, 271;
in passive aggression, 77; the
Pill, 272
Bitches, 274–75
Bonding: absence of, 29; touch,
see Touch bonding
Brain: limbic area, electrical
stimulation, 2–3; neocortex, 3
Buddhist movement, 265

Career women, 277, 281–84;
avoidance of sex, 73
Castration, fear of: and impaired
orgasm, 139; in paranoids,
83–84
Castration, loss of faculties as,
108
Children: dependence on parents, 44–45; in new sexuality,
296; and separation in mar-

riage, 30–31; and sexual
disorders of mothers, 160
Clitoris, erotic focus in, 161–65
Compensatory sexuality, 129
Compulsiveness, 65–75; fantasy
in, 221; and female sexual disorders, 119, 157, 159–60,
176–77; and male sexual disorders, 135, 138, 141–42; and
new sexuality, 303; obsessive,
128, 304; of women in domestic life, 70–72; see also
Obsession
Computer model of sexuality,
15–16
Coquetry, 54
Criminals, sexuality of, 93–94
Cyclothymics, 108–9

Death, 23; by orgasm, fear of,
175
Dependence, 19–21, 27–28, 34,
39–48; economic, 42–44; and
female sexual disorders, 119,
124, 157, 169–70; and male
sexual disorders, 138, 147; in
men and women compared,
100; new, 255–56; and new
sexuality, 305; pain, 40, 47;
parent-child relationship as
model, 44–45; on power, 44–
48; social, 40–42
Depression, 105–9; and impotence, 43, 107; loss of
sexuality as cause, 107–9, 117,
120, 121; mild, sexual disorders and, 129–30; neurotic
and psychotic, 106, 107
Desire, sexual, see Sexual desire
Detachment, 29–30; attachment
mixed with, 30–31
Divorce, 24, 262
Don Juans, 55, 100–101, 299–
300
Dyslexia, 123n

Economic dependence, 42–44
Ego function, 3

Ego psychology, 3
Ejaculation, disorders of, see Premature ejaculation;
Retarded ejaculation
Electrical stimulation of brain,
2–3
Erection: physiology of, 133–34;
and sexual disorders, 133–34,
141–42
Erikson, Erik, 205
Extended Sexual Orgasm (ESO),
304
Extramarital relationships: detachment and attachment in,
29–30; and separation, 31–33;
see also Sexuality, new

Fantasy, 217–30; absence of,
229–30; acting out, dangers
of, 227–29; in aggressives,
220–221, 228; and communication, 224–27; in
compulsives, 221; deviant,
226–27; guilt associated with,
222–24; in histrionics, 219–
20, 221, 228; and homosexuality, 138, 222–23, 224;
masochistic, 240–44; misuse
of, 217–18; in narcissists, 220,
228; in obsession, 220; parents
and, 218, 223–24; in passive
aggressives, 221; and passivity,
136–37; of personal relationships, 227; romantic, 225;
sadistic, 217–18, 223–24, 244–
45; in schizoids, 90–91, 221;
in sociopaths, 220; in therapy
for impotence, 196, 230; in
therapy of women, 198, 201;
in women's lives, 240–44
Father: of aggressive woman,
173; and female sexual disorders, 170–71, 174; and
impotence, 134; and male sexual disorders, 120, 124;
woman's choice of husband resembling, 237, 285

Freud, Sigmund, 16, 149, 258, 262, 303

Frigidity, discarding term known as, 113

G-spot, 161–62, 303–4

Herpes, 306

Histrionics, 49–57, 117, 129, 249, 252, 271; fantasy in, 219–20, 221, 228; female, 50–54, 100; and female sexual disorders, 124, 157, 177, 178; male, 50–51, 54–57; and male sexual disorders, 133–34, 138; marriage of histrionic woman and obsessional man, 212–14; and new sexuality, 298–300, 302; and separation, 31

Homosexuality, 18–19, 265–66, 306; and fantasy, 138, 222–23, 224; fear of, 138; histrionics in, 51, 55–56

Hypochondriasis, 108

Hypomanics, 103–5

Hysteria, sexual aversion in, 116–17

Hysterical "conversion," 51

Id, 15

Impotence, 126, 163, 250; and aggressive women, 98, 99; and depression, 43, 107, 120; discarding term known as, 113; in histrionics, 55; new, 255–68; in paranoids, 85; and premature ejaculation, 143, 144; and sexual disorders, 134–37, 140–42; therapy for, 194–96, 230

Incest and female sexual life, 119, 236–37

Indifference, sexual, 115, 118–21; female sexual disorders of, 119–20, 121; male sexual disorders of, 119, 120–21

Infants: sexuality, 20–21, 236; touching needed by, 20–21, 25–27

Inhibition, sexual: in histrionics, 51; in men, 150–53; in women, 155–65

Intimacy, 125–26, 128, 164; power and, 202–16

James, William, quoted, 15

Joyce, James, 17

Jung, Carl Gustav, 239

Kissinger, Henry, quoted, 45

Labile personalities, 109

Libido, 15; and economic dependence, 43; loss of, and depression, 106, 129, 130; low-libido syndrome, 43, 79

Literature of sex, 240, 280, 293–94

Love: falling in love, 13–14, 22, 235; and indifference, 119; in new sexuality, 295, 296; romantic, 232; in sexual difficulties, 203–5, 216; women's ideal of, 233–35

Manic state, 104

Marasmus, 20

Marriage: aggression in, 95–99; changing partners in, 228, 251, 259–61, 265–66; closed, 33; in conventional life-style, 275–78; detachment and attachment in, 29–30; and female sexual disorders, 158–60; histrionics in, 53–54; of histrionic woman and obsessional man, 212–14; and male sexual disorders, 135, 146–52; narcissism in, 60–61, 62; in new sexuality, for security, 305–6; open, 30, 32–33; passive aggression in, 77–80; of passive and dominant people, 206–11; separation in, 30–33

Masochism, pain dependence, 40, 47

Masochistic fantasy, 240–44

Massage parlors, 89–90

Masters and Johnson, 114, 192–93, 255, 304

Masturbation, 297, 298; female, and sexual disorders, 160, 162–63, 168, 169, 171, 172, 176; female, in therapy, 197–99; and inhibited orgasm in male, 151; and narcissism, 64; and paranoids, 82; in retarded ejaculation, 196–97; in schizoids, 89

Men: aggression against, 98–99, 119; fantasies of, see Fantasy; and female role, 50–51, 54–56; and literature of sex, 240, 280, 293–94; new sexuality and, 293–307; parents of, in sexual problems, 120, 124–25, 134–35, 150–51, 208, 209–10, 231, 236; psychosexual change and, 246–52; sexual disorders of, 111–86; sexual inhibition in, 150–53; sexual therapy for, 191–97; and transference neurosis, 233–35

Miniparanoids, 82; see also Paranoids

Mothers, 296; aggression as retaliation against, 95–96; of aggressive women, 173; and female sexual disorders, 169–70; and impotence, 174; and male disorders of orgasm, 150–51; and male sexual disorders, 120, 124; man's choice of wife resembling, 258–59; sons dominated by, 150–51

Narcissism, 29, 58–64, 125–26, 129; fantasy in, 220, 228; female, 61, 62, 63, 124; male, 60, 61–62, 63, 64; and new sexuality, 300–301, 302

New impotence, 255–68

New sexuality, 262–68, 293–307

Nymphomania, 130, 131, 132, 185, 281

Obsession, 65–75, 252, 282; fantasy in, 220; female compulsiveness and sexual obsession, 70–75, 125; and male sexual disorders, 140, 141–42, 145–46; male sexual obsession, 68–70, 267; marriage of obsessional man and histrionic woman, 212–14; and new sexuality, 303–4; and separation, 32

Oedipus complex, 16, 31, 236–37; maternally induced, 169

Open marriage, 30, 32–33

Orgasm, Extended Sexual (ESO), 304

Orgasm, female, 74–75, 113; delayed, 18, 200; disorders of, 138–39, 167–86; fear of dying by, 175–76; impaired, 178–82; incomplete, 180; inhibited, 126, 161–63, 168–78, 197–99; multiple, 130–31, 170, 185–86; multiple, inhibition of, 183–86; as petit mort, 73, 175; premature, 179–80, 199–200; therapy for disorders of, 197–201; vaginal vs. clitoral, 161–65; varieties of, 183–85, 186

Orgasm, male: disorders of, 142–54; impaired, 153–54; inhibited, 150–53; obsession with, 68

Orgasmic anesthesia: female, 179, 181, 200; male, 152–53

Orgasmic dysfunction, primary and secondary, 114

Pain, in new sexuality, 295, 302

Pain dependence, 40, 47

Paranoia, 28, 29, 305–6, 309–10; delusions and hallucinations in, 81

Paranoids, 33–34, 81–86, 127,
    249, 271; and female sexual
    disorders, 119, 165; and male
    sexual disorders, 135, 138–39;
    miniparanoids, 82; and new
    sexuality, 305–6; sexual fears
    in, 82–86, 125; single women,
    279
Paranoid schizophrenia, sexual
    aversion in, 116–17
Parents, 296–97; fantasy associ-
    ated with, 218, 223–24; faults
    of personality, 26–28; and
    female sexual disorders, 119–
    20, 124–25, 169–72, 174; and
    female sexual problems, 231,
    236–37, 241–42; and impo-
    tence, 135; and male sexual
    disorders, 120, 121, 124–25,
    134–35, 150–51; and male
    sexual problems, 208, 209–10,
    231, 236; and passivity, 205–
    6; personality affected by, 15,
    16, 19; separation from, 21,
    22–23, 26, 27; touching by,
    21; see also Father; Mother
Passive aggression, 76–80, 271,
    290, 292; fantasy in, 221; and
    female sexual disorders, 119,
    157, 171; and male sexual dis-
    orders, 124, 138, 147; and
    separation, 31–32
Passivity, 123–24, 128, 185; fear
    of, 136–38; and impotence,
    136–37; and masochistic fan-
    tasy, 240–41; therapy for
    passive patient, 205–12; and
    women's sexual liberation,
    272–74
Penis envy, 139
Personality: parents' effects on,
    15, 16, 19; and sexual behav-
    ior, 5–7
Personality traits, 37–102; basic,
    16–18
Pill, the, 272
Political Sexual Dysfunction,
    272–75

Pornography, 34, 119, 293–94,
    256–57, 297–98
Power: dependence on, 44–48;
    and intimacy, 202–16
Premature ejaculation, 142–49,
    250; and aggression, 147–49;
    and dependence, 146–47; in
    obsession, 70, 146; in passive
    aggression, 77–78, 147–48;
    primary and secondary, 144–
    45; in schizoids, 145–46; and
    sexual ambivalence, 126; ther-
    apy for, 191–94; women's role
    in, 145–49
Promiscuity: in new sexuality,
    129, 297, 298, 299, 304; and
    social dependence, 40–41
Psychosexual change, 246–52

Religion and sexual behavior, 35,
    44–45, 118, 142
Repression, sexual, in women,
    157–60
Retarded ejaculation, 150–53,
    250–51; therapy for, 196–97
Romance: in fantasy, 225;
    women's need for, 232

Sadistic fantasy, 217–18, 223–
    24, 244–45
Satyriasis, 131–32
Schizoids, 29, 32, 87–92, 250,
    252; arousal in, 126, 127, 128;
    avoidant behavior, 88–90; and
    avoidant personality, 87n; fan-
    tasy in, 90–91, 221; female,
    90, 91, 271; and female sexual
    disorders, 157, 173–74; male,
    89–90; and male sexual disor-
    ders, 138, 139–41, 145; and
    new sexuality, 301
Schizophrenia, 29; sexual, 207
Semans, James, 191–92, 193,
    200
Separation: in marriage, 30–33;
    from parents, 21, 22–23, 26,
    27

Separation anxiety, 14–15, 21–23

Sexual arousal, 122–32, 155, 164; excessive, 129–32; inhibition of, 115, 116, 128

Sexual desire, 113–21, 155; definitions of, 114–15; female disorders of, 155–67; inhibition of, 114–15, 129–30, 155; male disorders of, 118–42

Sexual disorders, 7–9, 111–86; female, 155–86; male, 118–54; see also names of specific disorders

Sexual dyskinesia, 123n

Sexual ego, 15

Sexual excitement, 155; female disorders of, 155–67; inhibition of, 113, 115, 125, 129–30, 155; male disorders of, 118–42

Sexual inhibition, see Inhibition, sexual

Sexuality: denial of, as obsession, 70–71; and depression, 43, 106–9; of histrionics, 52–56; life of mind versus pleasure of body, 69–71; in narcissism, 60–64; new, 262–68, 293–307; in older people, 266–68, 294; passive-aggressive, 77–80; publicity for, 256–58, 293–94; and touch, 20–22; understanding of, 3–4; in youth, 262–67, 294

Sexual revolution, 10, 131, 294–95, 305

Sexual schizophrenia, 207

Sexual selectivity and social dependence, 41–42

Sexual therapy, 9, 116, 187–252; expertise of therapist, 115, 202–3; fantasy in, see Fantasy; for female disorders, 197–201; for impotence, 194–96, 230; for male disorders, 191–97; for passive patient, 205–11; techniques, 189–201

Sherfey, Mary Jane, 170

Single people, disorders of arousal in, 127

Single women, 278–79

Social dependence, 40–42

Women: aggression against, 95, 96–97, 119, 134–35; bitches, 274–75; careers of, see Career women; conventional (passive) life-style, 275–78; cultural restrictions on, 239–41; family duties of, 237–38; fantasies of, 240–44; fear of assuming male role, 170; liberated, character sketch of, 284–86; and literature of sex, 240, 280, 293–94; love as ideal of, 233–35; middle-ground, character sketch of, 286–90; and new sexuality, 293–307; parents of, in sexual problems, 119–20, 124–25, 169–72, 174, 231, 236–37, 241–42; psychosexual change, 246–52; romance needed by, 232; sexual disorders of, 111–86; sexual freedom for, 235–36, 293–307; sexual problems of, 231–45; single, 278–79; "Total Woman" concept, 238–39; transference neurosis in, 233–35

Women's liberation, 269–70, 272; and aggressive men, 148; character sketch of liberated woman, 284–86; as sexual threat, 140–41

Women's sexual liberation, 116, 167, 269–92; transitional syndrome, Political Sexual Dysfunction, 272–75

About the Author

Avodah K. Offit, M.D., is a graduate of Hunter College and the University of Chicago. She majored in English and was elected to Phi Beta Kappa. She graduated from the New York University School of Medicine and is in the private practice of psychiatry and sex therapy. A consultant at Lenox Hill Hospital, she holds her clinical academic professorship at Cornell University Medical College in affiliation with the New York Hospital.

Her online address is: Virtualove@aol.com.